Education and the Historic Environment

The *Issues in Heritage Management* series is a joint venture between Routledge and English Heritage. It provides accessible, thought-provoking books on issues central to heritage management. Each book within the series is designed to provide a topical introduction to key issues in heritage management for students in higher education, and for heritage professionals.

The past is everywhere around us, and teaching about the past is a common trait of all societies. However, the choice of what past is taught, and how, is a complex decision. These chapters argue for the value of using the physical remains of the past – the historic environment – in teaching for every age group.

This evidence is not commonly used in education for a range of reasons, including lack of time and experience, so the introductory chapters show how and where the historic environment can be used to fit into and enhance learning. These guidelines are reinforced by case studies from a wide cross section of the heritage sector, which also prove that the physical heritage can not only be used to teach obvious subjects such as history but is also useful across the curriculum, from literacy and numeracy to citizenship.

Practical, inspiring and instructive, *Education and the Historic Environment* emphasises the contribution to both education and heritage that results from a positive relationship between the two disciplines. Teachers at all levels, and students, academics and professionals in archaeology and heritage management, will be able to use the case studies to reform and enhance their work.

Don Henson is Education Officer at the Council for British Archaeology.

Peter Stone is Director of the International Centre for Cultural and Heritage Studies, University of Newcastle.

Mike Corbishley was formally Head of Education at English Heritage and now lectures on heritage education at the Institute of Archaeology, University College London.

ISSUES IN HERITAGE MANAGEMENT
Published by Routledge in association with English Heritage

Series editor: Peter Stone, University of Newcastle

Education and the Historic Environment

edited by

Don Henson, Peter Stone and Mike Corbishley

Routledge
Taylor & Francis Group

LONDON AND NEW YORK

First published 2004
by Routledge
11 New Fetter Lane, London EC4P 4EE

Simultaneously published in the USA
and Canada by Routledge
29 West 35th Street, New York,
NY 10001

Routledge is an imprint of the Taylor & Francis Group

© 2004 English Heritage

Typeset in Bell Gothic and Perpetua by
Florence Production Ltd, Stoodleigh, Devon

Printed and bound in Great Britain by
Biddles Ltd, King's Lynn

British Library Cataloguing in Publication Data
A catalogue record for this book is available from the
British Library

Library of Congress Cataloging in Publication Data
Education and the historic environment/edited by
Don Henson, Peter Stone and Mike Corbishley.
    p. cm.
    1. Archaeology—Study and teaching—
Great Britain.   2. Historic sites—Interpretive
programs—Great Britain.   I. Henson, Don, 1956–
II. Stone, Peter G., 1957–   III. Corbishley, Mike
CC97.G7E37   2004
907′.1′041—dc22   2003014996

ISBN 0–415–28427–9 (hbk)
ISBN 0–415–28428–7 (pbk)

DEDICATION

Dedication

We should like to dedicate this volume to Professor Keith Branigan of the Department of Archaeology and Prehistory, University of Sheffield, a pioneer of 'archaeology and education'. In 1979, soon after his arrival in Sheffield, Keith began his service 'Archaeology in Education'. Over the twenty-one years it was run from the Department (and frequently his own home) hundreds of school teachers were helped to introduce their pupils to the fascinating world of archaeology through a regular newsletter; the provision of education packs, slides, and replicas; and an annual conference. The editors and many contributors to this volume have themselves been supported by Keith in a wide variety of ways. Always helpful, always supportive, always with a ready ear to listen.

CONTENTS

FIGURES

Tables

TABLES

CONTRIBUTORS

John Barnatt, Archaeology Service, Peak District National Park, Aldern House, Baslow Road, Bakewell, Derbyshire DE45 1AE.

Bill Bevan, Archaeology Service, Peak District National Park, Aldern House, Baslow Road, Bakewell, Derbyshire DE45 1AE.

Tim Copeland, International Centre for Heritage Education, University of Gloucestershire.

Mike Corbishley, Institute of Archaeology, University College London, 31–34 Gordon Square, London WC1H 0PY.

Fiona Davidson, Council for Scottish Archaeology, c/o National Museums of Scotland, Chambers Street, Edinburgh EH1 1JF.

Mike Dymond, Truro College, College Road, Truro, Cornwall TR1 3XX.

Mark Edmonds, Department of Archaeology and Prehistory, University of Sheffield, Northgate House, West Street, Sheffield S1 4ET.

Yannis Hamilakis, Department of Archaeology, University of Southampton, Highfield, Southampton SO17 1BJ.

Pippa Henry, 39 Matthews Way, Wooton, Abingdon OX13 6JX.

Don Henson, Council for British Archaeology, Bowes Morrell House, 111 Walmgate, York YO1 9WA.

Andrew Jones, York Archaeological Trust, 11–13 Ogleforth, York YO1 2JG.

Dave Jones, Bridgwater College, Bath Road, Bridgwater, Somerset TA6 4PZ.

Peter Lassey, 2 North View, Hollywell Green, Halifax HX4 9AT.

Gary Lock, Department for Continuing Education, Oxford University, Rewley House, 1 Wellington Square, Oxford OX1 2JA.

Graham McElearney, Learning Media Unit, University of Sheffield, Sheffield S10 2TN.

Caroline Malim, c/o Tim Malim, Gifford Consulting Engineers, 20 Nicholas Street, Chester CH1 2NX.

Sue Mitchell, Historic Scotland, Longmore House, Salisbury Place, Edinburgh EH9 1SH.

Vikki Pearson, Northamptonshire Heritage, PO Box 163, County Hall, Northampton NN1 1AX.

Paul Rainbird, Department of Archaeology, University of Wales, Lampeter, Ceredigion SA48 7ED.

Pippa Smith, Wessex Archaeology, Portway House, Old Sarum Park, Salisbury SP4 6EB.

Peter Stone, International Centre for Cultural and Heritage Studies, University of Newcastle upon Tyne, Bruce Building, Newcastle NE1 7RU.

Dave Weldrake, West Yorkshire Archaeology Service, Registry of Deeds, Newstead Road, Wakefield WF1 2DE.

Alex West, Wall to Wall Television, 8–9 Spring Place, Kentish Town, London NW5 3ER.

Damion Willcock, former Education Officer, Kilmartin House Trust, Dreva Cottage, near Broughton, Peeblesshire ML12 6HH.

Foreword

FOREWORD

This book is the third volume in the series *Issues in Heritage Management*. The series, a joint initiative between the English Heritage Education Service (EHES) and Routledge, is based on discussions at professional seminars and conferences where those involved in particular aspects of the heritage met and exchanged views, ideas and approaches. It is important to note that the seminars and conferences were conceived as educational, rather than policy-forming, events. The seminars that provided the information for the first two of these volumes (*Managing the Historic Rural Landscape* and *Managing Historic Sites and Buildings*) were organised and facilitated by the EHES. The majority of chapters in this book were first presented at the biennial education conference of the Council for British Archaeology. A few additional contributions, identified at the conference as being of major importance to the discussion, have been especially commissioned. The conference was supported by the EHES, for which the CBA offers its thanks.

The following chapters provide a 'snapshot' of policy and practice at the end of the twentieth century. They are intended to actively encourage debate of the issue of the relationship between heritage and education: from cradle to grave. They do not put forward a particular English Heritage view or policy but rather put the work of the EHES alongside that of many other organisations set within the wider context of education.

Peter G. Stone
International Centre for Cultural and Heritage Studies,
University of Newcastle, January 2003

ABBREVIATIONS

A-level   GCE advanced level
AQA   Assessment and Qualifications Alliance
ARC   Archaeological Resource Centre
AS-level   GCE advanced subsidiary level
ATF   Archaeology Training Forum
AVCE   Advanced Vocational Certificate of Education (formerly
           the advanced GNVQ)
BUAC   British Universities Archaeology Committee
CAA   computer-aided assessment
CBA   Council for British Archaeology
CCCAFU   Cambridgeshire County Council Archaeological Field Unit
CE   continuing education
Cert HE   Certificate of Higher Education
CMC   computer-mediated communications
CSA   Council for Scottish Archaeology
CSE   Certificate of Secondary Education (merged with GCE
           ordinary level into the GCSE)
DCMS   Department for Culture, Media and Sport
DfEE   Department for Education and Employment (later
           became the Department for Education and Skills)
DfES   Department for Education and Skills (formerly the
           Department for Education and Employment)
Dip HE   Diploma of Higher Education
DMV   deserted medieval village
EH   English Heritage
FE   further education
GCE   General Certificate of Education
GCSE   General Certificate of Secondary Education
GNVQ   General National Vocational Qualification
HE   higher education
HEC   IFA Higher Education Committee
HNC   Higher National Certificate
HND   Higher National Diploma

ICT	information and communication technology
IFA	Institute of Field Archaeologists
ITT	initial teacher training
JMB	Joint Matriculation Board
JQU	Joint Qualifications Unit (now the ABC Awarding Body)
LEA	Local Education Authority
LT	learning technology
LTSN	Learning and Teaching Support Network
MCQ	multiple choice questions
NEAB	Northern Examinations and Assessment Board
NHES	Northamptonshire Heritage Education Service
NTO	national training organisation (being merged into SSCs)
NVQ	National Vocational Qualification
OCR	Oxford, Cambridge and RSA Examinations Board
OFSTED	Office for Standards in Education
PG Cert	Postgraduate Certificate
PG Dip	Postgraduate Diploma
PGCE	Postgraduate Certificate of Education
PIC	Properties in Care Group
PPG 16	Planning Policy Guidance note 16
PPJPB	Peak Park Joint Planning Board
PTC	IFA Professional Training Committee
QAA	Quality Assurance Agency for Higher Education
QCA	Qualifications and Curriculum Authority
RBL	resource-based learning
RCHME	Royal Commission on the Historical Monuments of England (now merged into English Heritage)
SCACE	Standing Conference of Archaeology in Continuing Education
SCB	Scottish Conservation Bureau
SCCC	Scottish Consultative Council on the Curriculum (now merged into Learning and Teaching Scotland)
SCFA	Subject Committee for Archaeology (formerly SCUPHA)
SCUPHA	Standing Conference of University Professors and Heads of Archaeology (later became SCFA)
SGA	Scottish Group Award
SMR	Sites and Monuments Record
SNQ	Scottish National Qualification
SSC	sector skills council (being formed from NTOs)
SVQ	Scottish Vocational Qualification
TCRE	Technical, Conservation, Research and Education Group
TES	*Times Educational Supplement*
TTA	Teacher Training Authority
VLE	virtual learning environments
VR	virtual reality
WAC	World Archaeological Congress
WEA	Workers' Educational Association
WYAS	West Yorkshire Archaeology Service
YAC	Young Archaeologists' Club
YAT	York Archaeological Trust

INTRODUCTION: EDUCATION AND THE HISTORIC ENVIRONMENT INTO THE TWENTY-FIRST CENTURY

Peter Stone

> Their commitment to the project was high, and I am sure that the enthusiasm generated will last them the rest of their lives.
>
> Weldrake, Chapter 18, this volume

An anecdote and an apology

As a young, newly qualified history teacher working in what was (I think) the last Secondary Modern school in South Yorkshire in the late 1970s, I was faced with a syllabus that ran from 'Plato to NATO'. To say that the children, whose likely career path was at best 'down the pit' or working in the local supermarket, were less than interested is an understatement. And yet, when I took a piece of Anglo-Scandinavian pottery into class I had the pottery in one hand and the children in the other. 'Is it *really* that old?' 'Did some fella *really* make it?' 'Did they *really* eat out of it?' History – the past – had become real, tangible, and for those pupils a seed had been sown. I would be very surprised if any have become archaeologists – or even historians – but I do not think I would be far off the mark if I guessed that many of them are regular viewers of *Time Team* and perhaps a fair few members of English Heritage and/or the National Trust.

This anecdote, and the one quoted at the top of this introduction, could be repeated with minor modifications by all of the contributors to this book. When explored, the relationship between archaeology and education has always been an immediate one; a physical one – it provides us with Willcock's 'high octane fuel to the imagination' (Chapter 20: 216). Archaeology deals with the reality of the past – the everyday, and more specialised, things that those who have gone before us used. But, of course, it is also about much more than objects: rural and urban landscapes – indeed the whole *historic environment* or *heritage* – are grist to the archaeologist's mill. As such, archaeology encourages, essentially demands, that those involved in it engage with the past in an active, memorable way. Archaeology forces questioning, making its practitioners think about what happened in the past – how the past *worked* – and, crucially, it forces us to think of the people of the past.

Twenty-five years after teaching in South Yorkshire I find myself teaching postgraduate students studying for qualifications in the heritage sector about two parallel universes: Education and Heritage – which as suggested above includes (is, to my mind, in many ways, actually synonymous with) archaeology. I am sure my astronomical simile lacks any academic credibility, but one of these universes, Education, is far more powerful than the other, smaller and weaker Heritage universe. In fact, there is no need whatsoever for those living in the Education universe to take any notice of those living in the Heritage universe – and all too frequently they do not. As is frequently the case with unequal relationships, the weaker partner has to work much harder to keep the relationship alive.

Accepting this view of the relationship between heritage (archaeology) and education leads into the questions 'Why should people want to teach about the past in this way?' and 'Who should be taught?' As a committed heritage educator and professional, the answers to both questions are quite straightforward. I want to teach in this way because it is exciting, immediate, and real. It provides a more rounded view of the past than a history lesson constructed around documentary sources alone. As someone who has spent most of his life concerned with the preservation of the historic environment there is also a more evangelical reason: if people are taught of the value of the historic environment they will learn to appreciate it and support its preservation. An understanding and supportive public is an essential element in the battle to preserve the historic environment and is enough justification in itself for the teaching of the past through archaeology. So who should be taught? The implication from the last statement is that everyone should have the opportunity to be exposed to such an education. And so it should be. This does not mean, of course, that everyone should be forced to read archaeology at university or even for everyone to have to take archaeology at school. Rather, everyone should have the opportunity to discover and learn about the historic environment through archaeology within both formal and informal education – and from cradle to grave. Certainly some need the opportunity to read archaeology at a degree (and higher degree) level. The next generation of professionals need to learn about their subject and need to be trained. But perhaps far more important, and of more relevance to this book, is that the wider population should have the opportunity to be taught about the past through archaeology.

This has been the view of the Council for British Archaeology (CBA) for over fifty years (for example, CBA 1944, 1956). Over this time the CBA has striven to keep the relationship between archaeology and both formal and informal education alive, and to nurture and develop it (Henson and Davidson, Chapter 9; and see Corbishley and Stone 1994; Richardson 1989). More recently the CBA has been joined in these efforts by some of the national heritage organisations – English Heritage (Corbishley, Chapter 7), Historic Scotland (Mitchell, Chapter 8) and, for a short time (before the senior management inexplicitly and scandalously closed its education service), Cadw. Both English Heritage and Historic Scotland talk of the educational value of the 'historic environment' – a term essentially synonymous with the CBA's view of 'archaeology'. These national initiatives have been supported by countless regional and local initiatives by archaeology units and societies and even some universities – notably Sheffield and Southampton (see pp. 8–9). This volume is another weapon in the armoury of evidence to be deployed to further still greater integration. However, all of these organisations belong firmly in my Heritage universe and constantly find themselves on the outside asking for a small, walk-on role in the Educational universe.

The value of archaeology to education

Archaeology – as the study of the historic environment – forces teachers and students alike to ask questions of, and then interpret, the physical evidence of the past. Such questioning is, or should be, always enhanced by recourse to documentary sources where they exist. All too frequently however, such documentary sources do not exist and we are left to interpret the physical remains themselves. Such interpretation is at the core of archaeological enquiry. It is an enquiry that offers itself to multiple interpretation and – on occasion – manipulation and downright falsification (and see for example, Vargas Arenas and Sanoja Obediente 1990; Gawe and Meli 1990; Schmidt 1999; Sommer 1999). Such interpretation is also at the core of good education – where students of whatever age are taught to think critically and for themselves.

The acceptance of the possibility of multiple interpretation is also at the heart of history teaching. For example, in the English National Curriculum, 'pupils should be taught to recognise that the past is represented and interpreted in different ways, and to give reasons for this' (National Curriculum 2002). A number of contributors to this volume clearly demonstrate how their work can inform questioning of interpretation (for example, Bevan et al. Chapter 19; Copeland, Chapter 3; Weldrake, Chapter 18).

The argument is not that those who favour introducing more of the study of the historic environment into formal curricula in the UK (indeed globally) want to see the wholesale revision or expansion of the content of the curricula; rather, it is that they suggest a little more flexibility and the option of using the physical, and therefore tangible, elements of the past in the delivery of the existing requirements. Such an approach echoes the political aspiration for 'joined-up thinking' championed by the exponents of New Labour's theoretical manifesto. So what can be done? In the chapters that follow many of those who have been battling to include archaeology into the curriculum over the last thirty years and more review their work and show what has been achieved. I make a few additional comments below that are intended to provide a quick review and a context for where and how such efforts might be focused in the future.

The school curriculum: the continuing *excluded past*?

This unequal relationship between Education and Heritage is not confined to the UK. In the late 1980s Bob MacKenzie and I developed the concept of the 'Excluded Past' that related to the exclusion from curricula around the world of both prehistory and the past held true by many indigenous or minority groups (Stone and MacKenzie 1990). Examples from Australia to Argentina, from North America to Poland, and from Russia to Kenya testified to this exclusion and the unequal relationship between the universes of Education and Heritage. Four reasons for the exclusion were identified: overcrowded curricula; teacher ignorance; no relevance of heritage to modern society; and overt political manip-ulation (MacKenzie and Stone 1990: 3–4). While further international (Stone and Molyneaux 1994; Antiquity 2000) and national (Jameson 1997; Smardz and Smith 2000) reviews suggest a slight improvement in this situation in some countries, the reasons for exclusion are still there and still maintain the unequal relationship between my universes.

With respect to formal curricula in the UK, and accepting the reality that there are four national curricula within the UK (and see Henson, Chapter 1), some – no doubt oversimplistic and unfair – general comments can be made. First, there is still a major perception of 'overcrowded curricula'. Teachers, Local Education Authority staff, and the responsible national agencies, understandably continue to recoil at the prospect of introducing anything new to the curriculum that is not introduced from above. They therefore shut the door on the introduction of studying the historic environment – as opposed to documentary history – to their overworked lives. Despite some of the rhetoric of National Curriculum History that exhorts teachers to use 'a range of appropriate sources of information including . . . the media, artefacts, pictures, photographs, music, museums, buildings and sites, . . . as a basis for independent historical enquiries' (2002), most teaching is delivered relying almost entirely on written sources. Where used, objects and sites are used as a backdrop to illustrate. This is not surprising. Most of those teaching history in schools today were trained in a system dominated by a view of the past as driven by documentary history. Many are therefore uncomfortable with using the real historic environment, or with using objects from the past in any but the most superficial way. When I have said this in public a number of teachers and advisers have disagreed with me, citing examples of wonderful teachers able to use all evidence from the past with great skill. I have no doubt that there are many wonderful teachers out there willing and able to deliver such a high-quality education: unfortunately, my firm belief after being involved in In Service Teacher Training over the past twenty years is that such individuals are very much the exception and not the norm. I do not criticise those tasked with teaching about the past at any level; rather, I criticise the system that has trained them and the (at least perceived) rigidity of the system within which they have to work.

This perception, coupled with the government's reorganisation of initial teacher training (ITT) that lays significantly more emphasis on classroom practice at the expense of subject-specific knowledge and understanding, leads directly to the second reason for exclusion: just as those who have been teaching for a number of years, many newly qualified teachers are unsure of, and therefore uncomfortable with, using the historic environment in their teaching. This situation is made even worse by the real difficulty that those with first degrees in single honours archaeology have in being accepted on initial teacher training courses. A long-held view that only those with (since 1988 National Curriculum) subjects taught in school are suitable for selection to secondary ITT courses has long been criticised and opposed by the CBA and others. Recently the Teacher Training Authority (TTA), the body with responsibility for all ITT in England, had the opportunity to nail this particular misconception firmly while revising its general guidance to training institutions. Paragraph R1.8 of the final public draft of the revised guidance (TTA 2001: 16) stated that institutions providing ITT courses should 'recognise any degree of a United Kingdom higher education institution, or its equivalent, as an entry qualification for a postgraduate course of initial teacher training' and this was supported and praised by the CBA. On final publication, the recommendation had been removed. This does not imply any sinister Whitehall conspiracy against archaeology graduates, but it is another glaring example of the inability of the Heritage universe to impact upon the Education universe. We are left with the situation where graduates with single honours archaeology have to fight to be allowed onto both secondary and primary ITT courses. Those with joint honours fair better, as frequently they are accepted on the strength of their other subject.

The third element of the excluded past – that the historic environment has no relevance to modern society – is one that has been robustly questioned and countered by national heritage organisations. For example, the recent review of policies relating to the historic environment co-ordinated by English Heritage argued that the historic environment should be placed 'at the heart of education' (English Heritage 2000: 23). Recommendations (to be acted upon by government, the heritage and education sectors, and owners of historic properties) were made that would have facilitated such a positioning (2000: 23). Such a view has also recently been echoed by politicians. Writing in the Foreword of the government's response to *Power of Place*, the Secretaries of State for Culture, Media and Sport and for Environment, Transport and the Regions suggested that they needed to develop 'new policies to realise economic and educational potential' (DCMS/DETR 2001: 4). This DCMS/DETR report included no less than thirteen recommendations relating to realising the educational potential of the historic environment (2001: 16–23). Many of these will, no doubt, ensure that small steps are taken to enhance the educational potential of the historic environment. Unfortunately, as yet, I search in vain for the impact of such rhetoric on the daily delivery of history teaching and wonder if more might have been achieved had the Department for Education and Skills been involved in the drafting of the Report as well.

Finally, while it is not always particularly easy to see political interference in one's own backyard, there are obvious political implications of the choice of subject matter within the history syllabuses globally and, by implication, in the UK. One example will make the point. While prehistory is still essentially sidelined from the English history syllabus (only available as an option at Key Stage 2 as an example of local history) it is a strong element in the syllabuses in Scotland, Wales, and Northern Ireland. It has been suggested that such emphasis reflects an attempt by curriculum planners to establish national identity with its roots in a pre-union, pre-Christian world.

The above sounds overly pessimistic. There are significant and numerous opportunities for the integration of archaeology within the school curriculum. We have to be alert to such opportunities and move swiftly to make the most of them. Many archaeological units are already doing so (see, for example, Jones, Chapter 17; Malim, Chapter 15; and Smith, Chapter 16). Even developments that cause immediate concern, such as the usurpation of huge amounts of primary curriculum time by the literacy hour, can be turned into positive opportunities through the provision of literacy materials based on archaeology (see, for example, Northumberland National Park 2000). A number of agencies and, perhaps especially, museums are taking advantage of the requirements for pupils to have extensive Information Technology experience by developing interactive web materials (see for example, Cresswell Crags www.creswell-crags.org.uk/virtuallytheiceage; Museum of Antiquities available on: http://museums.ncl.ac.uk/archive/2002). In the English Curriculum 2000 the opportunities now provided by the Citizenship curriculum to introduce concepts of the value and implications of heritage may even begin to match those previously available through the broader-based curriculum in Scotland. We can only hope that the current review of the Scottish curriculum will not remove what has been a very effective opportunity. As a final example, the Green Paper on the revision of 14–19 education probably provides as many opportunities as it does threats. The real issue holding back the rapid expansion of archaeology within Further Education appears to be lack of trained staff rather than any lack of interest once courses are offered (and see Jones, Chapter 4). We must look to ways of nurturing and increasing a stock of archaeology tutors. At the same time, early discussions of the possibility of more practical and vocational 'hybrid' GCSE courses that might include elements of heritage alongside the more academic view of history should be seized upon and encouraged.

Higher education

The implications for higher education of the political aspiration to have 50 per cent of 18- to 30-year-olds involved in higher education by 2010 (DfES 2002) are still being assessed. What appears certain is that the significant increase in undergraduate student numbers that has been seen over the last few years, and that is set to continue if government pledges are to be achieved, can only deliver an educational standard comparable to the one that existed twenty years ago through a comparable increase in resources and staff. No such increases are apparent. As class size increases and staff size remains static (or in some instances actually drops) it is hard to see anything but a drop in standard. At the same time there appears to be a worrying downward trend in applications to study archaeology at undergraduate level. At present most archaeology undergraduate courses are meeting their (frequently increased) quotas – but from a reduced pool of applicants. Most university admissions tutors are understandably concerned, but argue that the quality of entrant has not (not yet at least) been affected. The real reasons for such a drop are hard to understand. Some point to an increased cautiousness amongst applicants in choosing degree programmes: if students are to graduate with a debt of some £10,000 or more (Davy 2002) they want to be sure that they will be able to pay off such a debt with some confidence. A glance at the opportunities afforded by the archaeology profession (average full-time wage of £17,079 (Aitchison 1999: 39), understandably puts some off. Many, perhaps encouraged by the present rash of television programmes (*Time Team, Meet the Ancestors,* and many others) that continue to equate archaeology essentially with excavation (and see West, Chapter 12), see an archaeology degree as a vocational qualification and not as what it frequently is: perhaps the most rounded general degree teaching critical thinking available in the twenty-first century. Whatever the reason, applications are falling and the profession should be more concerned than it appears to be.

My last sentence scratches at the surface of another major issue: I implied that the profession should be concerned with, and by extension might be expected to have an influence over, archaeology as taught within higher education. That an interest exists is clear (see, for example, Collis 2000). That influence exists is less clear as the fundamental obligation of those employed by universities to teach is to provide an education suitable for the majority of their students who will not spend the rest of their lives working within the profession. If university senior managers perceived archaeology at an undergraduate level to be a vocational degree, the number of archaeology departments in the country would be significantly reduced as quickly as redundancy or reallocation packages could be arranged for academic staff. Undergraduate archaeology cannot be expected to produce graduates able to move directly into any but the most junior posts within the profession. I know many colleagues within the profession who would argue that graduates from many, if not most, departments are not even suitably qualified for the most junior positions. The government-inspired increase in student numbers has only exacerbated a situation that has existed for a long time, and archaeology as a discipline has been trying to grapple with its role and function within higher education for many years (see Hamilakis and Rainbird, Chapter 5; Lassey, Chapter 11 and, for example, Stone 1983; Ucko 1983; Austin 1984; IFA 1987; Rainbird and Hamilakis 2001). In many ways the increase in student numbers has clarified the situation. Anecdotal evidence clearly indicates that a number of university archaeology departments are having to reduce the practical elements of their degree programmes as it is impossible to teach surveying, or technical drawing, or artefact handling to the number of 'customers' (students) being 'processed' (taught). Academic staff are in the process of radically overhauling not only their curricula but also the methodology of delivery and the whole pedagogical justification of teaching archaeology within Higher Education. McElearney (Chapter 13) reviews the developments in information and communication technology that offer some help in the restructuring and enhancement of learning, teaching, and assessment. However, while extremely valuable, especially in terms of generic key transferable skills, such ICT developments can never be the replacement for practical training in archaeological techniques.

As those teaching undergraduate degree programmes increasingly and honestly admit that they are not producing competent professionals the profession rightly questions where such training should, and can, be delivered. This debate has just had a new public airing as the new national 'Occupational Standards for Archaeological Practice' were revealed at the AGM of the Institute of Field Archaeologists in September 2002. It is a debate that will continue, quite correctly, over the coming years as the needs of the profession change. Only elements of this training requirement can be met by conventional degree programmes offered by universities, but the Occupational Standards will almost certainly have an increasingly important influence on the undergraduate curriculum. Other responses, such as continuing professional development courses, need to be designed and offered through collaboration between employers and training providers – including universities.

One response to the need for higher level and specialised professional training has been the significant increase in taught postgraduate programmes. The increase in such programmes appears to be welcomed both by university senior managers (as increasing postgraduate numbers bring in more revenue) and the profession as, at least in some cases, programmes are perceived to be tailored and structured with the needs of the profession in mind. My own university has seen such postgraduate provision expand from an initial intake of fourteen in 1994 to some hundred-plus students in 2002 across five specialised MA/M.Sc. programmes that range from Museum Studies to archaeological-based Geographical Information Systems. Gratifyingly, with respect to most of these particular degrees, the employment rate has been, and continues to be, some 80 per cent or more. Whether such a formula of delivering initial professional training through MA programmes will be flexible enough for future ever-changing professional require-ments, or economically viable given increasing student debt, remains to be seen. Certainly universities and employers need to develop closer working relationships to ensure that the needs of the sector are being met within a rigorous academic framework.

Lifelong learning

This book is not, however, only concerned with formal education. Sitting alongside the suggestion that the study of the historic environment can enhance the delivery of the school citizenship syllabus (Henson, Chapter 2) lies the long-held belief that archaeology can provide an important role within lifelong learning. Henry (Chapter 10) outlines the enormous success of the Young Archaeologists' Club (YAC) – a success that clearly demonstrates a continuing and developing interest in learning about the historic envi-ronment by a committed and increasingly large group of children. The Club aims to help develop 'inquisitive and well-rounded young people' (Chapter 10: 99) who will continue to have an interest in heritage issues throughout their lives. While some of these chil-dren do go on and carve out careers in the heritage sector (Club alumni include the present Chief Executive of English Heritage and the Director of the IFA) the real value of the Club lies not in the stimulation of the next generation of professionals but in the development of a concerned and supportive general public. An area that requires close attention and action, however, is the present situation where teenagers, who have to leave the Club at 16, are left without any form of continuing support. Provision of some form of support for the 16–19 age group is a crucial next step and is high on the CBA's agenda.

The nurturing of the development and stimulation of such concern and support is handed on by the YAC to those colleagues responsible for what used to be referred to as continuing education (Lock, Chapter 6). This is another area of education that has been radically modified through political intervention, with the most important (in this context) issue being the emphasis now placed on the delivery of formally assessed, accredited courses. Lock argues, however, that this emphasis should not mean that all lifelong learning needs to be formalised and accredited. There is certainly a place for accredited courses for adults but there is equally the need for opportunities to learn for learning's sake – for students, of whatever age, to enrol in courses that interest them and that will challenge them. Such an approach has, as Lock points out, a long tradition and secure theoretical educational credentials. For it to be discarded on the back of a political agenda that suggests *all* such learning be accredited through assessment would be a tragedy and a nonsense. Those fighting this political agenda are meeting with various levels of success but must be supported as much as possible: lifelong learning should not be hamstrung with the requirement that it *must* be accredited. Generations of people have and will continue to want to learn for the sake of increasing their knowledge and skills. While many may want formal recognition, many do not. To overtly, through government policy, or subversively, through funding arrangements developed as a knock-on effect of government policy, withdraw the opportunity to teach non-accredited programmes within adult/continuing education hits at the very heart of much extra-mural teaching of archaeology. Once again, the might of the Education universe flicks aside its weaker Heritage counterpart, perhaps not even realising the full implications of its actions.

The future

Two of the editors of this book (Henson and Stone) gave evidence in July 2002 to the All Party Parliamentary Archaeology Group (APPAG). APPAG was set up in 2001 by a group of cross-party MPs and Lords to carry out an enquiry into the current state of archaeology in the UK. A clear implication of the creation of the Group is that these politicians at least were less than satisfied with the (inadequate?) conclusions drawn in *Power of Place*. The Group, which numbers some 133 MPs and peers, has been hearing evidence from across the heritage sector and plans to publish its own report in late 2002. Questions ranged across the whole spectrum covered by this book, and our responses were listened to with care and consideration. Group members were struck with amazement when the current situation regarding access (or lack of it) for archaeology graduates to ITT courses was outlined. They also appeared sympathetic to our suggestion that some form of education or public outreach should be included within the new planning advice currently being revised and that perhaps Heritage Lottery Fund rules could be revised to allow for long-term revenue funding of education staff. Our overall impression was one of a supportive body of politicians ready to help whenever possible to attempt to deliver a closer relationship between my two universes. The Group will not, and cannot, change the world overnight and are concerned with the whole of archaeology within the UK, not just its relationship with education. However, those striving for wider teaching of the historic environment now have identifiable, influential supporters.

Through its various education committees the CBA has been fighting to strengthen the role of archaeology and the historic environment within lifelong learning for the past fifty years. Partly as the result of this work, the educational use of the historic environment has probably never been so secure. The following chapters demonstrate how it is supported by national heritage agencies, universities, and an increasing number of archaeological units. However, this does not mean that anyone involved in it should be complacent or that they should think the struggle is over. Generations of teachers were supported through the University of Sheffield's 'Archaeology in Education' project. The project ended, after twenty-one years, in 2000 (Brannigan 2000). A smaller impact was made by the 'Archaeology and Education' project run from the University of Southampton between 1985 and 1988 (Corbishley and Stone 1994: 385). The initiatives begun by these projects, and their influence, have been widespread – but no present university department has seen fit to continue their work. This is partly because their role has been supplemented by the many initiatives taken on by archaeology units. It is partly because of the work of English Heritage, the other national agencies, and the CBA and CSA; it is partly because of the pressures under which all university departments are at present. Regardless of the reasons, their demise should act as a warning to those interested in the teaching of the past through the historic environment. In exactly the same way, the history of Northamptonshire Heritage Education Service should serve as a constant reminder to us all of just how fragile even the best of local authority work can be (Pearson, Chapter 14). Given these warning signs, and the opportunities provided by an ever-changing education sector, there is much still to be done by the CBA.

The struggle goes on and no one should think that it is going to require anything but additional effort. We shall have to be inventive and seize every opportunity, however tangential to our core work. The following chapters reveal a success story delivered in adversity through long attrition and ingenuity. They should serve as a beacon to all of us to seize our chances to help facilitate and deliver the better, and integrated, educational use of the historic environment.

■ ■ ■

References

Aitchison, K. (1999) *Profiling the Profession: A Survey of Archaeological Jobs in the UK*, London: Council for British Archaeology, English Heritage, Institute of Field Archaeologists.

Antiquity (2000) Special section: Archaeology in education. In *Antiquity* 74: 122–218.

Austin, D. (1984) *Archaeology Courses in British Universities: A Report by the British Universities Archaeology Committee*, Lampeter: St David's University College.

Brannigan, K. (2000) 'All good things come to an end . . .', *Archaeology in Education* newsletter, May.

Collis, J. (2000) Towards a national training scheme, *Antiquity* 74: 208–214.

Corbishley, M. and Stone, P. (1994) The teaching of the past in formal school curricula in England. In P.G. Stone and B.L. Molyneaux (eds) *The Presented Past: Heritage, Museums and Education*, London: Routledge, 383–397.

Council for British Archaeology (1944) Preliminary report of the Sub-committee on Archaeology and Education for submission to the Executive Committee of the Council for British Archaeology. Unpublished.

Council for British Archaeology (1956) Unpublished report on conference on schools and archaeology, CBA: London.

Davy, P. (2002) Red alert. In the *Guardian* 2002, 1 October. Available online: http://money.guardian.co.uk/creditanddebt/studentfinance/story/0,1456,798018,00.html (accessed 7 October).

Department for Culture, Media and Sport and Department for Environment, Transport and the Regions (2001) *The Historic Environment: A Force for Our Future*, London: DCMS.

Department for Education and Skills (2002) 14–19: Extending opportunities, raising standards. Available: http://www.dfes.gov.uk/14–19greenpaper/ (accessed 7 October).

English Heritage (2000) *Power of Place: The Future of the Historic Environment*, London: HMSO.

Gawe, S. and Meli, F. (1990) The missing past in South African history. In P.G. Stone and R. MacKenzie (eds) *The Excluded Past: Archaeology in Education*, London: Unwin Hyman, 98–108.

Institute of Field Archaeologists (1987) *Archaeology in the Universities: Submission to the UGC Arts Sub-Committee Working Party from the Institute of Field Archaeologists*, Birmingham: University of Birmingham.

Jameson, J. (ed.) (1997) *Presenting Archaeology to the Public: Digging for Truths*, Walnut Creek, Calif.: AltaMira Press.

MacKenzie, R. and Stone, P.G. (1990) Introduction: the concept of the excluded past. In P.G. Stone and R. MacKenzie (eds) *The Excluded Past: Archaeology in Education*, London: Unwin Hyman, 1–14.

Museum of Antiquities (2002) Available: http://museums.ncl.ac.uk/archive/ (accessed 7 October).

National Curriculum for England (2002) Available: http://www.nc.uk.net (accessed 7 October).

Northumberland National Park (2000) *'The Lost Palace' Resource Pack*, Hexham: Northumberland National Park Authority.

Rainbird, P. and Hamilakis, Y. (2001) *Interrogating Pedagogies: Archaeology in Higher Education, Lampeter Workshop in Archaeology 3*, BAR International Series 948, Oxford: Archaeopress.

Richardson, W. (ed.) (1989) *CBA Education Bulletin 6* (Papers presented to the Archaeology Meets Education conference, Southampton, 1987), London: CBA.

Schmidt, M. (1999) Reconstruction as ideology: the open air museum at Oerlinghausen. In P.G. Stone and P. Planel, *The Constructed Past: Experimental Archaeology, Education, and the Public*, London: Routledge, 146–156.

Smardz, K. and Smith, S. (eds) (2000) *The Archaeology in Education Handbook*, Walnut Creek, Calif.: AltaMira Press.

Sommer, U. (1999) Slavonic archaeology: Grob Raden, an open air museum in a unified Germany. In P.G. Stone and P. Planel, *The Constructed Past: Experimental Archaeology, Education, and the Public*, London: Routledge, 157–170.

Stone, P.G. (1983) Unpublished report to the British Universities Archaeology Committee Working Party on the state of archaeology in British universities.

Stone, P.G. and MacKenzie, R. (eds) (1990) *The Excluded Past: Archaeology in Education*, London: Unwin Hyman.

Stone, P.G. and Molyneaux, B. (eds) (1994) *The Presented Past: Heritage, Museums and Education*, London: Routledge.

Teacher Training Agency (2001) *Requirements for the Provision of Initial Teacher Training*, London: Teacher Training Agency.

Ucko, P. (1983) Unpublished chairman's report to the British Universities Archaeology Committee Working Party on the state of archaeology in British universities.

Vargas Arenas, I. and Sanoja Obediente, M. (1990) Education and the political manipulation of history in Venezuela. In P.G. Stone and R. MacKenzie (eds) *The Excluded Past: Archaeology in Education*, London: Unwin Hyman, 50–60.

PART ONE

The Present State of Education in the United Kingdom

Chapter 1

THE EDUCATIONAL FRAMEWORK IN THE UNITED KINGDOM

Don Henson

There have been major changes to the structure of education in the last twenty years and the pace of change has shown no signs of slowing down. It is only possible here to highlight a selection of the reforms and developments. Much is omitted and anyone wanting to go into more detail should consult books such as Chitty (1999) and Mackinnon and Statham (1999).

The organisation of education in the United Kingdom

There is no single education system in the United Kingdom as a whole. While the United Kingdom parliament retains control of education in England, control in the rest of the country has been devolved to the Scottish Parliament, the Welsh National Assembly and the Northern Ireland Assembly. Within each of these areas there is a complex hierarchy of organisations and structures that covers education from school up to higher education (Figure 1.1). Some organisations cover only one part of the United Kingdom while others operate more widely. Figure 1.1 is very much a summarised picture with many organisations omitted (e.g. OFSTED and the new Adult Learning Inspectorate). The most divergent of the nations within the United Kingdom is Scotland, which has historically kept its own education system even before devolution. It can be expected that the differences between the various parts of the United Kingdom will increase now that devolution has been put into place.

The framework of qualifications (Table 1.1) is also complex, with Scotland again differing from the rest of the United Kingdom.

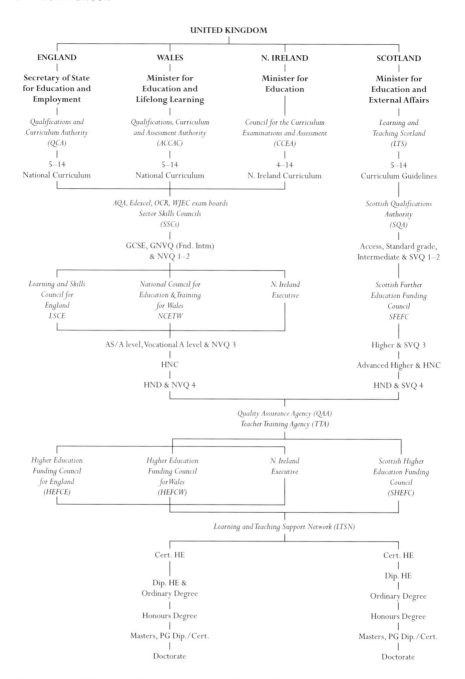

Figure 1.1   Educational frameworks in the United Kingdom

Table 1.1 Qualifications frameworks in the United Kingdom

England, Wales, N. Ireland

Level	Qualifications and Stages		
School curriculum	Key Stage 1		
	Key Stage 2		
	Key Stage 3		
Entry	Certificate of Achievement		
Foundation	GCSE D–G	GNVQ – foundation	NVQ 1
Intermediate	GCSE A*–C	GNVQ – intermediate	NVQ 2
Advanced	GCE – AS/A level	AVCE	NVQ 3
HE1	Cert. HE, HNC		
HE2	Dip. HE, HND, Ordinary Degree, Foundation Degree		NVQ 4
HE3	Honours Degree		
HE4	PG Cert., Dip., Masters		NVQ 5
HE5	Doctorate		

Scotland

Level	Qualifications and Stages		
School curriculum	P1–3		
	P4–6		
	P7–S2		
1	SNQ – Access 1		
2	SNQ – Access 2		
3	Standard – foundation	SNQ – Access 3	
4	Standard – general	SNQ – Intermediate 1	SVQ 1
5	Standard – credit	SNQ – Intermediate 2	SVQ 2
6	SNQ – Higher		SVQ 3
7 (HE1)	SNQ – Advanced Higher, Cert. HE, HNC		
8 (HE2)	Dip. HE, HND		SVQ4
9 (HE3)	Ordinary Degree		
10 (HE4)	Honours Degree (incl. MA)		
11 (HE5)	PG Cert., PG Dip., Masters		SVQ 5
12 (HE6)	Doctorate		

Much of the complexity has arisen in recent years with the development of vocational qualifications at 14+, and the attempt to relate these to existing educational levels. In higher education, there is a great deal of variety in the terminology for qualifications used by different institutions. The Quality Assurance Agency has recently devised a national framework which it is hoped will help to standardise terminology in the future, although the framework is not mandatory. While responsibility for validating NVQs, HNC and HND courses lies with organisations dealing with school and further education, they can be equated with university level qualifications, which adds further complexity to the system. For example, the Advanced Higher grade of the Scottish National Qualification is rated as equivalent to HNC but is also widely regarded as equivalent to A-level, which is definitely rated lower than HNC in the rest of the United Kingdom.

The place of archaeology in the scheme of qualifications is outlined in Table 1.2. Although this focuses on the place of archaeology by name, it is important to realise that archaeological skills may also be taught outside named archaeology or history topics. It is particularly important to accept that archaeology has cross-curricular applications in schools, and that many new initiatives in teaching can and should be targeted for archaeological input (e.g. education for sustainable development).

5–14 education

The advent of the National Curriculum (implemented firstly in England in 1988) saw some advance for archaeology in the teaching of history. All the curricula orders and guidelines in the different parts of the United Kingdom stressed the importance of using non-documentary evidence for history. In England, Wales and Northern Ireland this took the form of stipulating the use of artefacts, buildings and sites. It is only possible to study the whole range of evidence for the past by using written documents alongside visiting the historic environment to see archaeological remains and actively engage in historical enquiry. It is, however, noteworthy that the word 'archaeology' was only used in the section of the original history orders in England that dealt with ancient civilisations (e.g. ancient Egypt). There were some interesting differences between the different history curricula. The curriculum in England began with the Romans, with no mention of prehistory other than the example of the neolithic revolution at Key Stage 3. In this respect, the National Curriculum marked a retrograde step since the Ministry of Education pamphlet of 1952 which noted that most schools were including prehistory among the topics taught in first year of secondary school. In contrast, in Wales, perceived continuity with the 'Celtic' Iron Age led to a curriculum that began with prehistoric hunter-gatherers. Scotland, covering areas that lay mostly outside the Roman province of Britain, likewise began with the ancient world, although this would be interpreted mostly as dealing with ancient civilisations rather than northern British prehistory. The National Curriculum also saw the entrenchment of many previous

Table 1.2 Archaeology qualifications in the United Kingdom

Level of education	Qualification or stage	Archaeology
School curriculum	Infants	History (England): artefacts, historic buildings, museums and sites under historical enquiry
	Juniors	History (England): archaeologists mentioned under historical interpretation; artefacts, historic buildings, museums and sites under historical enquiry; prehistoric settlers under local history study; Hadrian's Wall, Sutton Hoo, Jorvik and Tudor buildings are also mentioned elsewhere; Ancient Greece and a world history study (e.g. ancient Egypt etc.)
	Secondary	History (England): archaeologists mentioned under historical interpretation; artefacts, museums, buildings and sites under historical enquiry; the neolithic revolution under European study before 1914; art and architecture 1066–1500 and 1500–1750; a world study before 1900 (e.g. Peruvian or Islamic civilisations)
Foundation and Intermediate	GCSE	AQA GCSE Archaeology at 72 colleges and schools
	GCSE	Schools History Project GCSE Assignment – History around Us can include artefacts, buildings and sites, and must be based on a visit to a historical site
	Intermediate 2	SGA Land and Environment optional unit D84211 – Field Archaeology
	NVQ 1–2	JQU Environmental Conservation unit 940–08 – Field Archaeology 1 JQU Environmental Conservation unit 940–09 – Field Archaeology 2 *Note: these are not NVQs but are notionally equivalent to NVQ levels 1 and 2*
Advanced	AS/A level	AQA AS/A level Archaeology at 128 colleges and schools *Note: 174 colleges and schools offering GCSE or AS/A level*
	GNVQ	GNVQ Leisure and Tourism: additional unit 25 – Heritage Tourism
	Higher	SGA Land and Environment optional unit D84212 – Field Archaeology

Table 1.2 continued

Level of education	Qualification or stage	Archaeology
Higher education – initial	Cert. CE	15 certificates from 10 universities
	Cert. HE	38 certificates and 7 diplomas from 28 universities
	HNC	4 HNCs from 4 institutions
Higher education – middle	Dip. HE	7 certificates and 12 diplomas from 12 universities *Note: 31 universities offering certificates or diplomas through CE*
	HND	6 HNDs from 6 institutions *Note: 8 colleges or universities offering HNC or HND*
Honours degree	BA, B.Sc., MA (Scot.)	69 single honours degrees from 33 universities +250 possible joint or combined honours degrees from 40 universities; archaeology as modules in other degrees from 8 universities
Postgraduate	MA, M.Sc., M.Litt., M.Phil.	155 taught Masters degrees from 41 universities *Note: 77 departments in 54 universities teaching archaeology to honours degree or postgraduate level*
Other	No qualifications	Leisure courses offered by university CE departments, the WEA and other providers

ideas about teaching history. In particular, the periods taught ranged from the Romans to the twentieth century, with increasing emphasis on more modern history at the higher age ranges of secondary education.

The revised curriculum orders from 2000 in England are more positive for archaeology. For the first time, prehistoric settlers have been mentioned at Key Stage 2 and the work of archaeologists is recognised as contributing towards an understanding of how we interpret the past. The new orders have been backed up by exemplar schemes of work which will become the blueprint from which many teachers (if not most) will derive their lesson plans. It is unfortunate therefore that, as noted above, the schemes for Key Stage 3 are much more focused on the use of classroom-based written or photographic sources than those for Key Stages 1 and 2.

Post-14 education

Education at post-14 has also undergone great change in recent years. The landscape of education at this level was set by the development of academic-style qualifications, the General Certificate of Education (GCE) Ordinary (O) and Advanced (A) levels in 1951, and the Certificate of Secondary Education (CSE) in 1965. A wide variety of other non-academic qualifications were also offered but suffered from lesser status than the GCE. The O level and CSE were later combined as the General Certificate of Secondary Education (GCSE). The number of students taking archaeology at this level has increased dramatically. There were just twenty-five students nationwide studying for the archaeology A-level in 1970. By 2000, archaeology was available as a GCSE, AS and A-level, with 1,227 students sitting exams in one of these. The development of a new modular structure for AS and A-level, with students being encouraged to study more AS-level subjects in their first year, should benefit popular subjects like archaeology. Although it is too early to tell, there are indications that numbers studying archaeology will increase within the new structure. Scotland has seen the recent establishment of a new National Qualification to provide an equivalent to GCSE and A-levels, which combines flexibility with a complexity that makes the English system seem simple. It is too soon as yet to see how this new system will operate in practice, or how it will need to be modified in the future. However, it is encouraging that archaeology is present as a module at both Intermediate 2 and Higher level in the Scottish National Qualification.

A major development has been the creation of a national system of vocational and semi-vocational qualifications as an alternative to the traditional academic style pathway. The high levels of unemployment suffered in the 1980s led to an increased recognition of the need to improve potential employees' skills and provide more job-related training. One result of this was the General National Vocational Qualification (GNVQ), which since 1993 (now called the Advanced Vocational Certificate of Education, or vocational A-level, at advanced grade) has offered a flexible approach to learning about vocational areas and provided key skills required by employers. Archaeology can be offered as part of an optional unit within the Leisure and Tourism GNVQ. Parallel to the GCSE/GCE and GNVQ is the National or Scottish Vocational Qualification (NVQ/SVQ), designed to demonstrate competence in work-based tasks for people in employment or on work placements. Although national standards for the development of archaeology NVQs were created, NVQs in archaeology were not taken up. The development of the new qualification came too soon for archaeology, which had not at that time assessed its training needs as a profession. Since then, the Archaeology Training Forum has been set up by the leading archaeological bodies to co-ordinate an archaeological approach to training which will eventually lead to training opportunities appropriate to the profession.

Higher and continuing education

Access to university education had expanded slowly since the nineteenth century with the foundation of universities outside Cambridge, Oxford and the four ancient Scottish universities of Aberdeen, Edinburgh, Glasgow and St Andrews. Fifteen new universities were established between 1824 and 1926, but the major expansion was the creation of twenty institutions between 1961 and 1967, alongside the Education Act of 1962 that put in place a system of mandatory maintenance grants for undergraduate study through Local Education Authorities. University education thus became more accessible to students from a wider range of social backgrounds. Further expansion followed, with the founding of the Open University in 1969 providing courses through distance learning for adult students. However, the world of higher education has been transformed in recent years. Student loans have now replaced maintenance grants and students have been charged tuition fees since 1998. The number of universities has expanded greatly since 1988 with the raising of polytechnics and colleges of higher education to the same status as universities. Archaeology has benefited from this expansion of institutions and student numbers. The first CBA guide to archaeology in universities (Roe 1979) listed twenty-four archaeology departments and thirty-four universities teaching some sort of undergraduate archaeology. In the latest guide (Henson 1999), this had increased to twenty-eight archaeology departments and a further forty-five other departments in fifty-two universities teaching undergraduate or postgraduate archaeology. One of the growth areas has been in continuing education (what used to be termed 'university extra-mural teaching'), where the tradition of universities offering liberal adult education courses has been largely replaced by a range of qualifications available by part-time study. In the academic year 1999–2000, there were fifty-four archaeology certificate courses, twenty-five diplomas, nine undergraduate degrees and two postgraduate degrees available through continuing education. In addition, there were over a thousand course units available for study, most of them credit bearing. The number of people studying archaeology by this method rivals the number studying by traditional full-time higher education.

■ ■ ■

References

Chitty, C. (1999) *The Education System Transformed*, Tisbury: Baseline Books.

Henson, D. (1999) *2000 CBA Guide to Archaeology in Higher Education*, York: Council for British Archaeology.

Mackinnon, D. and Statham, J. (1999) *Education in the United Kingdom: Facts and Figures*, London: Hodder & Stoughton and the Open University.

Roe, F. (1979) *Guide to Undergraduate University Courses in Archaeology*, London: Council for British Archaeology.

Chapter 2

ARCHAEOLOGY IN SCHOOLS

Don Henson

> The errors of former times are recorded for our instruction
> in order that we may avoid their repetition.
>
> William Gladstone, 1879, from a speech
> given in Midlothian

Introduction

Archaeology is not a topic that features as a separate subject within
the school curricula in the United Kingdom. However, archaeological evidence and techniques have to form part of history and also
contribute towards aspects of geography and science. Enterprising
teachers will also be able to make use of archaeology within most
other subjects taught in school. In this chapter, I will concentrate
on the use of archaeology within history teaching, since this is
currently where the bulk of archaeological evidence is actually used
in schools. Henson (1997) should be consulted for information
about archaeology within other subjects.

The frameworks for teaching history

It needs to be pointed out that there is no national curriculum for
schools in the United Kingdom. Instead, there are four separate
curricula for the individual nations within the United Kingdom:
England, Scotland, Wales and Northern Ireland. The curricula in
England, Wales and Northern Ireland are very similar in structure
and share much common content. That for Scotland is very different

in both structure and content. In addition, the Scottish curriculum is issued as non-mandatory guidelines, whereas the curriculum is statutory in the rest of the United Kingdom. The Scottish curriculum guidelines refer to history as 'people in the past' within environmental studies, alongside 'people and place' and 'people in society'. The major differences between the curricula are listed in Table 2.1. The Scottish curriculum is currently being revised. References here are to the existing guidelines unless otherwise stated. The curriculum in Northern Ireland is also undergoing revision.

Archaeology and history are both concerned with studying the evidence of the past, and share many aims (cf. Elton 1967; Rahtz 1985). The most comprehensive statement of the aims of studying history in schools is contained in the revised curriculum orders for England (DfEE and QCA 1999a, 1999b), which offer a statement outlining the distinctive contribution of history to the school curriculum ('The Importance of History'). These aims can be grouped into three sets based on what we learn from our study of the past. The three sets are:

● Learning about the past: knowledge and understanding of the events and features of past times.

Table 2.1   Major differences between the history curricula in the United Kingdom

England	Wales	Northern Ireland	Scotland
Statutory			Guidelines only
Knowledge, understanding and skills include chronology, historical content, change, nature of evidence, interpretation, enquiry, communicating the results of an enquiry			The same, plus developing informed attitudes, considering the meaning of heritage and ways of preserving the past
The medieval period begins in the eleventh century			Medieval begins in 400
Periods topics begin with the Romans	Period topics begin with prehistory		
Local history occurs at Key Stage 2	Local history occurs at Key Stages 2 and 3	Local history is optional	Local history is not specifically mentioned as a topic
Non-period topics include European and world history, including ancient Greece	Thematic topics, e.g. seafaring, castles and cathedrals, exploration and encounters, migration and emigration	Choice of thematic topics, European or world history	Pupils must look at Scottish, British, European and world contexts

- Learning from the past: deriving lessons for the present from the past and from using historical methodology.
- Learning to use the past: the past used as heritage in the present.

The aims as given in the distinctive contribution statement broadly reflect the opinions of the original History Working Group in 1990 who produced a list of reasons why history should be studied in schools (Bourdillon 1994: 27–40). The relationship between the two is shown in Table 2.2. The most important change since 1990 is that only one of the Working Group's aims concerned learning *about* the past, while the new orders have reinforced this with two further statements. This has reduced the importance of learning *from* the past, which was the strongest element within the Working Group's aims. If learning about the past is reinforced at the expense of learning from the past, then the effect is to increase the separation of the past from the present. History becomes a voyeuristic exercise whose major purpose is simply to accumulate knowledge of 'what happened when'. This could result in history being seen as little other than entertainment with little relevance for people living now. Thus, there will be a danger that those disciplines that study the past – history and archaeology – will be seen as having little social utility.

There is one notable feature missing from the curricula in England, Wales and Northern Ireland that has an important place within the Scottish guidelines. A concern for the past as a physical heritage to be preserved for future generations is reflected in the attainment target 'developing informed attitudes' laid down for the social subjects within environmental studies. Part of this attainment target states that pupils should 'appreciate and take a responsible part in preserving records, evidence and experience of the present and past as aspects of the character and heritage of the local and wider community' (the proposed revision waters this down to 'the importance of preserving their social and cultural heritage'). The presence of this attainment target in the history curriculum in Scotland can be readily understood by comparing the aims of history in the two countries. The document *Scottish History in the Curriculum* in 1997 laid down a set of aims which closely mirrored those for England apart from one important exception. This was that a key aim for history in Scotland was to underpin Scotland's tourist and heritage industries (SCCC 1997: 3). This is not surprising, given Scotland's greater degree of national self-consciousness, as compared to that in England, and the marketing of an explicitly Scottish cultural identity within the tourism industry. While its absence in England may therefore be understandable, it is perhaps surprising that the curricula in Wales and Northern Ireland also lack a dimension dealing with the issue of caring for heritage.

Putting aims into practice

How the aims of teaching history are incorporated in the curriculum orders will tell us a great deal about how the teaching of history is carried out in practice,

Table 2.2 The aims of history in the English National Curriculum

History Working Group 1990	2000 curriculum: the distinctive contribution of history	Learning
Arouses interest in the past	History fires pupils' curiosity about the past in Britain and the wider world	About the past
	As they do this, pupils develop a chronological framework for their knowledge of significant events and people	About the past
Helps understand the present in the context of the past	Pupils consider how the past influences the present	From the past
	Pupils consider what past societies were like, how these societies organised their politics, and what beliefs and cultures influenced people's actions	About the past
Contributes to knowledge and understanding of other cultures	They see the diversity of human experience	From the past
Helps give pupils a sense of identity and understanding of their own cultural roots	They understand more about themselves as individuals and members of society. What they learn can influence their decisions about personal choices, attitudes and values	To use the past
Prepares pupils for adult life	In history, pupils find evidence, weigh it up and reach their own conclusions. To do	From the past
Trains the mind by means of disciplined study and introduces pupils to the methodology of historians	this they need to be able to research, sift through evidence, and argue for their point of view – skills that are prized in adult life	From the past

and so how pupils' ideas of history (and by extension archaeology) will be formed. I will take the new curriculum in England as a test case. Comparing the distinctive contribution statement with the curriculum content reveals an interesting pattern (Table 2.3). Curriculum content is divided into 'knowledge, skills and understanding' and 'breadth of study'. It is noteworthy that the 'knowledge, skills and understanding' address either historical methodology or the content of knowledge about the past. Even the period and area topics within the breadth of study largely address those aims which are concerned with teaching about the past itself, rather than helping pupils understand the connections between past and present. How this is to be achieved is not made explicit within the new orders. It is assumed

Table 2.3   Comparing aims of history with curriculum content

Aims	Curriculum content	
Distinctive contribution of history to the school curriculum	Knowledge, skills and understanding	Breadth of study
History fires pupils' curiosity about the past in Britain and the wider world		All areas
As they do this, pupils develop a chronological framework for their knowledge of significant events and people	● Chronological understanding	All areas
Pupils consider how the past influences the present		
Pupils consider what past societies were like, how these societies organised their politics, and what beliefs and cultures influenced people's actions	● Events, people and changes in the past	All areas
They see the diversity of human experience		Local, British, European and world studies
They understand more about themselves as individuals and members of society. What they learn can influence their decisions about personal choices, attitudes and values		
In history, pupils find evidence, weigh it up and reach their own conclusions. To do this they need to be able to research, sift through evidence, and argue for their point of view – skills that are prized in adult life	● Historical interpretation ● Historical enquiry ● Organising and communicating	

that somehow pupils will understand how the present and future depend on a knowledge of the past through a knowledge simply of 'what happened when'. It is clear that the narrative story of past events dominates thinking about teaching history, with the effect of obscuring the wider social utility of the subject.

It is in the new citizenship dimension of the National Curriculum in England that a wider justification for archaeology can be found. There are citizenship guidelines for Key Stages 1 and 2, and statutory orders for citizenship as a mandatory subject at Key Stages 3 and 4 from 2002. Archaeology can be used to teach various aspects of the guidelines and orders. For example, the guidelines for Key Stage 1 state that children should be taught 'what improves and harms their local, natural and built environments and about some of the ways people look after them'. The recent events surrounding the discovery and excavation of the timber circle on the Norfolk coast, the so-called 'Seahenge' (Champion 2000), and the resulting TV and media interest, would have been an ideal topic to use at Key Stage 3 where there is a requirement to 'think about topical political, spiritual, moral, social and cultural issues, problems and events by analysing information and its sources, including ICT-based sources'.

However, it is worth noting that the citizenship guidelines and orders make no specific reference to archaeological heritage (unless included under 'built environment' or just 'environment'). Therefore, the use of archaeology as a basis for teaching citizenship will not be obvious to most teachers. We will need to exercise some ingenuity in persuading teachers we can offer them the resources for teaching the subject. Reference is made in the guidelines and orders to the environment and sustainability. These are issues to which archaeology can contribute and are aspects of the wider social utility of the subject. That the curriculum has not specifically included the historic dimension of the environment, or applied the notion of sustainability explicitly to historic cultural resources, is perhaps a demonstration of the marginal position of archaeology in the consciousness of those responsible both for the education system in England and for environmental management.

Lessons for archaeology

There are lessons in the above for archaeology. Most writers identify archaeology simply with the study of people's behaviour through material culture (Wheeler 1954; Clarke 1968; Shanks and Tilley 1992). However, a more encompassing definition is that of Rahtz, though we would now replace 'man' with 'people' or some other non-gender-specific term:

> Archaeology is the study of material culture in its relationship to human behaviour . . . It is also concerned with the environment in which mankind has developed and in which man still lives.
>
> (Rahtz 1985: 1)

This wider definition, with its inclusion of the environment, provides archaeology with a link to current environmental concerns, including issues of sustainability. It is a strength of archaeology that it can inform us about the mutual interaction of people with their environment over the long timescales necessary for disentangling climatic from human factors. It is thus well placed to provide a historical dimension to environmental issues and put current ecological concerns into a wider perspective. As we have seen, history is treated as part of environmental studies in the Scottish school curriculum, whereas in England and Wales the historical disciplines are not linked with studies of the environment. Indeed, it is common to find schools forcing pupils to decide between history or geography as mutually exclusive options for GCSE.

Understanding that the environment is ever-changing and that even supposedly 'natural' landscapes are the result of thousands of years of human exploitation should be a major message of archaeology. Unfortunately, in many people's minds archaeology is still simply the study of the material remains of the past. Even some archaeologists seem to forget Wheeler's words (1954: 18): 'Too often we dig up mere things, unrepentantly forgetful that our proper aim is to dig up people.'

The concentration of archaeologists on material remains, perhaps best exemplified by Clarke's approach to archaeological theory in his *Analytical Archaeology* of 1968, is matched by the media's obsession with spectacular finds like the 'ice man, Ötzi', or exotic civilisations like ancient Egypt or the Aztecs. In spite of the best efforts of programmes like *Time Team* and *Meet the Ancestors*, it is the perceived domination of archaeology by artefacts and sites which serves to hide the wider behavioural and environmental concerns of the discipline.

This misapprehension of purpose is also shared by history, where the aim of the discipline is often seen as deriving from the past a narrative story of what actually happened. Narrative is easy to understand; it often involves interesting events and, above all, involves named individuals with whom people can identify. In this way learning *about* the past becomes the dominant perceived aim of the subject while learning *from* the past is hidden behind the seductive appeal of the narrative. It is not surprising, therefore, that the teaching of history in schools is based so strongly on period-specific study, nor that archaeology is mainly seen as contributing material evidence to support the creation of historical narrative through the requirement to use artefacts, buildings and historic sites as sources of evidence for the past. It also provides one possible reason for the absence of mandatory prehistory in the English history curriculum, since prehistory is incapable of supplying narrative content.

The wider purposes of archaeology are poorly represented in the way that many archaeologists communicate with the public. The emphasis on the publication of site reports, the studies of particular places, the monographs on particular artefacts or types of site, and even the period-based accounts of how people lived at particular times in the past all fail to get across why archaeology is important (how it helps us to learn from the past). Archaeology and history are often seen as mere 'back-looking curiositie' (Camden, in Bahn 1996: 2). This has meant that the actual practice of teaching the past in schools tends to focus on describing 'what happened when' rather than linking past and present to derive lessons for the future. This leads to a view of archaeology and history as interesting subjects but of marginal importance to society as a whole.

Linking archaeology with learning

Some way of relating archaeology to present-day society is needed if the discipline is to be accepted as important. The need for archaeology to justify its existence has been amply demonstrated by the actual and proposed cuts made to archaeology services in recent years (Morris 1999). There are many politicians and journalists who would undoubtedly agree with Bahn (1996: 6) that 'Archaeology is undeniably a "luxury" subject, which constantly needs to justify its existence . . .'

I suggest that archaeologists, and historians, need to differentiate clearly between the objects and the results of their studies. The main object of study is the past itself; a set of objectively verifiable facts. These are things that can be described and measured with greater or lesser degrees of accuracy. Analysis of these 'facts' leads to the production of histories; interpretations that seek to explain the past by producing accounts of the reasons for change or motivation behind events. Both the remains of the past and of previous interpretations exist as objects in the present and together form the heritage of a community or society. These three categories – the past, histories and heritage – can be linked through the processes of recovery, interpretation and creation to three different kinds of educational process; that is, we learn about the past, we learn from histories and we learn to use heritage. An example of how such a scheme might work in practice is given in Table 2.4, based on the wooden circle found in 1999 off the Norfolk coast ('Seahenge').

This threefold scheme can be used to help make archaeology better understood by society at large (Table 2.4). It helps us to clarify what we do and focuses our attention on the different aspects of the discipline. Archaeologists commonly communicate the past and the histories we base on that past. However, we also need to ensure that we involve people more in the recovery of the past and the creation of their own heritage. The past itself cannot be owned; it happened and is now gone, but its previous existence is there to be shared by any with an interest in it. The remains of that past (the physical heritage), however, are owned by individuals and by organisations. Conflicts over this ownership are common (e.g. the Elgin Marbles, the Lewis chessmen or the Lindisfarne Gospels). Archaeology has a great responsibility to recognise that communities often regard the physical remains of the past as part of their own heritage and need to involve people fully in the curation of that heritage. By involving people in the recovery of evidence of the past and the curation of physical heritage, we are also involving them in the transmission of the interpretations we place on the remains of the past (their intellectual heritage). However, this is not all. We also need to empower people to create their own histories (their own interpretations of the past) and to create their own heritage, both physical and intellectual. We need to do this to avoid falling into the trap of intellectual and professional arrogance, assuming that we as archaeologists have sole rights of investigating and owning the past and its remains. We cannot be accepted by society as a useful discipline, worth fostering and protecting, if we set ourselves above that society as the intellectual few acting on behalf of the ignorant many. In this, we need to learn the lessons of the school curricula, which seek to equip pupils not just with historical knowledge but also with the skills to make their own judgements and interpretations (see Table 2.5).

■   ■   ■

Table 2.4   The past, histories and heritage at 'Seahenge'

The past	Histories	Heritage
The physical remains – sites, artefacts, manuscripts, pictures (e.g.: a ring of wooden posts and central upturned tree base)	Set interpretations of periods or events, creating a reconstruction (e.g.: a mortuary structure linked to solar mythology or a point of religious power linking humans and the natural/spiritual world)	Heritage sites, artefact collections, historical myths (e.g.: *past* – a site to be contested between local and national concerns; *history* – an interpretation debated between archaeologists and others)

The above are processed as follows:

Recovering the evidence (e.g.: excavation, survey)	Interpreting the evidence (e.g.: chronology, method of construction, alignment)	Creating historical commodities (e.g.: the *past* – creating a reconstruction of the site; *history* – adoption of the site as a symbol of human–earth relationship by modern 'druids')

The above processes can be used for the following types of learning:

Learning about the 'facts' of the past (e.g.: planning the site, measuring the posts, describing the axe marks on the surface of the timbers, finding out how it was built)	Learning from the events and features of the past (e.g.: appreciating different views to our own of the treatment of the dead, valuing simple technological capabilities)	Learning to use the past and our created histories for pleasure, profit or to justify the present (e.g.: *past* – the basis for a peak time TV programme; *history* – using the site to make a point about present-day lack of care for the environment)

Table 2.5   Processes involved in archaeological education

Education = communication, involvement and empowerment through:
- recovering remains of the past in order to learn about the past
- analysing the evidence to produce interpretive histories in order to learn from the past
- converting remains into commodities as heritage to enable people to make use of the past

References

Bahn, P. (1996) *Archaeology: A Very Short Introduction*, Oxford: Oxford University Press.

Bourdillon, H. (1994) *Teaching History*, London: Routledge.

Champion, M. (2000) *Seahenge: A Contemporary Chronicle*, North Walsham: Barnwells Timescape.

Clarke, D.L. (1968) *Analytical Archaeology*, London: Methuen.

Department for Education and Employment and Qualifications and Curriculum Authority (1999a) *The National Curriculum: Handbook for Primary Teachers in England*, London: HMSO.

Department for Education and Employment and Qualifications and Curriculum Authority (1999b) *The National Curriculum: Handbook for Secondary Teachers in England*, London: HMSO.

Elton, G.R. (1967) *The Practice of History*, London: Fontana Press.

Henson, D. (1997) *Archaeology in the English National Curriculum*, York: Council for British Archaeology.

Morris, R. (1999) Birdsong returns, but history is lost, *British Archaeology* 42(15) (March).

Northern Ireland Office (1994) *Curriculum (Programme of Study and Attainment Targets in History) Order (Northern Ireland)*, Belfast: HMSO.

Rahtz, P.A. (1985) *Invitation to Archaeology*, Oxford: Blackwell.

Scottish Consultative Council on the Curriculum (1997) *Scottish History in the Curriculum*, Dundee: Scottish Consultative Council on the Curriculum.

Scottish Consultative Council on the Curriculum (1999) *Environmental Studies 5–14: Society, Science and Technology Consultation Draft*, Dundee: Scottish Consultative Council on the Curriculum.

Scottish Office Education Department (1993) *Curriculum and Assessment in Scotland National Guidelines: Environmental Studies 5–14*, Edinburgh: Scottish Office Education Department.

Shanks, M. and Tilley, C. (1992) *Reconstructing Archaeology*, London: Routledge.

Welsh Office Education Department (1995) *History in the National Curriculum: Wales*, Cardiff: HMSO.

Wheeler, Sir R.E.M. (1954) *Archaeology from the Earth*, Oxford: Oxford University Press.

Chapter 3

INTERPRETATIONS OF HISTORY:
CONSTRUCTING PASTS

Tim Copeland

Introduction

The idea that the past is open to different interpretations – that we can construct different pasts from the same evidence – can be bewildering to both teachers and children as well as to the general public. This appears to be recognised by many publishers and heritage presenters, as often the past is portrayed in a positivistic manner, the dominant image being almost a photograph of reality (Lewthwaite 1988: 86). It is noticeable that of the Key Elements in the National Curriculum History Orders (DfEE 1995) it is the 'Interpretations of History' element that causes the most problems for teachers. Perhaps the major influence on teachers has been their own positivistic experience of history during their own schooling. Heritage presenters wish to attract school parties to their attractions and often do not want to disturb teachers and children by showing various interpretations of the same event or place, or at least not drawing attention to them. However, the National Curriculum recognises the fact that there are differing interpretations of the past and Key Element 3 Interpretations of History at Key Stage 2 requires that children are able to identify and give reasons for different ways in which the past is represented and interpreted. The purpose of this chapter is to highlight the challenging possibilities of meeting the requirements of Key Element 3 and also giving the various audiences of archaeology a more valid way of looking at the past. Throughout, the term '(re)constructions' is used rather than 'reconstructions' as the latter presupposes that we can get at exactly what the past was like. However, there is no way of testing our attempts against past realities (Copeland 1998; also see Stone and Planel 1999: 1–2).

National Curriculum requirements

There are two strands to Key Element 3 at Key Stage 2:

● children make their own interpretations of history;
● they analyse others' interpretations.

Within this dual context differentiated levels of achievement can be identified (see Table 3.1).

Pupils need to be given a 'vocabulary' so that they can make sensible comments about interpretations. They can be taught that interpretations differ because of:

● access to evidence;
● purpose and intended audience;
● background of author.

Pupils will progressively see:

● that people put their own ideas into history;
● that disagreements and differences in versions of history do not mean that one account is right and the other is wrong;
● that history cannot cover everything, so some kind of selection is needed.

The implications for this view in terms of archaeology are:

● there is more than one way of viewing the past when using archaeological sources;
● accounts of the past differ because archaeological evidence can be ambiguous and is capable of being interpreted in more than one way, so since we cannot report self-evident truths we have to use informed creativity;
● some of the interpretations based on this sort of material will inevitably reflect an individual's own beliefs and political standpoint.

A constructivist approach

It would appear that the National Curriculum can be delivered using a constructivist approach to the past. In order to provide activities and experiences that are congruent with the curricular requirements is it is necessary to explore what such an approach entails.

Table 3.1 Differentiated levels of achievement

Elementary level	Pupils identify differences between interpretations
Medium level	Pupils can explain how interpretations are produced and how differences come about
High level	Pupils can evaluate whether interpretations are accurate

Lewthwaite has likened a constructivist approach to the past to

> a painter attempting to construct the likeness of a subject faithful to the orig-
> inal, capturing the 'character' or 'personality' rather than merely the profile,
> despite the singular inconvenience of the sitter's being hidden behind a
> screen and assisting the artist in his interpretation only by answering
> such specific questions that are put to him (and in an unfamiliar tongue, to
> boot).
>
> (Lewthwaite 1988: 87)

and Fowler has suggested that:

> Then, although it has happened, and cannot change itself, far from being dead
> the past is dynamic, for essentially it is a construct of our minds. In a very
> real sense it is our past (wherever we may be born or live), for, to a degree,
> we fashion it as we will rather than just accepting it as it is, never mind what
> it was.
>
> (Fowler 1992: 5)

Elsewhere (1998) I have suggested that a constructivist approach to the History
Orders, especially to interpretations of the past, is more valid in terms of the
nature of the subject.

Individual constructions

The past is inaccessible, but the remaining evidence can be examined. In order to
bring children's previous experience of evidence and help them select aspects of it
to explore the source they are using, we need to set up a 'cognitive dissonance'
by posing a question to make the 'dumb' evidence 'speak', and put the children
in an unfamiliar mindset. This key question frames an activity to be carried out
using the evidence. The result will be a construction, an interpretation, of the
evidence that we need to have communicated in some way, speaking, drawing,
writing, in order to evaluate it. Asking further questions of the evidence refines
the construction, especially as new skills are developed through the questions.
Working with the evidence forms a progressive spiral of constructions.

Using other people's constructions

When children are faced with a textbook, picture or (re)construction, they are
using the results of someone else's construction process. This 'someone' might
be a fellow pupil, an 'expert' or an interested adult. Children engaging in identifying the type of interpretation, explaining the differences and evaluating the
source, need to ask a range of questions to make their own construction of
the interpretation. These questions will help them to think and provide unfamiliar
ways of interrogating the source, causing a 'cognitive dissonance'. Again, the

children's view of the interpretation can be refined and become increasingly sophisticated through progressive questioning of the source. If it is the intention of the primary interpreter to make the source more intelligible to his or her audience then the 'loop' goes back to the original evidence and the primary interpreter can alter the interpretation in the light of audience comment (Copeland forthcoming).

Two aspects are important in this view of the learning about the past:

- children need to be given a range of interpretations of the same event or place (see Table 3.2);
- they should be introduced to the 'vocabulary' of a range of key questions about interpretations that they can use to cause the 'cognitive dissonance' that will help them understand how pasts are constructed and presented and differ.

Progressive questions

These are focused on archaeological sources (sites, buildings and artefacts) related to Historical Interpretation. Most questions can be posed at different key stages, depending on the context.

To identify different ways in which the past is represented

- Where else have we seen pictures of this object or structure?
- How many books or pictures about this place or thing can we find?
- How have we represented this aspect of the past: in words, as a drawing, as a model?
- How many ways is this aspect of the past represented in this museum/on this site: reconstruction models, life size reconstructions, living history, models, pictures, CD-ROM, sound commentary, guidebooks, video?

Table 3.2   Range of possible interpretation formats

Advertisements	Pictures/portraits/paintings
Artists' illustrations	Pupil work
Cartoons	Poetry
Computer simulations	Radio
Diaries	(Re)constructions
Drama and plays	(Re)enactments
Fiction	Replicas
Film and video	Sites
Historians' opinions – books, television, radio	Songs
Museum displays	Teacher accounts
Oral accounts	Television

To give reasons for different ways in which the past is represented

- Why did the person decide to use this format?
- Did they want to describe (words and pictures), classify (topic web, Venn diagram, matrix), compare (bar chart), order in time or type (timeline, list, flowchart), position in space (map, plan, scale drawing, scale model), show similarities with other pieces of evidence (table, graph, histogram)?
- Why didn't they use another form of representation?
- Who is the representation meant for?
- Why do they need it?
- What will they do with it?

To identify ways in which the past is interpreted

- How does this interpretation differ from the original source?
- Where do the interpretations differ? Is it in looking at the remaining evidence, or is it in reconstructing missing pieces?
- Has anything been added to the original source; has anything been left out?
- How is the information in this representation different from the information in others?
- Where do these sources of information disagree or agree?

To give reasons for the different ways in which the past is interpreted

- Who made these interpretations? Do you think they are different because they were made by different people? Why do you think this?
- Do you think that the person who made this interpretation has visited the site or building or seen the artefact?
- Are the interpretations of the same age? Make a timeline of them. How have they changed?
- Why do you think the interpretations disagree? Is it because there was more information? Did ideas about this period change?
- How many ways can you think of interpreting a site, building or object? Why have you chosen the one you have used?

To analyse and evaluate interpretations

- What is the effect of this interpretation? What did the person who made this (re)construction want to say about the place? What effect did the person who made this interpretation intend it to have? Which parts of this interpretation were intended to influence people in that way?
- Did the interpreter want to have a particular effect for a purpose, such as politics, belief, or tourism?
- Is the interpretation as it is because of what the interpreter did or who they were?
- Is the author of this source being fair to the site or object?

- Which parts of this interpretation could we not know from the archaeological sources? Do you think that historical evidence has been used to complement the archaeological evidence?
- Which of these interpretations do you find most convincing and why? Which interpretation do you like most and why? What does your choice say about how you interpret, or would like to interpret, archaeological sources?

Interpretation activities

The constructivist approach lends itself well to developing interpretation activities. Each activity needs a key question and a range of interpretations. The activities can be differentiated for differing abilities by:

- the level of the question;
- the demands of the activity;
- the number and type of source used;
- the method of communication (talking, drawing, writing).

The 'template' activities suggested here also offer possibilities for the use of numeracy and literacy.

Interpretations of events or people

Provide a range of interpretations of an event or person; for example, Boudicca. This might include contemporary sources, pictorial sources of statues, cartoon impressions, textbook illustrations (if possible from a variety of dates).

Key questions:

- What things do all the accounts have?
- What is different about them?
- Why are they different?

Children might begin by comparing two pictorial accounts. They could make a list of the attributes of each source. Then, using a Venn diagram, they might see what in the overlapping set indicates what is similar about the accounts. The details not in the overlapping set will be the differences between the accounts. A high-level activity using this information will be to suggest reasons why the accounts differ. Is it because of the audience? Is it because of the time they were compiled? Is it because more information was available to the compiler of one of the sources?

For some children communication might just be through talk; others will complete the formal recording using the Venn diagram; the most able will write a report about the reasons for the differences.

Interpretations of (re)constructions of sites

Many sites and buildings are depicted in a wide range of two- and three-dimensional imaginative visual (re)constructions showing the structure at some time during the past. These are valuable sources for a range of interpretation activities. The date the sources were made needs to be identified and they need to be complemented by an illustration of the location in the present.

Key question:

● How was this (re)construction made?

Put one source in the middle of a sheet of white paper and annotate around it using different colours for each task:

(a) evidence that came from the site
(b) evidence that might have been got from previous visual sources
(c) evidence that the maker used personal imagination
(d) things that are useful about this visual construction
(e) things that are not useful about this visual construction

The report can be written in the first instance using the colours employed in the initial analysis. This helps children to see the use of discrete paragraphs for similar information. It will also help later when comparing the analysis from a range of interpretations. If the source being used is a verbal description of the site or building then the sentences or parts of sentences can be underlined using the same colours and (d) and (e) can be a written commentary alongside the source.

This activity can be repeated with a range of sources, and children can begin to detect where sources have repeated previous conceptions of the site or where new information has been retrieved and included in an interpretation.

Interpretations of pictorial sources

There are many visual interpretations of 'life at the time' that can be analysed by children. It is possible to use 'scaffolding' in the form of 'writing frames' which suggest 'sentence stems' with any type of interpretation, but it is most effective when using pictorial representations:

● Interpretations of life in . . .
● This interpretation shows . . .
● It was made to . . .
● The person who made it found out about life then by . . .
● I think several types of sources were used to make this picture . . .
● Archaeological sources were used to . . .
● Picture and documentary sources were used to . . .
● Where evidence was not available I think the person who made this interpretation . . .
● This interpretation is useful because . . .

Conclusion

'Interpretations of History' is perhaps the most difficult key element for teachers to tackle, but children seem to have few difficulties with the concept if it is presented to them carefully. The idea of constructed pasts can be threatening to some adults or empowering and liberating to others. However, it is perhaps the most valid way for viewing the conclusions that are made from archaeological evidence and as such we should take every opportunity of engaging our audiences by taking them into our professional confidence rather than give them just one, fixed view of the past. It is only by encouraging questioning that we can engender reflection on the representation and interpretation of taken-for-granted pasts, and foster understanding of the strengths and limitations of archaeology.

■   ■   ■

References

Copeland, T. (1998) Constructing history: all *our* yesterdays. In M. Littledyke and L. Huxford (eds) *Teaching the Primary Curriculum for Constructive Learning*, London: David Fulton.

Copeland, T. (forthcoming) Presenting archaeology to the public: constructing insights on-site. In N. Merriman (ed.) *Public Archaeology*, London: Routledge.

Department for Education and Employment (1995) *History in the National Curriculum*, London: HMSO.

Fowler, P. (1992) *The Past in Contemporary Society: Then, Now*, London: Routledge.

Lewthwaite, J. (1988) Living in interesting times: archaeology as society's mirror. In J. Bintliff (ed.) *Extracting Meaning from the Past*, Oxford: Oxbow Books, 86–98.

Stone, P. and Planel, P. (1999) Introduction. In P. Stone and P. Planel (eds) *The Constructed Past: Experimental Archaeology, Education and the Public*, London: Routledge, 1–14.

Chapter 4

ARCHAEOLOGY IN FURTHER EDUCATION

Dave Jones

Introduction

Archaeology in further education (FE) is at a crossroads. The present wide-ranging alterations to further education regarding both its relationship with higher education and the revisions to the A-level (GCE advanced level) and GNVQ (General National Vocational Qualification) syllabuses through the government's curriculum 2000 initiatives, present the discipline with many golden opportunities in the twenty-first century. However, should these opportunities be missed, then archaeology in further education could suffer a serious downturn in recruitment. This would, of course, have far-reaching consequences for the discipline as a whole. The future of archaeology in further education is very much in the hands of the further education providers, and, more specifically, the lecturers themselves.

A-level archaeology

So where does the subject stand at present? Not surprisingly, archaeology in further education is still dominated by the traditional pathways, AS- (Advanced Subsidiary) and A-level, but GCSE (General Certificate of Secondary Education), Access and increasingly higher education provision are also proving very popular.

A-level qualifications have undergone a great deal of change recently and are now modular, with a first year of three modules, which can be 'cashed in' for an AS-level qualification, or built on by a further three modules in the second year for a full A-level.

These changes have meant a rewriting of syllabus content and structure by all examination boards. Previously, there were two archaeology courses, offered by the AQA and OCR examination boards. The OCR board decided to withdraw its archaeology provision, leaving the AQA as the sole provider of archaeology at A-level. The AQA specification is radically different to that of the old OCR syllabus. The AQA syllabus, adopting a theme-based style, is a little harder to resource, requiring a wider range of case-studies in order to meet its aims.

It is interesting to note that the OCR have fully revised their Classical Civilisation syllabus in response to the loss of archaeology. This new syllabus, which includes such topics as 'The Archaeology of Roman Britain', 'Archaeological Methods', together with a coursework option which can be entirely archaeological in its approach, is a very important development, as lecturers with a historical background who are at present delivering the OCR syllabus may find it a viable alternative. Furthermore, it provides the AQA with some welcome competition.

The advantage of the new modular system for archaeology is that there could be an increase in students taking AS-level. Archaeology stands to benefit from this as a highly attractive additional subject. Indeed, figures from the Council for British Archaeology for the first intake of students show that while 513 students took the last of the old A-level syllabus exams in 2001, the same year saw 806 students taking the new AS-level.

The quality of teaching at AS- and A-level depends not just on the backgrounds of the tutors but also on the quality and quantity of the syllabus support meetings and materials provided by the AQA. It is also the responsibility of the CBA and similar organisations to provide opportunities for archaeology lecturers to meet and share ideas at further education conferences. Most importantly, lecturers themselves must take advantage of any opportunities provided. If the support offered is not utilised, we will only have ourselves to blame if our classes fail to recruit or retain numbers.

Curriculum 2000

It is very important to stress at this stage that the changes demanded by Curriculum 2000 are not all negative. In fact, overall Curriculum 2000 offers further education archaeology some golden opportunities. The first, and most obvious opportunity, is the broader subject base offered to students in their AS year. At present, students tend to do three A-level subjects in their first year. This will increase to four or even five in some institutions. This is where a minor subject such as archaeology has the chance to recruit quite large numbers onto its AS programme. It is then down to the subject lecturer to keep them interested into the second year.

Curriculum 2000 will also allow candidates to combine AVCE (Advanced Vocational Certificate of Education) and A-level modules to produce wide and varied portfolios of study. Archaeology has the opportunity to offer modules to AVCE

Science and Leisure and Tourism students. These courses already recruit very healthy numbers: archaeology must surely be in a position to benefit.

Archaeology has one other significant advantage over many AS- and A-level subjects in that it is an ideal medium for delivering all of the key skills at level 3. Not only the 'hard' skills of numeracy, IT and communication, but also the 'soft' skills of problem-solving, working with others and improving own learning. The 'Personal Study' is the most obvious way in which these skills can be satisfied, but many of the other elements of the AQA specification lend themselves to key skills delivery. With clever marketing by the AQA, centres offering archaeology and the archaeology staff themselves, the subject can be promoted as one of the few specifications able to cover all of the key skills. It could even be offered as an alternative to General Studies in some centres, which is proposed to be the main medium for key skills provision in most institutions. If this opportunity is to be seized, it is up to the AQA to signpost very clearly the key skills in their materials.

Finally, it is essential to stress the need to include all staff in any training and development which may be offered in response to the changes mentioned above. Archaeology is taught by many part-time members of staff who often miss out on such training opportunities. These lecturers must insist that they are included in any staff development sessions.

Access, GCSE and higher education courses

There is often a danger that any discussion of academic provision in further education concentrates wholly on AS- and A-level. There are a variety of other courses on offer in further education which warrant discussion. The first of these is Access, often referred to as Access to Higher Education. These Access courses are especially important as they offer learners the opportunity to study archaeology at levels 1, 2 and 3. Access Archaeology provision can be combined with already established programmes such as Access to Science or Access to Social Science; these archaeology options often prove very attractive to adults who have never studied the subject before.

Access courses are becoming increasingly accepted by many higher education institutions. Well-written and well-planned units can be catered to match either (a) a partner higher education institution's entry requirements and/or (b) the strengths of the subject staff and resources at the further education institution. Moreover, it is these Access students who often provide the majority of recruits onto higher education courses offered at the further education institution itself.

Imaginative timetabling has enabled some further education institutions to offer AS- or A-level archaeology as part of an Access programme. If AS- or A-level numbers are low, this has the effect of increasing the viability of the subject. As stressed earlier, it is often the use of initiative and imagination that ensures the survival of minor courses in today's competitive world.

GCSE Archaeology is still an important element of the subject's provision in further education. Since the beginnings of the GCSE in 1988, the number of students taking archaeology has averaged 530 each year – a significant number for a minor subject. The syllabus is offered by the AQA, and feeds nicely into their A-level. However, it does provide a sound introduction into the subject in its own right. It is possible to increase the uptake of the GCSE at further education level by offering it as more than simply an enrichment course for students sitting other A-levels, or as an evening class to adult learners. Colleges should be encouraged to offer GCSE Archaeology as part of their overall resit programme. The subject has the advantage of being hugely popular, due to television programmes such as *Time Team*, but, more importantly, it is not something which most resit candidates will have already failed at school. This could, obviously, have a significant bearing on pass rates and grade profiles. If archaeology tutors stress this final point to line managers, the chances of the course being supported are much improved.

It is in the area of higher education provision that some FE colleges are now focusing their attention. Archaeology is an ideal subject to offer at higher education level in an FE college. It is exactly the type of course which will attract adult learners who wish to study for a course (a) locally, (b) part-time, and (c) which is unusual and interesting.

The government is keen to encourage HNC (Higher National Certificate) and HND (Higher National Diploma) provision through further education institutions, leaving the honours degrees to the universities. This is an opportunity which several colleges have already seized upon, in partnership with local universities. In southern England, for example, the University of Bournemouth has made enormous progress in developing HNC and HND courses in partnership with local colleges, building on the work of Yeovil College which ran a very successful HND in Practical Archaeology. Other colleges in the region offering, or about to offer, HNDs or HNCs in archaeology in partnership with a university are Salisbury College and Bridgwater College with the University of Bournemouth, and Truro College with Exeter University. Somerset College of Arts and Technology offers a HND validated through the Edexcel exam board.

It is important to stress that the success of these courses is based on careful planning, adequate resourcing and, very often, a successful further education programme, such as A-level, from which to recruit numbers. If higher education courses in the further education sector are to succeed, quality must be at the forefront of all provision. This is essential to guarantee the interest and support of the universities and the profession. Under-funded, poorly taught courses will do nothing more than undermine the success and standing of the already established, high-quality courses mentioned above.

Fieldwork, networking and resources

For these higher-level courses to succeed (and to make A/AS-level programmes more relevant) FE college students need greater access to fieldwork opportunities in the form of both excavations and surveys. Excavations are often very expensive or simply use students as 'trowel fodder', providing no training at all. Quality, low-cost experiences do exist, but these are very hard to find, and places are at a premium. If the universities wish to recruit quality students and the profession wishes to employ adequately trained personnel, then they must play their part in providing the fieldwork opportunities.

However, the further education providers must also take some initiative. Many local archaeological societies carry out high-quality fieldwork on a regular basis. Liaising with these organisations can bring mutual benefits. If a college ensures that all of its archaeology students join the local society, this will (a) introduce them to a network of interested and experienced people, (b) provide many fieldwork opportunities, (c) increase the membership of the society, (d) open up a new market for recruiting on to the college's archaeology courses, and (e) give access to expert speakers at the society symposiums, etc. Perhaps these societies could be encouraged to set up sub-branches at the further education institution, offering, in particular, a service which is relevant to the 16–19 age range. At present the Young Archaeologists' Club provides an excellent service for under-16s, and the societies themselves provide many opportunities for the 20+ age group. The Time Team Club is perhaps another avenue for providing the post-school, pre-university age group with something. The majority of societies which the author has been in contact with are very keen to become involved with local colleges for the reasons mentioned above.

It is equally important that further education archaeology taps into the local professional set-up. The County Archaeologist, Archivist and Museums Officer are often very keen to be of assistance. They are sometimes able to suggest fieldwork topics and/or offer work experience placements. The author must stress, however, that conversations with further education providers lead him to the conclusion that the amount of co-operation at this level is very uneven. The author's county, Somerset, is one of the lucky ones, with students and lecturers being given the fullest assistance. There are certainly councils that could take a lead from Somerset – after all, these students are the future of archaeology.

Fieldwork opportunities are not the only resources which need to be addressed. Much of further education archaeology is offered on a part-time/evening class basis, often by a part-time member of staff with less than satisfactory access to a college's learning resources (the same being true for other minor subjects). The examination boards need to be fully aware of this situation simply because some lecturers are discouraged from offering the subject due to problems in obtaining adequate resources. In addition, due to the time constraints imposed upon part-time and evening class provision, high-quality resources which can be freely duplicated under a site licence would be a real asset. Curriculum 2000 provides the AQA with a golden opportunity to provide high-quality syllabus support material in order to recruit new centres to their subject.

These are exciting times for resourcing for archaeology. A new textbook, aimed at A-level/HNC/HND students, has already been published in 2001 by Routledge as *The Archaeology Coursebook*. The Internet also provides a wonderful opportunity for the production and circulation of ideas and resources. The CBA's website is already proving to be of great assistance to lecturers as well as to the public.

The structure of the further education sector

Since further education was removed from the control of local education authorities and colleges were made independent (known as the incorporation of the sector), the sector has been forced to compete for numbers in a quasi-marketplace. I will not comment on the rights and wrongs on incorporation, but it does throw up a significant problem for archaeology. A subject like Archaeology will always recruit smaller numbers than, say, Geography. If it is offered in only one or two local colleges, then there are enough numbers to go around. What is happening increasingly, however, is that institutions are battling to recruit limited numbers. In reality, rather than one course of twelve students running, two or three smaller classes fail to happen. This is, of course, very unfortunate. It is up to further education providers to make sensible arrangements between themselves to ensure the continuation and success of minor courses.

Finally, reference must be made to the outcomes and results-driven ideals which now dominate the further education sector. There was a time when general interest courses which did not necessarily lead to any certification were offered at further education colleges on a regular basis. It is increasingly true that lecturers are being encouraged to consider results and outcomes rather than the enjoyment and discussion of their subject. If we are not careful, this attitude could be the death of adult education and evening class provision.

Chapter 5

INTERROGATING PEDAGOGIES: ARCHAEOLOGY IN HIGHER EDUCATION

Yannis Hamilakis and Paul Rainbird

In this chapter we outline and discuss the context, the framework and themes of the workshop 'Interrogating Pedagogies: Archaeology in Higher Education' (Lampeter 5–7 September 2000), co-ordinated by the authors. This was, to our knowledge, the first conference in Britain to be devoted exclusively to the teaching of archaeology in higher education. The first section of the chapter deals with the context and the rationale behind the workshop (YH), whereas the second section outlines some of the themes and ideas which emerged from the debates (PR).

The context, aims and rationale

The workshop took place against the background of some significant developments in higher education in Britain and worldwide. Obviously, as with everything in education, there is no objective way to outline these developments, and depending on where you stand you may see them as catastrophic or as beneficial. There are certain developments, however, which need restating.

A financial crisis characterises most universities in the world, save for some elite institutions relying on private endowments, mostly in North America. Partly as a result of this crisis, higher education has experienced the commoditisation of knowledge, the privatisation of the remaining public aspects of the university, and the intensification of links between university research and private capital, a phenomenon which some describe as 'the corporatisation of the University' (see Miyoshi 2000; Castree and Sparke 2000). To give some examples from the United Kingdom, major corporations such as Shell, BP and Glaxo now fund academic posts and research centres in universities, thus shaping the research agenda by promoting specific topics – e.g. research on oil rather than renewable resources (Monbiot 2000). In archaeology this trend is not so prominent as yet, but we have recently observed the major sponsorship of fieldwork projects by international corporations (Shell, British Airways, Visa, etc.) and, in one case, the direct interference of a corporation in the direction of research, and the interpretation and presentation of its results. In this instance, Visa, a major sponsor of the excavation at Catalhöyük, requested an exhibition on the 'evolution of the credit card' from prehistory to the present (Hodder 1999; Hamilakis 1999).

Despite the continuing financial crisis and cuts in public funding, student numbers have vastly increased in recent years in Britain and elsewhere. In the British context, state funding has been linked to student numbers. This has partly fuelled the expansion, but has also led to competition, not only between different institutions but also, in some cases, between different academic units within institutions.

As the result of the above developments, universities have now acquired many of the characteristics of a service industry, where students and their families are seen as customers who demand that the product they are buying should be quality assured. As a further consequence, we have seen the development of what some have described as an 'audit culture' (cf. Shore and Wright 1999), with the mass expansion of bureaucratic procedures which are supposed to safeguard the quality of the delivered product. Many academics have internalised the discourse of accountability and have adopted a managerial, supposed neutral communicative code in the quest for 'efficiency' and 'excellence'.

The proliferation of higher education provision (in Britain expressed through the acquisition of university status by the former polytechnics), coupled with decreasing public resources and the demand of the 'market' to opt for 'quality-assured' products, has led to the establishment of league tables for universities. Research output is increasingly seen as the main distinction mechanism for universities and the main tool through which the remaining state research funding is allocated. Competition for high scores in the audit procedures, such as the Research Assessment Exercise, has led to the devaluation of teaching (which is seen as a low-prestige and almost punitive process), the creation of a poorly paid, academic underclass who carry a significant part of the teaching workload (postgraduate students, teaching fellows, lecturers on short-term contracts), and the divorce of teaching from research.

At the other end, employers in areas such as archaeology, the 'heritage industry' and the 'cultural resource management' sector (an industry that has expanded vastly recently, replacing in some ways traditional industries) operate in a similar culture of cost-effectiveness and capitalist microeconomics. They thus demand that their employees should be well qualified and equipped with the necessary skills to carry out the prescribed tasks in the minimum possible time and at the minimum possible expense. As stakeholders, employers, as well as professional bodies, propose changes to university curricula so that their employees can satisfy these criteria.

Thus universities have recently implemented, or are currently implementing, a series of drastic changes as a response to financial constraints, the introduction of capitalist maximisation strategies and pressures from employers. What is amazing in all this is how little discussion and debate have been engaged in prior to the implementation of these changes, which may alter the profile of pedagogy – in our case archaeological pedagogy – beyond recognition. The whole issue seems to be treated as simply a matter of objectified, neutral administrative developments, rather than of contested, context-specific and power-related approaches. The language of efficiency and accountability, and the discourse of excellence, seems to be omnipresent, overshadowing most critical approaches. There is another paradox in this situation which needs pointing out. While we know, at least within the Anglo-American tradition, that archaeological theory has become a major and important concern which permeates all aspects of our research, the philosophy and method-ology of archaeological teaching and pedagogy seem to have remained immune and unaffected by these theoretical developments. So, for example, while the content of our teaching often concerns theories advocating plurality and multivocality, para-doxically our pedagogical practice, more often than not, subscribes to a monologic, authoritative discourse. Furthermore, while in our research many of us have under-mined the premises of objectivism, constantly emphasised the knowledge–power nexus, and have rejected the application of maximisation principles in the study of prehistoric economies and societies, in our educational and pedagogical practice (and in our life as academics) we seem to have endorsed these ideas. We sit back and listen to countless speeches by university administrators on efficiency and maximisation, or we willingly implement the policies of self-policing through struc-tures which are supposed to guarantee accountability, seen in an objectified and neutral manner. Since we are not advocating an image of the university as an 'ivory tower' (an image which is a caricature anyway, since universities operate in the public sphere), we can admit we are accountable; but how often do we stop and ask accountable to whom? We would also prefer to replace accountability (implying a narrow view based on quantification) with responsibility, reinforcing the question: who are we responsible to?

In spite of earlier attempts to address educational issues in archaeology in the United Kingdom (e.g. Austin 1984; Richardson 1989) and internationally (e.g. Stone and MacKenzie 1990; Stone and Molyneaux 1994; Jameson 1997; Smardz and Smith 2000) we still believe that there has been relatively little recent debate on pedagogy. The gap between the sophisticated approaches in our research and the objectivist and supposedly neutral approaches to our teaching practice and admin-istration was the main reason which led us to organise the workshop 'Interrogating Pedagogies'. It is instructive for a moment to compare archaeology with other disciplines in this respect. Geographers have had since 1977 an international and highly respected journal devoted to the teaching of geography in higher education, and they organise regular meetings. A recent issue of this international journal, *Antipode* (32(3)), was devoted exclusively to this matter, with a range of important papers. Anthropologists in the United Kingdom have for years had an anthropology teaching network which organises regular meetings, and a number of recent critical interventions in their premier journals (e.g. Shore and Wright 1999; Gudeman 1998; Di Giacomo 1997) is an indication of how seriously they take the whole issue. Archaeologists are thus lagging considerably behind. To be fair, there has been some discussion in national (e.g. as organised in Southampton in 1987 – and see Richardson 1989; and by the CBA in 1999 and 2001) and international (e.g. all of the major World Archaeological Congresses) conferences, and other forums, on these issues (cf. a special section on education in *Antiquity*: e.g. Collis 2000). However, many of the recent initiatives in archaeology seem to be driven by the needs and concerns of professional organisations (Chitty 1999). The Society for American Archaeology has been particularly active with task forces, meetings and publications (e.g. Bender and Smith 2000). The European Association of Archaeology is only just now starting to address the issue. To return to Britain, the recent benchmarking document statement (Quality Assurance Agency for Higher Education 2000) which we discussed extensively at the workshop offers an opportunity to debate these issues further. The establishment of the Subject Centre for Archaeology, Classics and History is an interesting development in that respect, as is the establishment of the Archaeology Training Forum.

One of the aims of this workshop was to emphasise that archaeological pedagogy, like all pedagogy, is much more than training – it is concerned with philosophy, reflexivity, politics, the critical engagement with the world, life experiences, and not simply with training transferable skills. We hoped that the workshop would ignite the debate, therefore, on archaeological pedagogy and education, and not simply archaeological training, by encouraging debate:

- on education as a life transforming experience rather than simply as an instrumentalist notion (cf. Coleman and Simpson 1999; Heyman 2000);
- on linking critical archaeological theories with critical archaeological pedagogies;
- on teaching not only skills, methodologies, chronologies and cultural sequences but also, primarily, critical thinking, the ability to question, interrogate seeming common sense and the accepted order of things, and the ability to not only understand but also change the social conditions of someone's life and experience (cf. Freire and Faundez 1989; Giroux 1988, 1991, 1992 from a large bibliography on critical and reflexive education).

We also hoped that the debate would cover more specific but equally important things as well. To take just one example. It is surprising that we all more or less use in our first-year teaching a well-known and highly successful textbook now in its third edition (Renfrew and Bahn 1999), and yet apart from one or two engaging book reviews, there is almost no discussion on its epistemological and ideological foundations, on its pedagogical premises, on its authority (on textbooks and authority see Johnston 2000).

The workshop

The workshop took place in early September 2000 at the University of Wales, Lampeter, and it was funded by the United Kingdom Council for Graduate Education. As noted above, it aimed to discuss and debate issues relating to current bureaucratic changes in the higher education sector that may effect the provision of archaeology, and this included the Quality Assurance Agency (QAA), especially as expressed through 'benchmarking', the formation of the Subject Centre for Classics, History and Archaeology, and a number of recent documents from British archaeology's professional institutions expressing concerns and hopes regarding expected 'outcomes' for students of archaeology. To this end academic archaeologists from Britain were joined by representatives of the Council for British Archaeology (CBA), the Institute of Field Archaeologists (IFA), the Subject Centre, Cadw – Welsh Historic Monuments, English Heritage, and the Society for American Archaeology. The discussion in the Workshop raised a number of themes and issues, a few of which we report here.

The mix of academics and 'employers/professionals/practitioners' at the meeting proved extremely fruitful and, although illustrating the diversity of practice within archaeology, it did provide common ground in identifying consensus in regard to all participants' commitment to the subject and interest in its future. In terms of the provision of archaeology in higher education a presentation by Henson (CBA) revealed that there are twenty-eight full departments of archaeology in Britain, but almost three times that number of departments actually teach archaeology in one form or other at degree level. This rather brought into question how SCFA (the Subject Committee for Archaeology) can be regarded as fully representative of academic archaeology.

The 'benchmarking' statement produced by SCFA for the QAA provided the focus of much discussion. A number of participants heralded the document as providing much-needed definition for the project of archaeology inside and outside of academia, although others noted that archaeology itself was only thinly defined. It was noted that the SCFA members, in preparing this document, appeared to be restricting the teaching of archaeology to departments from which their members are drawn. Many of the non-archaeology departments and non-traditional methods of higher education provision (e.g. distance learning) may fall outside of the broad, although not ultimately prescriptive, requirements of the 'benchmark'. Vehement concerns were raised that although not prescriptive at present, the documentation and tabulation of expected 'standards' could easily, and perhaps ultimately, turn into a checklist of absolute minimum requirements assessed by the QAA. It was also noted that some departments had immediately put into effect changes to their curricula to meet the perceived needs of the document. The Workshop was in general agreement that the benchmarking document requires far greater circulation, and basic debate, prior to its expected revision in three years' time. As noted above, this bureaucratisation of archaeology teaching has already had an effect on the current delivery of undergraduate courses and must lead to different expectations of graduate students and employers. A number of participants raised concerns that processes such as these threatened to homogenise the provision of archaeology in higher education and, in so doing, reduce the diversity that makes archaeology such a vibrant subject for study.

Continuing professional development was considered a necessary component for all undergraduates choosing to pursue a career in archaeology. Some of the participants from outside academe requested more vocational training in the undergraduate degree, but the question had to be asked 'what would then be left out?' An outcome of these discussions was that undergraduates needed to be made aware at an early stage in their courses what skills and experience they would need to demonstrate if they wished to go straight into the 'profession'. The IFA are unwilling to recommend the taught Masters degree as a requisite to entering the 'profession' as this would imply extra cost to the student who, in most cases, would need to self-finance the degree. Although sympathetic to student financial difficulties, it was pointed out that taught postgraduate degrees had become increasingly popular and that, due to successive legislative changes, the burden of debt was already present within the undergraduate degree structure.

Further issues related to career development and the specifics of teaching archaeology in HE were also presented at the meeting (see Rainbird and Hamilakis 2001). Due to the preliminary nature of such an exciting range of perspectives, much of the final session, rather than coming to a final set of conclusions, involved discussion for future collaboration.

Afterword

Archaeology is not alone in having to face a future where the only certainty is that there will be changes and that these might be dramatic. It is clear that the role of university education as a means of providing experience and opportunity, based on the development of educated critical awareness, is being eroded rapidly by a global system related to 'costs' and 'outcomes'. Our experience of the workshop has shown us that the death of the wide provision of archaeology in higher education would be a rapid outcome of a homogenised vocation-led teaching strategy. Archaeology in higher education has only in the last twenty years or so been able to take its place alongside the other humanities and social sciences as a mature discipline that can bear not only internal debate but also contribute to wider debates in such areas as cultural politics. The current moves to bureaucratise higher education have the potential to return archaeology in British universities to the situation prior to the 1960s when it was regarded as a degree only available to those of independent means.

Clearly these are important issues, and the Lampeter Workshop, it is hoped, has ignited discussion and debate that will continue through further meetings to be arranged through a new Steering Committee for Archaeology in Higher Education. The necessary further discussion and debate is also enhanced by the recently set up Internet discussion list for academic archaeologists at <www.jiscmail.ac.uk/lists/ arch-ac-UK/>.

A serious debate on the teaching of archaeology in higher education has been long overdue. It is about time we start reflecting not only on what we teach but also on how we do it and under which pedagogical framework, as well as on the consequences and effects for students, for us, for society. It is about time that we reclaim the space of archaeological pedagogy colonised by the administrative and bureaucratic logic. This workshop was only the beginning.

■ ■ ■

References

Austin, D. (1984) *Archaeology Courses in British Universities*, Lampeter: St David's University College.

Bender, S.J. and Smith, G.S. (eds) (2000) *Teaching Archaeology in the Twenty-First Century*, Washington, DC: Society for American Archaeology.

Castree, N. and Sparke, M. (2000) Professional geography and the corporatization of the university: experiences, evaluations and engagements, *Antipode* 32(3): 222–229.

Chitty, G. (1999) *Training in Professional Archaeology: A Preliminary Review*, Carnforth, Lancashire. (Commissioned by English Heritage on behalf of the Archaeology Training Forum.)

Coleman, S. and Simpson, B. (1999) Unintended consequences? Anthropology, pedagogy and personhood, *Anthropology Today* 15(6): 3–6.

Collis, J. (2000) Towards a national training scheme for England and the United Kingdom, *Antiquity* 74(283): 208–214.

Di Giacomo, S.M. (1997) The new internal colonialism, *Critique of Anthropology* 17(1): 91–97.

Freire, P. and Faundez, A. (1989) *Learning to Question: A Pedagogy of Liberation*, Geneva: WCC Publications.

Giroux, H.A. (1988) *Teachers as Intellectuals: Toward a Critical Pedagogy of Learning*, New York: Bergin & Garvey.

Giroux, H.A. (1991) Democracy and the discourse of cultural difference: towards a politics of border pedagogy, *British Journal of Sociology of Education* 12(4): 501–519.

Giroux, H.A. (1992) *Border Crossings: Cultural Workers and the Politics of Education*, New York: Routledge.

Gudeman, S. (1998) The new captains of information, *Anthropology Today* 14(1): 1–3.

Hamilakis, Y. (1999) La trahison des archéologues? Archaeological practice as intellectual activity in postmodernity, *Journal of Mediterranean Archaeology* 12(1): 60–103.

Heyman, R. (2000) Research, pedagogy and instrumental geography, *Antipode* 32(2): 292–307.

Hodder, I. (1999) *The Archaeological Process*, Oxford: Blackwell.

Jameson, J.H. (Jr) (1997) *Presenting Archaeology to the Public: Digging for Truths*, Walnut Creek, Calif.: Altamira Press.

Johnston, R. (2000) Authors, editors, and authority in the postmodern academy, *Antipode* 32(3): 271–291.

Miyoshi, M. (2000) Ivory tower in escrow, *Boundary* 27(1): 7–50.

Monbiot, G. (2000) Masters of the universities, *The Guardian*, 11 September.

Quality Assurance Agency for Higher Education (2000) *Archaeology*, Gloucester: Quality Assurance Agency for Higher Education.

Rainbird, P. and Hamilakis, Y. (2001) *Interrogating Pedagogies: Archaeology in Higher Education*, Oxford: Archaeopress.

Renfrew, C. and Bahn, P. (1999) *Archaeology: Theory, Methods and Practice* (3rd edn), London: Thames & Hudson.

Richardson, W. (ed.) (1989) *CBA Education Bulletin* 6.

Shore, C. and Wright, S. (1999) Audit culture and anthropology: neo-liberalism in British higher education, *Journal of the Royal Anthropological Institute* NS 5: 557–575.

Smardz, K. and Smith, S.J. (2000) *The Archaeology Education Handbook: Sharing the Past with Kids*, Walnut Creek, Calif.: Altamira Press.

Stone, P.G. and MacKenzie, R. (1990) *The Excluded Past: Archaeology in Education*, London: Unwin Hyman.

Stone, P.G. and Molyneaux, B. (1994) *The Presented Past: Heritage, Museums and Education*, London: Routledge.

Chapter 6

ROLLING BACK THE YEARS: LIFELONG LEARNING AND ARCHAEOLOGY IN THE UNITED KINGDOM

Gary Lock

Introduction

The notion of lifelong learning is rapidly becoming the dominant paradigm within the United Kingdom educational establishment. Within its first eighteen months in power, the new Labour government had commissioned three advisory reports relevant to post-compulsory education, and published responses to them. These all emphasised the importance of creating a national learning culture within which learning at any age is valued and nurtured. In this chapter, I will briefly review this government view of lifelong learning and attempt to fit it into a wider field of concern. I will attempt to differentiate between formal and informal learning contexts, and the implications of this for university delivered adult, or continuing, education.

Essential to creating successful lifelong-learning situations is an understanding of how and why adults learn, and the relationship between learning and teaching. Based on my own experiences of working with adult learners in a variety of archaeological situations over the last twenty years, I will suggest that archaeology is particularly well suited to this new paradigm. Archaeology as a humanistic discipline creates scenarios in which individuals can establish links between their own present and a version of the past that draws meaning from within their own life experience. The challenge facing university adult educators in archaeology is the integration of this student-centred contextual approach to learning into the traditional and changing formal constructs within which we work.

The governmental framework

During 1997 and early 1998 the United Kingdom government received three commissioned advisory reports which are relevant to university continuing education and published a response to each. These were the Kennedy Report, *Learning Works: Widening Participation in Further Education* (Kennedy 1997), and its response *Further Education for the New Millennium* (Department for Education and Employment 1998a); the Dearing Report, *Higher Education in the Learning Society* (National Committee of Inquiry into Higher Education 1997), and its response *Higher Education for the 21st Century* (Department for Education and Employment 1998b); and the Report of the Fryer Committee, *Learning for the Twenty-First Century* (Fryer 1997), and its response in the form of a Green Paper, *The Learning Age: A Renaissance for a New Britain* (Department for Education and Employment 1998c). These six documents obviously contain a large amount of detail relevant here; space allows only a brief review.

The essence of government thinking is encapsulated within *The Learning Age* (Department for Education and Employment 1998c), and it is this which will probably form the basis for future legislation. Central to this is the theme of lifelong learning – to such an extent that it will impact on all aspects of individuals, communities and the economy. It claims that learning throughout life must become the norm and defines lifelong learning as 'the continuous development of the skills, knowledge and understanding that are essential for employability and fulfilment' (ibid.: 16). The way of achieving this is seen as being via a cultural shift to create a learning society, 'a culture of self-improvement for the many and not the few' (ibid.: 28). A whole series of mechanisms is suggested to bring these big ideas into practice, not least the widening of educational provision at post-compulsory level for people of any age and the strengthening of equal opportunities policies. Extra government funding is to be available, although the establishment of Individual Learning Accounts will encourage people to invest financially in their own learning. New relationships between higher education institutions and employers are proposed, with the establishment of the University for Industry focusing on basic skills and vocational courses. A National Grid for Learning will harness the power of the Internet to create structured good-quality electronic resources that are available for learners at all levels and accessible from all schools, colleges, universities and public places such as libraries. Many of these proposals are already underway (see the DfEE United Kingdom Lifelong Learning website at: http://www.lifelonglearning.co.uk/index.htm).

While the main aims of these proposals have been generally well received by the educational world in the United Kingdom (Department for Education and Employment 1999), points of concern within university continuing education remain. These are centred on access, participation rates and rising numbers, funding, accreditation, standards and quality, marketing and management. Within formal university structures that are driven by funding and at the mercy of political ideology, these are valid and important issues, but in many ways they miss the exciting and positive points of what lifelong learning really means. We need to take a wider view to appreciate the complexities of the challenge.

Types of learning

A typology of adult learning situations has been suggested (Rogers 1996): the formal, the extra-formal and the non-formal. Formal structures comprise the educational system of statutory and non-statutory agencies such as schools, colleges and universities. These are hierarchically ordered and chronologically graded, all of which form the main focus of the government thinking outlined above. Extra-formal courses and classes are run by formal agencies outside the educational system, such as commercial bodies and training agencies, but still have identified learners and learning objectives. These are also included within government proposals, often for the delivery of work-based training rather than education. The non-formal sector is the diverse range of learning opportunities provided by voluntary agencies and informal groups (Elsdon *et al.* 1995). Within this category the concept of self-directed learning is central, whereby individuals recognise their own learning needs and through individual or group action devise strategies for meeting them. This is the truly lifelong process that enables individuals to acquire values, skills and knowledge from daily experience. It is the integration of these three sectors that will create the learning society that the government proposes, and to this end we need to set formal continuing education into the wider research context of how and why adults learn.

This raises the conflict between theory and practice. While the former is embedded within academic constructs, influenced by wider debates concerning philosophy and social theory, the latter is determined by government policy and funding. Not surprisingly, the two do not always match, as is the case here to a large extent. In terms of theoretical progression, the functionalist models of the 1950s and 1960s that saw education as a means of fitting individuals more effectively into society, gave way in the 1970s and 1980s to more radical ideas of education as individual and group empowerment and autonomy (Rogers 1996). In policy and funding terms, however, the 1980s and 1990s under the right-wing Conservative government were dominated by economic-driven models which viewed learners as human capital. Direction within learning recognises an individual's powers of critical awareness and responsibility for their own learning. To a certain extent, Houle's classic study of 1961, *The Inquiring Mind*, pre-empted this by identifying three types of adult learner: those who were goal-oriented, having very specific interests often to do with work; those who were activity-oriented whose main incentive was social interaction; and, third, the learning-oriented who are the self-directed learners seeking out learning opportunities in everyday experiences. Ideas were formalised by Knowles, initially in 1970, in his theory of andragogy, 'a distinctive theory of adult learning':

> The move from pedagogy to andragogy is seen as a necessary stage in the adult's development in learning, i.e. the move from dependency on a teacher to self-direction: adult acquires a new status . . . this self-concept becomes that of a self-directing personality . . . Adults tend to resist learning under conditions that are incongruent with their self-concept as autonomous individuals.
>
> (Knowles 1983: 56)

Individual learning

Recognition and respect of adulthood, maturity and self-direction is not just a theory of education but almost a moral philosophy, and one which underpins much of the thinking on adult learning today. A series of empirical research projects and publications, mainly in the USA in the late 1960s and through the 1970s, expanded and reinforced these ideas (Percy *et al.* 1994). These recognised that adults construct rational models of self-directed learning based on planning, choice and aims by having 'learning projects' and going through 'learning episodes'. An illuminating study by Penland (1979) based on interviewing 1,501 American adults found that 80 per cent of them considered themselves to be continuing learners, and yet only 2.9 per cent were engaged in taught courses. More than three-quarters of those interviewed had planned one or more learning projects in the previous year and the mean time spent on these had been 156 hours per person. It was also established that the years spent in formal education, and qualifications gained there, were poor predictors of adult learning activity and that minority groups are much more likely to learn informally because of the social and cultural barriers within formal education. The three top-ranked reasons in support of self-directed learning, rather than taking a course, were the ability to set one's own learning pace, learning style and flexibility of effort.

Similar recent findings in the United Kingdom have confirmed the importance of informal learning (Elsdon *et al.* 1995). Studies show that a considerable amount of self-initiated and self-directed adult learning goes on which is completely outside the formal educational structures. By 1991, Candy was able to talk of lifelong learning as being a broad, diverse and nebulous concept dependent upon two components: vertical integration (learning opportunities from the cradle to the grave) and horizontal integration (learning opportunities in a variety of contexts). The ways that these two components impinge upon an individual's life-space construct opportunities for learning, and formal learning is not always the most attractive option.

It is important to recognise that learning is a complex process that has exercised the minds of educational theorists for generations. At one level, learning is the very essence of being human as an individual learns through action and by pursuing related actions. It may be that a sequence of actions cannot proceed without learning taking place, although the person involved may not be consciously 'learning' or have made a decision to learn. It is at this level of daily social praxis that lifelong learning both creates social life itself and is created by social life. That constant learning is essential for a satisfying existence based on interpreting and making sense of the material and spiritual world around and within us has already been suggested.

Within a wider theoretical scheme of development, behaviourist theories have given way to humanist theories. The former emphasise the active role of the teacher who dispenses knowledge compared to the more passive role of the student who receives it. Knowledge often equates with truth, is independent of both teacher and learner and is the same for all learners. Humanist theories, on the other hand, are largely post-modern and reject the positivism of empirical research and locate learning within the complexities and uncertainties of the individual learner's social context. Again, however, the conflict of theory and practice has been evidenced by the competence drive via qualifications frameworks imposed on university continuing education over the last decade. The classic position of starting where the learner is, championed by liberal adult education for many decades, has been forced to fit within models based on concepts of providers and clients more akin to commerce than education. In practice, therefore, the shift could be seen as from humanist to behaviourist.

Humanist models embed learning within the individual's experience and within the resources and conditions of the learner's situation, including interpersonal relationships. Consequently, learning is not determined by external influences but created within each of us as we observe and reflect on experience to construct meaning and sense which is applied to the world around us. This is the learning cycle suggested by Kolb (1984): from experience through critical reflection on experience to action which creates new experience ready for the next cycle. Embedded within this are individual intentions, goals and decisions concerning the reasons for learning. It follows, then, that knowledge is not an external reality waiting to be handed on by a teacher but is the personal construction of new perceptions. The archaeological result of this process is that we construct various acts of knowing that are always contingent and provisional, so that rather than validating knowledge itself we are left with the task of establishing criteria by which we can judge the questions asked and the answers arrived at in each specific case. One way of doing this is by assessing which acts of knowing carry personal experiential validity (i.e. make sense within our individual experience). I suggest that this is particularly relevant to learning archaeology for at least two reasons. First, archaeology is about people and about being human. Post-processual theory emphasises the experiential aspects of being in the world and of constructing meaning within ourselves, whether now or in the past. A humanised past connects with the present through commonality because knowledge, the construction and use of knowledge, has always been and still is the essence of being human. For neolithic people, just as for ourselves, knowledge was mediated between experience, personal and cultural bias of what is important and relevant, and future aims, needs and goals.

The second reason why this is of relevance to learning archaeology is because of the importance of analogy. Analogy has always been central to archaeological inter-pretation: houses look like houses and axes look like axes, etc. Humanist approaches to learning and to archaeology shift the emphasis of analogy from an understanding of the material record to an understanding of the human condition. Within each of us analogy combines with personal experience to create the reservoir needed for critical reflection. It is the depth of this reservoir that often makes adult students more demanding to work with than those straight from school: they have more life experience against which to test and question new ways of knowing. To take a training excavation as a single example of an archaeological learning situation, the learning cycle and use of analogy are central as students make sense of the material and construct meaning from the archaeological record. As Hodder has recently argued (1999), excavation is interpretation at the trowel's edge; his hermeneutic spiral equates with Kolb's (1984) learning cycle so that interpretation and learning merge into one. Both are based on the reworking and modification of 'pre-knowns', and it follows that a 50-year-old student is likely to have a richer reservoir than an 18-year-old. I know from experience, for example, that the hermeneutics of interpreting the construction, use and abandonment of a timber-framed roundhouse benefit from having experienced carpenters and thatchers in the discussion group. Much of the power and fascination of archaeology is based on this perceived commonality with aspects of the past, of 'us' and 'them' all being human together and facing the demands of practical problem-solving together with abstract conceptualisation.

Structuring learning

Is all learning, especially incidental learning that we all encounter every day of our lives, the same as education? Most people would say not and agree that education requires some form of structure and is a more integrated process that requires planning. Rogers (1996) suggests that three characteristics differentiate education from informal learning: education is both sequential and cumulative, it progresses through making connections between pieces of information and experiences; the educational process operates within general principles so that methods and conclu-sions can be applied elsewhere within an established framework of knowledge; the educational process is at the same time both capable of being completed and yet remains incomplete. Individual learning episodes can be completed with goals reached, satisfaction attained and a sense of fulfilment achieved, and yet there is always a next stage – new doors open; there is always more to learn. Surveys have shown that one way individuals use to create 'educational' structure within self-directed learning is through joining interest groups, societies and clubs (Penland 1979; Brookfield 1981; Elsdon et al. 1995). Belonging to a 'community of learning' provides the support, interaction and exchange of expertise that can overcome some of the disadvantages of individual self-directed learning such as a lack of resources and following intellectual dead-ends. In this context it is no coincidence that amateur county archaeological societies were the first large-scale organisations within United Kingdom archaeology. For example, the Surrey Archaeological Society, formed in 1854, had 365 members in its first year with the object of studying and preserving the county's antiquities by 'encouraging individuals in making researches and excavations, and afford them suggestions and co-operations' (*Surrey Archaeological Collections*, Volume 1, 1855). The Sussex Archaeological Society was inaugurated in 1846 and had ninety members within its first three weeks (*Sussex Archaeological Collections*, Volume 1, p. 1, 1847), while the Wiltshire Archaeological and Natural History Society had nearly three hundred people at its first meeting in Devizes Town Hall in 1853 (*Wiltshire Archaeological and Natural History Magazine*, Volume 1, Preface, 1854). Rules of these societies were, and still are, quite explicit in encouraging all, regardless of class, to participate in mutual learning and understanding. This was to be achieved through regular lectures, field trips and using publications as the medium of communication, with costs kept low so as to 'reach all classes of people' (ibid.). Discussion of religious and political topics was specifically forbidden and seen as a distraction from the business in hand. The emphasis was on unity through the understanding of a shared past, which was only possible by ignoring a diverse and fragmented Victorian present. Local societies still play an important role in the structures of archaeological learning and county journals form the articulated backbone of the national archive.

Social reforms of the Victorian period which are relevant here include university extension classes that began the long tradition of adult education within British universities. It was, ironically, Oxford and Cambridge, those two bastions of elitism, that started what would now be called outreach work when in the 1870s they established extension classes whereby dons travelled the country giving a series of lectures on topics of scientific and literary interest aimed at the general public (Goldman 1995). In 1888, the first-ever summer school was held in Oxford and attended by over nine hundred students, based on principles of egalitarian learning within an intensive group situation. Two years later, in 1890, the archaeologist Sir Arthur Evans gave the first archaeological input to an extension class. The motivation for these pioneers was based largely on a personal political commitment to the early Labour movement, but also on a respect for people's ability to learn regardless of their social background, a sentiment that most people working in continuing education today would still agree with.

Changes in continuing education

Is there a future for continuing education? University continuing education courses of today in the United Kingdom are the legacy of these Victorian social reformers and are currently facing their greatest challenges since those early days. Within the last few years CE funding has been 'mainstreamed', resulting in many CE departments being absorbed into mainstream departments, together with the courses offered. The merger has also been at the philosophical level with increasing concern over standards and accreditation. This has imposed upon CE the traditional formality of university ideology based on the quantification of quality and success. The positive benefit of this is that within these formal structures are immensely widened access opportunities to higher education through part-time award-bearing courses within a national transferable credit framework. The negative aspect is the reinforcement of the divide between formal and informal learning, with the strengthening of the bureaucratic system based on setting targets, keeping records, performing tests and identifying outcomes. There is a great danger that these demands will exclude more people than they include: people who benefit through learning in ways that are not easily quantifiable, who recognise achievement in ways other than paper statements, who gain fulfilment through participation and seek learning because it is a pleasure and personally enriching (Hayes 1998). The 'traditional liberal adult-education classes' of CE, which are rapidly disappearing because of the funding emphasis on accredited classes, appeal to these values and often provide a pathway into the more formal learning structures.

Conclusion

Despite the rhetoric of New Labour, lifelong learning is not something they have invented or recently thought of. There is an existing body of theory and empirical research that suggests reasons why adults learn and how we learn most productively and satisfyingly. Learning is a spectrum merging from the incidental learning, which is the daily practice of engaging with the world, through informal goal-oriented learning often within interest groups, to the formal structures of the educational system. Archaeology is well integrated into both the formal and informal systems, and the major challenge facing university CE educators lies in the integration and engagement of these two sectors. Traditionally, CE has been more flexible and able to respond to social change than mainstream university departments, and it is essential that this distinctiveness is retained, valued, and utilised to the full. Learning is for life and there is no reason why archaeology should not be so as well.

Acknowledgements

I would like to thank the Committee for Archaeology and the Department for Continuing Education, University of Oxford, for funding my participation at WAC4, Cape Town, South Africa, in January 1999, where an earlier version of this chapter was first given an airing. Thanks are also due to Professor Maria Slowey (Glasgow

University) who read and commented on an earlier draft, and to Judy Brown (Oxfordshire County Council, Department of Lifelong Learning) who made me realise how peripheral universities are within the learning strategies of most people. The views expressed in this chapter, however, are entirely my own.

■   ■   ■

References

Brookfield, S. (1980) Independent adult learning, *Studies in Adult Education* 13(1): 15–27 (National Institute of Adult Education, Leicester).

Candy, P.C. (1991) *Self-direction for Lifelong Learning*, San Francisco: Jossey-Bass.

Department for Education and Employment (1998a) *Further Education for the New Millennium: Response to the Kennedy Report*, London: HMSO.

Department for Education and Employment (1998b) *Higher Education for the 21st Century: Response to the Dearing Report*, London: HMSO.

Department for Education and Employment (1998c) *The Learning Age: A Renaissance for a New Britain* (Green Paper) Cm 3790, London: HMSO.

Department for Education and Employment (1999) *The Learning Age. The Response*, London: HMSO.

Elsdon, K., Reynolds, J. and Stewart, S. (1995) *Voluntary Organisations: Citizenship, Learning and Change*, Leicester: NIACE (The National Organisation for Adult Learning) and The Continuing Education Press.

Fryer, R.H. (1997) *Learning for the Twenty-First Century. First Report of the National Advisory Group for Continuing Education and Lifelong Learning*, Belfast: NICATS.

Goldman, L. (1995) *Dons and Workers. Oxford and Adult Education Since 1850*, Oxford: Oxford University Press.

Hayes, C.D. (1998) *Beyond the American Dream: Lifelong Learning and the Search for Meaning in a Postmodern World*, Wasilla, Ark.: Autodidactic Press.

Hodder, I. (1999) *The Archaeological Process: An Introduction*, Oxford: Blackwell.

Houle, C. (1961) *The Inquiring Mind*, Madison: University of Wisconsin Press.

Kennedy, H. (1997) *Learning Works: Widening Participation in Further Education*, Coventry: FEFC.

Knowles, M.S. (1970) *The Modern Practice of Adult Education: Andragogy versus Pedagogy*, New York: Association Press.

Knowles, M.S. (1983) Andragogy: an emerging technology for adult learning. In M. Tight (ed.) *Adult Learning and Education*, Beckenham: Croom Helm.

Kolb, D.A. (1984) *Experiential Learning: Experience as the Source of Learning and Development*, Englewood Cliffs, N.J.: Prentice-Hall.

National Committee of Inquiry into Higher Education (1997) *Higher Education in the Learning Society (The Dearing Report)*, London: HMSO.

Penland, P. (1979) Self-initiated learning, *Adult Education Quarterly* 29(3): 170–179 (Washington, DC: American Association for Adult and Continuing Education).

Percy, K., Burton, D. and Withnall, A. (1994) *Self-directed Learning among Adults: The Challenge for Continuing Educators*, Lancaster: Association for Lifelong Learning.

Rogers, A. (1996) *Teaching Adults*, Buckingham: Open University Press.

Surrey Archaeological Collections 1 (1855).

Sussex Archaeological Collections 1 (1847).

Wiltshire Archaeological and Natural History Magazine 1 (1854).

PART TWO

National Organisations

Chapter 7

ENGLISH HERITAGE EDUCATION: LEARNING TO LEARN FROM THE PAST

Mike Corbishley

> The cities that Europe can offer are too full of rumours from the past. A practised ear can still detect the rustling of wings, the quiverings of souls. We feel the dizziness of centuries, of glory and of revolutions.
>
> Albert Camus, *Noces suivi de l'été*

Introduction

While each country's many heritages are defined in ways particular to that country, the 'heritage providers' have two broad duties. One is to care for the physical remains of those 'rumours from the past', quoted above (Camus 1959). The other is to make those heritages accessible in various ways, both physically and intellectually, in reality or virtually through interpretative media.

English Heritage is the United Kingdom government's adviser on all aspects of the built heritage in England. It was established as The Historic Buildings and Monuments Commission for England by the National Heritage Act 1983 and began work in April 1984. English Heritage is sponsored by the government's Department for Culture, Media and Sport, which has overall responsibility for heritage policy in England. It also works closely with the Department for Transport, Local Government and the Regions, which is responsible for planning, housing and transport. This department, and the Department for Environment, Food and Rural Affairs, provides the constitutional framework within which most decisions affecting the historic environment are made.

In April 1999, English Heritage merged with the Royal Commission on the Historical Monuments of England to become the lead body in the heritage sector. The work of English Heritage falls, broadly, into four categories: identifying buildings of historic or architectural interest and ancient monuments for protection under the law; surveying historic buildings and archaeological sites and making this record available through the National Monuments Record; assisting owners of historic buildings and monuments with conservation responsibilities to secure the future of England's historic environment; and helping the public to appreciate, understand and enjoy their heritage.

Within this fourth category of work is English Heritage's main educational work – considered by English Heritage's governing body, the Commission, and by government to be a fundamental part of English Heritage's work and crucial if we are to create a climate in the future which will be more sympathetic to the historic environment. The English Heritage Commission has established a department of education with full-time education officers working in each of its nine regions, an officer responsible for further and adult education, and an officer based at the National Monuments Record. All the education officers have teaching qualifications and service or experience in heritage education.

The historic environment context

The context in which English Heritage Education operates defines what its policies and strategies are. There are two separate contexts in which it must work. One is the context of the historic environment. While the definition of the historic environment might seem obvious to those working within it, the public, and in particular different sections of the public, now have a variety of views. The views of television viewers have certainly been influenced by programmes such as *Time Team* and *Meet the Ancestors*. However, the view of what the historic environment is and what it means in these television programmes is, essentially, that of the archaeologists who write and present the programmes. If you substitute the word 'heritage' for historic environment, then there will be different responses. A recent opinion poll (MORI 2000), commissioned by English Heritage, quotes the following taken during a focus group discussion around the question 'what is the heritage?':

> Everybody's heritage is different. The environment you grow up in gives you your heritage.
>
> (Asian female)

The research revealed that 98 per cent of those interviewed thought that heritage was important for teaching children about the past and that all schoolchildren should be given the opportunity to find out about England's heritage. To the question 'If you were given £100 to put towards one aspect of the heritage which aspect would you choose?', the greatest percentage chose 'education programmes for schools'.

More than half those interviewed said that they were as interested in learning about other people's cultures as their own.

Anyone working in heritage education needs to be aware of changes to people's attitudes towards heritage or the historic environment. English Heritage expects that the recent review of the historic environment, published as *Power of Place* (English Heritage 2000), which the government asked it to carry out, will lead to a redefinition of 'heritage' and shape future policies in the light of the widespread public consultation that contributed to the review.

The curriculum context

The other context in which English Heritage education operates is defined by the curriculum. It has always taken the view that any service, or provision of resources for education, at whatever level, needs to be firmly based on published curricula. The author has discussed this before (Corbishley and Stone 1994), but curricula at different levels in education have since changed, in particular in post-16 provision (Jones, Chapter 4; Hamilakis and Rainbird, Chapter 5) and in lifelong learning (Lock, Chapter 6). The government's 'Learning Journey' will have an effect at all levels of education, both formal and informal.

However, it is still the National Curriculum, and in particular the History curriculum, which defines much of the work of heritage educators, including English Heritage. Each version of the History curriculum has been fraught with controversy. At the time of the second version of the National Curriculum, an *Evening Standard* leader (quoted in Corbishley 1999) voiced the concerns and views of some people, saying that:

> The teaching of history has to be based on imparting facts. Without the basic framework of constitutional and political history – that is to say, kings and queens, battles and parliaments – even a rudimentary understanding of the subject is not possible.
>
> (Corbishley 1999: 75)

The leader went on to 'accuse the people who drew up the curriculum' of recommending a curriculum which is heavily dependent on social trends, economic development and non-European cultures:

> One knows, of course, what this will involve: imaginative compositions about the home life of Anglo-Saxon villagers, coloured drawings of the domestic implements of medieval Londoners, subjective accounts of his experience by a young protester at Peterloo . . . Of course it's much easier to let children speculate about everyday life in the remote past than to teach them, say, about the Reformation.
>
> (Corbishley 1999: 75)

This rather quaint view, which betrays the leader writer's lack of understanding about both the nature of historic evidence and about the way in which children learn, was still being voiced at the latest version of the History curriculum. However, to a large extent, 'the people who drew up the curriculum' have resisted the demands for 'back to basics' history teaching in 'Curriculum 2000'. The latest National Curriculum documents (DfEE/QCA 1999) still contain the requirements to teach periods of history to Key Stage 1, 2 and 3 pupils, using a variety of real sources of evidence from a variety of viewpoints.

Many people now agree that some of the best and most imaginative history teaching and learning is taking place in primary schools. Pam Stephen's work (Stephens 2000) of encouraging learning by primary pupils with special educational needs is just one example of the good work that is going on.

Supporting teachers

English Heritage education's main role is to support teachers. As a national organisation, with responsibilities for promoting the whole of the historic environment in England, and recognised by government as the leading heritage education organisation, it feels that 'teaching teachers' is the most effective way of ensuring that the historic environment is used in teaching not just history but a variety of other subjects. We support teachers in five main ways.

First, we try to influence government thinking about the inclusion of the historic environment in published curricula. We have always commented on drafts of the National Curriculum, public examinations and post-16 qualifications, for example, often in association with other interested bodies such as the Council for British Archaeology. The fact that pupils in primary and secondary schools can be found handling real objects, visiting real historic monuments, deciphering real documents and examining the bias in artists' impressions is testimony to the influence the major heritage education organisations have had.

Second, we provide free advice and in-service training courses for teachers (INSET) – from introductions to particular sites to residential courses which examine aspects of the local historic environment. Because students training to become primary teachers receive so little help with evidence-based history teaching, we have concentrated effort and resources on teacher-trainers, teacher-trainees, and newly qualified teachers, producing specific publications for them (English Heritage 1997).

Third, we have devoted large parts of our annual budget, since our formation in 1984, to the publication of a range of resources for teachers and tutors at various levels in education. Part of this is commitment to free material ranges from a termly magazine, *Heritage Learning*, to booklets on a large number of the historic sites in our care. The resource material includes books, poster packs, CD-ROMs, and videos covering all major aspects of the historic environment – for example, school buildings (Purkis 1993) or prehistory (Corbishley *et al.* 2000), and curriculum-based studies of the historic environment such as art (Lockey and Walmsley 1999) or English (Collins and Hollinshead 2000). We have also published a range of specialist book and video resources for GNVQ students and tutors.

Fourth, we offer free visits to all the sites in our care to any educational institution, provided that the visit is curriculum-based. At some sites we provide on-site facilities for education groups. We always provide resource material with ideas for making effective use of the site. We never provide on-site teaching for pupils as we feel that the teacher should be supported to make visits both to our sites and to the greater historic environment on his or her own. We do provide a programme of on-site workshops to cover specific areas of the curriculum, such as the literacy and numeracy strategies.

Fifth, we are concerned that pupils, and the communities they are part of, begin to think about what kind of environment they want to grow up in. Part of the research quoted above (MORI 2000) brings this out in answer to questions about attitudes to heritage:

> The future, so our kids can grow up and there is something to show, to look back and say, 'yes we had that and we have looked after it'.
>
> (Asian female)

We have organised projects in every one of our nine regions to research and publish ideas for using the historic environment to teach citizenship at both primary and secondary levels. This initiative builds on another, 'Schools Adopt Monuments', which English Heritage has been managing nationally at sixty-two schools across the country. Summer 2001 saw the culmination of linking literacy and historic sites at summer schools held at two of our sites. These summer schools were funded by the Department for Education and Employment (DfEE, now DFES).

Future developments

There are a number of areas which English Heritage Education is now moving into. The service has concentrated very much on addressing the needs of formal education. We will be widening our work through an integrated strategy for Education, Events and Outreach. We will be developing new and improved resources on our own sites to support informal learning by children visiting as part of family groups, as well as within formal education groups. We are developing specialist parts of our website especially for children. The web will, increasingly, become a major resource in providing information, advice and learning materials.

English Heritage now has a social inclusion policy. The education department has helped put that together and is publishing a guide for teachers, called *Cultural Connections* (Corbishley 2000), addressing the issues of the many cultures and peoples from across the world who have influenced British history, society, landscapes, buildings and objects.

Finally, we have begun to provide very specific help to other heritage organisations who care for parts of the historic environment but look to English Heritage to advise on, and in some cases (for example the Churches Conservation Trust and the Historic Houses Association) provide, an actual education service. In addition, the publication of the government's response to English Heritage's review of the historic environment (DCMS 2001) has given us the task of developing the place of education within the historic environment sector, in particular producing specific curriculum-based resources and developing lifelong learning opportunities, together with the Learning and Skills Council.

■   ■   ■

References

Camus, A. (1959) *Noces suivi de l'été*, Paris: Gallimard.

Collins, F. and Hollinshead, L. (2000) *English and the Historic Environment*, London: English Heritage.

Corbishley, M. (1999) The National Curriculum: help or hindrance to the introduction of archaeology in schools? In J. Beavis and A. Hunt (eds) *Communicating Archaeology*, Oxford: Oxbow Books.

Corbishley, M. (ed.) (2000) *Cultural Connections: Using the Evidence of Historic Sites*, London: English Heritage.

Corbishley, M. and Stone, P.G. (1994) The teaching of the past in formal school curricula in England. In P.G. Stone and B. L. Molyneaux (eds) *The Presented Past*, London: Routledge.

Corbishley, M., Darvill, T. and Stone, P. (2000) *Prehistory*, London: English Heritage.

Department for Culture, Media and Sport (DCMS) (2001) *The Historic Environment: A Force for Our Future*, London: DCMS.

Department of Education and Employment (DfEE) and Qualifications and Curriculum Authority (QCA) (1999) *The National Curriculum*, London: DfEE/QCA.

English Heritage ([1997] 2000) *Learning Beyond the Classroom. Information for Newly Qualified Teachers* (revised edn), London: English Heritage.

English Heritage (2000) *Power of Place: The Future of the Historic Environment*, London: English Heritage.

Lockey, M. and Walmsley, D. (1999) *Art and the Historic Environment*, London: English Heritage.

Market and Opinion Research International (2000) *Attitudes Towards the Heritage*, London: English Heritage/MORI.

Purkis, S. (1993) *Using School Buildings*, London: English Heritage.

Qualifications and Curriculum Authority (2000) *Evaluation of Parents' Leaflets*, London: QCA Research Team.

Stephens, P. (2000) Romans for a day. *Heritage Learning, Autumn 2000*, London: English Heritage.

Chapter 8

HISTORIC SCOTLAND AND EDUCATION: A HOLISTIC APPROACH

Sue Mitchell

Introduction

Scotland's built heritage is a rich tapestry which illuminates the nation's history from the earliest times. The thread reaches from prehistoric standing stones to medieval castles and formal great gardens through to Georgian houses, Victorian factories and Second World War defences. This fascinating built heritage has an important role in promoting a wider understanding and appreciation of Scottish culture. As an education resource it is truly inspiring!

Historic Scotland was created as an agency in 1991 and is part of the Scottish Executive Education Department, which embraces all aspects of the cultural heritage. As part of the Scottish Executive, Historic Scotland is directly accountable to Scottish Ministers for safeguarding the nation's built heritage, and promoting its understanding and enjoyment.

Reflecting the dual roles enshrined in the mission of the agency, educational objectives are embedded into its internal and external activities: first, in terms of acquiring and continuing to develop the technical knowledge and skills needed to conserve the built heritage; second, in terms of developing informed and positive attitudes to the built environment through a range of informal and formal education programmes and communication initiatives.

Whilst there is an Education Unit in Historic Scotland dedicated to the development of structured learning and teaching initiatives, the activity of this department is only part of the story. Education lies at the heart of the agency, rooted within an organisational structure that facilitates the fulfilment of its broad educational objectives.

Developing skills to safeguard the nation's built heritage

The potential for Scotland's built heritage to motivate learning and teaching is remarkable, and safeguarding its future is essential. Under the direction of the Director and Chief Executive, knowledge developed within the Historic Buildings and Ancient Monuments Inspectorates informs the work of the Heritage Policy Directorate. The implementation of policies apropos the agency's role in safeguarding the nation's built heritage is supported by the Technical, Conservation, Research and Education Group (TCRE). Formed in 1993, TCRE works to improve the standard of conservation carried out on Scotland's built heritage through research, the development of skills relating to conservation of the built heritage, and by raising standards of conservation practice among owners, trade and professional groups.

TCRE both undertakes conservation projects through the Historic Scotland Conservation Centre and co-ordinates specialist training opportunities through the Scottish Conservation Bureau (SCB), the three main training programmes being Interns, Fellows and Quinque Fellows – a mid-career exchange placement by the Quinque Foundation in America. The SCB is also a central enquiry point for advice and information on conservation in Scotland. The Director of TCRE chairs the Scottish Conservation Forum in Training and Education. Meeting six-monthly, this body includes representatives of colleges and universities, as well as those involved in the building industry and related professional bodies. Furthermore, TCRE is currently leading a UK-wide initiative to integrate more closely the different accreditation schemes for professionals in building conservation.

TCRE publishes Technical Advice Notes, Practitioners' Guides, Research Reports and Conference Proceedings, and arranges the official issue of all its technical publications to university and college libraries, and to participating members of its various other conservation liaison groups.

Promoting understanding and enjoyment: opportunities for informal learning

Working alongside Heritage Policy and TCRE is the Properties in Care Group (PIC) which provides the main channel of communication between Historic Scotland and the general public. PIC looks after the conservation and presentation of some 300 historic monuments and buildings in state care. Its activities are wide ranging and encompass the work of both the Education Unit and the new Interpretation Unit, amongst others. The remit of the Interpretation Unit covers the presentation of the properties and the provision of informal learning opportunities.

In presenting its properties in care Historic Scotland seeks to provide a number of learning opportunities and engage with a variety of audiences. A mix of interpretative media, each having an appeal to different age groups, intellectual interests and abilities, delivers a range of informal learning experiences.

All sites open to the public are provided with interpretative panels, which present an introduction to the site and its history, and highlight features of archaeological and/or architectural interest. Staffed sites offer additional learning opportunities. These may include guidebooks, sound guides, guided tours, costumed interpretation, audio-visual displays, exhibitions, interactive displays and programmes, all of which require on-site management and supporting services.

Interpretation is not only used to communicate the history of the site and its archaeological or architectural significance but also to explain active conservation projects at properties in care. The use of explanatory interpretative panels, specialist talks and guided tours, as well as craft skills demonstrations, ensures that conservation values are highlighted during any such on-site works, raising awareness of the importance of preserving our cultural heritage and promoting positive attitudes.

One of the most successful and dynamic ways Historic Scotland has engaged with its visiting public, especially families, over the last ten years has been through the development of an annual events programme. Since its inception in 1993, this programme has provided endless opportunity to re-present the built heritage and its history to the people of Scotland and its visitors. Bringing sites to life through re-enactment, music and drama, it has successfully brought many tens of thousands of visitors to the properties at weekends and evenings.

Another avenue for promoting enjoyment and understanding of the built heritage is the membership organisation, Friends of Historic Scotland. A quarterly magazine advertises forthcoming events, offers special Friends activities and features editorial on a range of topics relating to the work of Historic Scotland. Friends of Historic Scotland plays a key role in generating informed and positive attitudes to the built heritage among the Scottish population, with overseas Friends and supporters.

On-site learning opportunities are augmented by Historic Scotland publications. Since 1993, jointly with educational publishers, Historic Scotland has produced two series of publications, each with a different learning market. Working with B.T. Batsford, the Chief Inspector of Ancient Monuments has been series editor of a range of books aimed at interpreting the principal archaeological and architectural monuments to a broad audience. Titles include *Prehistoric Scotland*, *Viking Scotland* and *Pilgrimage in Medieval Scotland*. A further series of publications called *The Making of Scotland* has provided for younger audiences, or those whose requirement is for easy accessibility, a colourful range of books full of photographs of sites and artefacts and associated reconstruction drawings, maps and plans. The aim of this series is described as providing 'lively, accessible and up-to-date introductions to key themes and periods in Scottish history and prehistory'. Both series make sure that the value of the archaeology and the built heritage as sources of evidence for the past take their place alongside other publications looking at themes in Scottish history. Teachers and lecturers have been particularly appreciative of these publications, but they have also appealed to a much wider audience. Titles are now sold in shops at major Historic Scotland sites and, perhaps more importantly, in bookshops in High Streets throughout the country.

Beyond the needs of the visitor and the High Street, Historic Scotland produces a range of other publications based on research topics within the Inspectorates, TCRE or other specialist departments. Historic Scotland staff also write regularly for professional magazines and journals about their work.

The Education Unit: opportunities for structured learning

If a distinction is to be made between the work of the Education Unit and that of the Interpretation Unit, it must be that the Education Unit focuses on providing opportunities for structured learning and teaching more so than informal learning. That is not to say that the Education Unit has no role to play in developing interpretation. Education Officers with knowledge of different learning styles contribute both to the interpretative planning process to identify audience needs and to the development of a range of interpretative media to ensure that those needs are met. Traditionally, however, the main principle behind the work of the Education Unit has been to establish Historic Scotland as a serious contributor of education materials for use in schools and at historic sites.

In recent years the Education Unit has seen an increase in the number of education officers and supporting administrative staff. The result has been an expansion of the service it provides to include the delivery of an annual programme of activities for schools at selected sites, in-service training for teachers, and the generation of a number of special projects each year which support national initiatives. Research undertaken by the Inspectorates, TCRE and other divisions underpins the development of all formal education opportunities provided by the Unit.

The Free Educational Visits Scheme is fundamental to the Education Unit's service provision. Visits to historic sites provide a context for unique and imaginative learning opportunities, and Historic Scotland is keen to encourage their use by a range of education groups. This scheme helps to fulfil Historic Scotland's commitment to social justice, offering free entry to qualifying groups. The accompanying teacher or group leader generally leads visits booked through the Free Educational Visits Scheme. The success of the visit, therefore, is dependent on good planning and the use of high-quality resource materials. The Education Unit encourages teachers and group leaders to make a free preparatory site visit to gather essential information about facilities and plan appropriate on-site activities. If a planning visit is impractical due to difficulties of distance or time, teachers and group leaders can visit the Historic Scotland website to find out more about the property they are visiting and download selected resource materials. Awareness-raising courses both for practising teachers and for teachers in training are carried out at a number of sites throughout Scotland each year to encourage effective use of the sites to support studies across the curriculum.

The Education Unit has produced a variety of resource materials targeted at the schools audience, but which can also help other educational groups in their planning.

These resource materials include: basic site profiles; site-specific resource packs; packs dealing with types of site, such as castles and abbeys; and packs which focus on themes such as heraldry or how to besiege a castle. The packs advocate use of the site as a context for learning, developing investigative skills and informed attitudes about social and environmental responsibility as well as knowledge in specific subject areas. They are always developed in collaboration with educational professionals who know the curriculum, have used the sites and understand their potential to support studies across the curriculum. The authors of the packs follow recognised good practice, structuring background information and creative ideas into suggestions for pre-visit, on-site and post-visit activity at different levels.

Each year, at selected sites, Historic Scotland offers a varied programme of activities specifically for school groups. There is a small charge to cover costs for these activities, which include themed tours, costumed role-play, drama, storytelling, re-enactments, art and design, traditional crafts, medieval music and dancing, delivered either by Historic Scotland Education Officers or other heritage education specialists.

A great favourite with schools is the costume activity offered at a number of castles throughout Scotland, which aims to increase understanding of castle life. Historic Scotland Education Officers have developed activities around two periods: the sixteenth century, popular with schools studying Mary Queen of Scots; and the thirteenth century, popular with schools studying the Wars of Independence. Once in costume, children are encouraged to look for the clues to discover who would have dressed as they are, and why they dressed in this way. Clothes tell stories of hierarchy and power (or lack of it), and the children develop their own way of behaviour appropriate to their 'character'. Role-playing a banquet or dancing the paean in the Great Hall contributes to the children's experience of life for their castle 'character'.

An activity can focus pupils on details they can see on and in the buildings of the site they are visiting. At Edinburgh Castle the Education Officer leads pupils on a heraldry trail, directing observation to various coats of arms connected to the Wars of Independence which can be found on display in the Great Hall, in the decoration of the stained glass windows and in the relief panels around the castle. Pupils start by looking closely at and discussing the statues of Robert the Bruce and William Wallace located at the drawbridge of the castle. As they follow the heraldry trail pupils are introduced to the significance of colour, shape and symbols in the coats of arms they encounter – learning which is reinforced as pupils design their own coats of arms and manufacture these designs in clay. As an extension activity pupils take their clay heraldic shields back to class with information on how to paint them and ideas for creative writing.

The schools programme can sometimes link to significant Historic Scotland projects, such as ongoing archaeological excavations, offering school groups the chance to tour the site with an archaeologist and examine artefacts found on the dig. The opportunity to be so close to working archaeologists and to see discoveries being made while they watch is rare and engrossing. A resource pack helps teachers prepare for the visit and gives ideas for follow-up activity back in the classroom. A recent such project happened at Cadzow Castle in Lanarkshire. In this instance, interactive pages about the dig were available on the Historic Scotland website. Schools were also invited to post their classroom work on the website to be seen by other schools and visitors to the dig.

The Education Unit undertakes a number of special projects each year. These target a range of audiences and are often originated to support national initiatives. Amongst these have been contributions to National Construction Week, organised by the Construction Industry Training Board; the Big Draw, a national campaign to promote interest and develop skills in drawing; the Archaeology Fair co-ordinated by the Council for Scottish Archaeology (CSA); and careers events conducted by Careers Scotland. The Education Unit continues to develop its audience base to embrace learners of all ages and plans are afoot to support Adult Learners Week, organised in Scotland by the Scottish Adult Learners Partnership.

One of the most successful and exciting special projects undertaken in recent years was a three-day Gaelic education event held at Stirling Castle, the result of a collaborative project between Historic Scotland and Comunn na Gàidhlig, established with Scottish Office support in 1984 as a co-ordinating Gaelic development agency. More than three hundred pupils aged eight to eleven years, from nineteen Gaelic medium schools across Scotland, visited the castle for activities, which included lessons in medieval life and the history of Stirling Castle. Gaelic-speaking 'Jon the Jester', played by actor and television presenter Tony Kearney, made the lessons fun and accessible for children. Activities such as these raise the profile of Gaelic and work on both an educational and linguistic level.

Conclusion

It has not been possible in a few thousand words to cover all educational activity being undertaken within Historic Scotland, or even within the Education Unit, but hopefully this chapter will have given a flavour of the agency's holistic approach. Accordingly, the content of this chapter has been developed with contributions in thoughts or words from a few of those people whose work has been highlighted. Thanks must therefore go to Ingval Maxwell, Director of TCRE; Dr David Breeze, Chief Inspector of Ancient Monuments; Genevieve Adkins, Head of Interpretation; and not least to Marion Fry, former Education Manager of Historic Scotland. If you wish to find out more about Historic Scotland you can log on to the website on www.historic-scotland.gov.uk

Chapter 9

THE COUNCIL FOR BRITISH ARCHAEOLOGY AND THE COUNCIL FOR SCOTTISH ARCHAEOLOGY

Don Henson and Fiona Davidson

The early years

The Council for British Archaeology was founded in 1944 and is an independent charitable trust consisting of more than 450 organisations and institutions, and over 5,000 individual members. Its aim, as laid down in its Memorandum and articles of association, is:

> To advance the study and practice of the archaeology of or pertaining to Great Britain and Northern Ireland and in particular to promote the education of the public in British archaeology and to conduct and publish the results of research herein.

Although educating the public is fundamental to many of the CBA's activities, its work in relation to formal education is co-ordinated by its Education Committee. One of the CBA's first acts in 1944 was to set up an education sub-committee to develop an education policy. This proposed, among other things, the need to include archaeology in teacher-training, producing a bibliography for teachers, working closely with museums, encouraging archaeological organisations to co-operate in educational matters, involving universities in the training of archaeology teachers, encouraging the BBC to cover archaeology, and having a CBA standing committee on education. Education was also discussed at a CBA meeting in 1948, where Jacquetta Hawkes noted that archaeology had great potential for teaching not just history but also geography and English, and that it could also be used to strengthen people's attachment to their locality, improve people's aesthetic sensibilities, teach greater understanding for different cultures and enable greater life choices in the present (all of which points have been reflected in more recent debates about the nature of the school curriculum and government policies in relation to the historic environment). Another speaker, Philip Corder, noted the importance of contacting the non-specialist audience through popular literature and the 'new media' (in 1948 these were broadcast radio and film). Some of the proposals were adopted, while others had to wait for some time before being acted upon (e.g. having a permanent education committee), while some were taken up much later by others (e.g. the archaeology in education service at Sheffield University, run by Professor Keith Branigan to help train teachers). The early education work of the CBA concentrated on producing introductory booklists for teachers (three between 1949 and 1976), and holding a conference on archaeology and schools in London in 1956.

Providing an education service

In spite of the 1944 committee's recommendation, it was not until 1975 that a permanent set of education committees under an Education Board was established. It is clear that without a committee the ability of the CBA to be active in the educational field between 1944 and 1975 was limited. The establishment of the Education Board enabled the CBA's role in formal education to achieve a greater strategic purpose. The first Chairman of the Board was Professor J.D. Evans. He outlined the need for greater education in archaeology in his inaugural lecture as head of the Institute of Archaeology in the same year:

> Despite its great and growing popularity it seems to me that archaeology is still a widely misunderstood subject (not least by some of its friends, and even of its practitioners), and as a result of this it is still far from having achieved the place, either in formal education or in the general consciousness of society, to which its achievements, and its relevance to our human condition, entitle it.

The Board defined its aims as 'to make the general findings of archaeology, especially prehistoric archaeology, a part of the intellectual equipment of all members of society'. The Board's remit was the whole field of formal education, including schools, further, continuing and higher education. An early concern of the Board was the need for an education officer to be employed by the CBA. The first such officer was appointed in 1977. Unfortunately, funding difficulties meant that the post was not continuously filled on a full-time basis. However, support for education came from the CBA structure review of 1991 (the Cramp Report). This identified education as a core function of the CBA and stated that the educational workload was such that the appointment of a full-time education officer was essential; the post has been full-time since 1994. This enabled the CBA to be much more effective in achieving its educational goals. Indeed, the CBA continues to be the only body with a general overview of educational provision for archaeology in the United Kingdom. The CBA's education officers have been:

- Mike Corbishley, 1977–1984 (full-time to 1981)
- Gill Heyworth, 1985–1988 (honorary)
- Gareth Binns, 1988–1991 (part-time)
- Peter Halkon, 1992–1994 (part-time)
- Donald Henson, 1994–present (full-time)

Much of the Board's work was devolved to committees dealing with the various education sectors: the Schools Committee, the Further Education Committee and the British Universities Archaeology Committee. The Schools Committee was the longest-lived and most active of these. This structure was replaced by a single Education Committee in 1992. The Committee has been able to devise education strategies for the CBA with clear priorities for action. Shortly after this, the CBA regional and national groups were urged to appoint their own volunteer education liaison officers to provide a local point of contact for teachers and students.

The Council for Scottish Archaeology

The Council for Scottish Archaeology originated as the Scottish Group of the CBA in 1950. It reinvented itself in 1988 as an independent voluntary body, recognising the need for Scottish issues to be addressed directly from a Scottish base. One of its core principles is 'to advance the education of the public concerning Scotland's archaeological heritage', and its aim within that is 'to demonstrate that archaeology has a role to play within formal and informal education, in a great variety of subjects, at all levels and for all ages'.

There was no direct provision for education in the staffing of CSA until 1995 and the appointment of a part-time assistant director with a remit for education, although the part-time nature of the post meant a limit as to how active a role could be taken. In 1996 the post was elevated to a full-time basis and the benefits in scope and quality of the CSA's educational efforts was marked. However, until funding for another member of staff with a remit dedicated solely to educational initiatives is found success in the education field will remain diluted. The assistant directors so far have been:

- Jane Fletcher, 1995–1999 (part-time until 1996)
- Fiona Davidson, 1999–present

Also in 1996 an Education Committee was formed as a sub-committee of the CSA Executive Committee, its role being to support the educational work of the assistant director and act as a forum for exchange of good practice. It began looking at producing a proposal for a resources index for Scotland. The work of the CSA is linked with that of the CBA through having a representative sit on the Education

Committee of the CBA. This allows an interchange of ideas and experience between Scotland and the rest of the United Kingdom.

The scope of education

It is important to emphasise that the scope of education at the CBA and CSA has never been restricted to schools and children. The current fashion for lifelong learning (see Lock, Chapter 6) was foreshadowed very early by the CBA, which has always considered archaeological education to be a continuous process from childhood to post-retirement, with multiple opportunities to learn about, and become involved in, archaeology. This has been reflected in the structure and membership of its various committees dealing with education, and in the various education strategies and priorities developed by the Education Committee. The CBA has sought to influence the nature of the school curriculum, the content and structure of 14+ examinations, and has engaged in debates about the nature of higher and continuing education. Its publications have been aimed at school teachers, archaeologists and potential higher education students. The education officer supports the work of teachers and lecturers in schools, colleges and universities, and handles enquiries from students and parents covering all ages from primary school children to retired people. Promoting opportunities to study archaeology throughout a person's life is a key part of the CBA's approach to education. Likewise, the CSA has always considered education to encompass more than simply the school curriculum, and has put a lot of work into developing educational elements within its projects and initiatives, such as Adopt a Monument and, currently, Shorewatch. From early on, it has provided opportunities for incorporating archaeology in informal education, through its annual summer school and the Scottish field school of archaeology. The CSA is keen to involve youth groups, school groups and Young Archaeologists' Club branches to take part in these projects. Taking archaeology to the wider public has been achieved through initiatives like Scottish Archaeology Month (previously National Archaeology Days in Scotland) which encourages people in Scotland to investigate, explore and present their own heritage, and the bi-annual Archaeology Fair. The CSA also maintains an Outreach element to its work which is under increasing demand. Participation in a number of national and regional public events, such as the Edinburgh International Science Festival, Shetland Science Festival, East Lothian Festival of Science and Nature, Aberdeen Techfest, Countryside Fairs, and Environmental Fairs has helped raise the profile of archaeology.

Higher education

In 1979, the Universities Committee compiled a guide to university archaeology courses (Roe 1979), the first of a series that continues to be published to the present day (Roe and May 1983; Austin 1990; Heyworth 1995; Henson 1999). A striking feature of the CBA's involvement in higher education over the years has been the recurrence of several key issues. It is interesting to note that as early as 1976 the Universities Committee was noting concern about the lack of fieldwork training opportunities for undergraduates. A major concern, which led to the recon-stitution of the Committee in 1980 as the British Universities Archaeology Committee (BUAC), was the closure of archaeology departments in 1982/83 and the impact of financial cuts within universities (Austin 1990). By 1987, the BUAC was also engaged in talks with the IFA about the provision of training in archae-ology; still a concern at the present day. The BUAC was eventually replaced by the Standing Conference of University Professors and Heads of Archaeology (SCUPHA), an independent body, for which the CBA provided secretarial services. This has now become the Subject Committee for Archaeology (SCFA). The Universities Committee was also worried in 1982 about the acceptance onto PGCE courses of archaeology graduates. This continues to be a concern of the present Education Committee. In spite of archaeology providing a good, well-balanced degree with the ability to relate to many areas of the school curriculum, and covering many key transferable skills, some universities will only accept graduates on PGCE programmes with a degree in a school curriculum subject for such courses, and this does not include archaeology. The Education Committee after 1992 has continued to be concerned about higher education – for example, making a lengthy submission to the Dearing Inquiry into Higher Education.

Continuing education

The Further Education Committee eventually changed into the Adult Education Committee and was concerned to monitor adult continuing education courses in archaeology. Since 1993, the CBA has co-ordinated a yearly meeting of continuing education tutor organisers, the only such subject forum within continuing educa-tion. The tutors have now set themselves up as the Standing Conference of Archaeology in Continuing Education (SCACE), which has allowed this sector to become more visible and involved in current developments in archaeological training. A valuable part of the CBA's work has been the maintenance of a national database of all continuing education courses. Occasional early efforts at compiling data have been replaced by a regular compilation of information since 1994. This allows the CBA to have a nationwide picture of the provision of public education in archaeology at this level.

Schools and further education

The work of the Schools Committee between 1975 and 1992 soon settled down into certain areas, which continue to be important work for the current Education

Committee, although the areas of work have been broadened in scope to be wider than simply education in schools.

Influencing the curriculum

The Schools Committee was heavily involved in the preparation of syllabuses for education at 14+. These included a CSE Mode 1 syllabus and the JMB (later the NEAB and now AQA) A-level Archaeology. The CBA continues to be involved in the work of the AQA subject committees for archaeology which prepare and vet the exam papers each year for GCSE, AS and A-level. The Qualifications and Curriculum Authority (QCA), alongside the Curriculum and Assessment Authority for Wales, has also sought input from the CBA into the preparation of the school curriculum at 5–14. Right from the beginning of the curriculum, the CBA has been forcefully making the case for archaeological input into children's education. It produced *Archaeology 5–16* in an attempt to highlight the contribution archaeology could make to education in schools. Early on, there was concern over the lack of prehistory as a period of study in the curriculum in England, apart from the neolithic revolution as a suggested topic in Key Stage 3 (unlike in the rest of the United Kingdom). CBA pressure has had some success, and the latest version of the curriculum orders for England being taught from 2001 now include reference to prehistoric settlers as part of local studies in history, and to archaeologists by name under interpretations of history. This is the first time that either has been mention in the orders. Furthermore, countering a threat to local studies in the early drafts of the latest orders was an important part of the CBA's submission to QCA, and this element of the history curriculum was eventually restored in the final version of the new orders published in 1999. The separate nature of the curriculum in Scotland requires specific input from within Scotland to ensure that the place of archaeology is enhanced. The CSA has been keen to encourage the greater use of archaeology within history topics, and in other appropriate areas of the curriculum, through responding to consultation documents. Responses have been made to consultations on *Culture in the Curriculum*, *Scottish History in the Curriculum*, and *Changes to Environmental Studies in the 5–14 Curriculum*.

Helping teachers find resources

Adequate teaching of archaeology at all levels depends not only on having teachers and curricula, it also needs proper resources for the teachers to use. The CBA produced a booklist for teachers in 1949 (Fox 1949) and a more comprehensive guide to resources in 1979 (Corbishley 1979). This continues to be an important part of its work (Halkon *et al.* 1992; Henson 1996). Other publications for teachers have included a *Bulletin of Archaeology for Schools* (1977–1985), a Lloyds Bank-sponsored series of booklets on various themes (1982 and 1985)[1] and the *Education*

Bulletin (1985–1989). The Education Officer also helped to establish the Audio-Visual Media Working Party, jointly between the CBA and the British Universities Film and Video Council. This has sought to publicise the existence of audio-visual resources for the teaching of the subject, and as part of this administers the Channel 4 Film Award for archaeology. The CSA also provides information on resources for teachers, but it also provides its own interactive kits and activity packs. Although the CSA is acting mostly only in a reactive role in this area of work, the demand for these resources is currently outstripping staff time and resources. The hands-on nature of these kits have a broad educational benefit. The resources prove especially popular with student teachers who find archaeology a valuable medium for teaching a whole range of subjects in the primary school curriculum. The interactive kits have also provided a stimulus for history for pupils with learning and behavioural disabilities.

Networking and sharing of ideas

As a national organisation, the CBA is in a key position to provide a focus for networking between practitioners of archaeological education. This helps people to share ideas, information and expertise, and so raises the overall level of education work. Early attempts at networking focused on the production of serial publications, e.g. the *Education Bulletin*, and occasional conferences (for example Richardson 1987). There was also a short-lived schools award for archaeological education in schools. Publications included one-off works designed to stimulate thinking about the teaching of archaeology and to show examples of what could be done. An early work was *Peopling Past Landscapes* (Steane and Cox 1978), while a CBA Research Report followed later (Cracknell and Corbishley 1986). The advent of the centrally organised school curriculum led to the production of guides to the use of archaeology in teaching in both England and Wales (Corbishley 1992; Howell 1994; Henson 1997; Pearson 2001). With the reinstatement of a full-time education officer in 1994, a more regular series of workshops and conferences has been possible. These have included a series of one-day workshops at various venues around the country, and longer weekend conferences for particular educational sectors, e.g. GCSE and A-level tutors. National conferences covering the whole spectrum of education were organised in 1987, 1999 and 2001. The 1987 conference was organised jointly with the Archaeology and Education Project of the University of Southampton (Richardson 1987). The later conferences were organised with the support of English Heritage, and in 2001 also by the Learning and Teaching Support Network. These will become a regular feature of the CBA's work, to be held every two years. Within Scotland, the CSA has sought to ensure that archaeology is properly represented within environmental education networks, e.g. the Scottish Environmental Education Policy Forum, and the Built Environment and Education Working Group.

Training

The CBA has long been concerned about the provision of training in archaeology. Apart from advertising field opportunities in the Briefing section of *British Archaeology*, it used to administer its own qualification, the Diploma in Practical Archaeology. This ran from 1979 to 1989, latterly in association with the Dorset Institute of Higher Education. Provision of courses in archaeology at all levels has greatly increased since then and there is no longer a role for the CBA in providing training directly. Likewise, the CSA used to run its own programme of training events and seminars but has more recently decided to continue in an advisory capacity, encouraging other groups to promote archaeological education. In-service training has been provided for countryside rangers, university students and student teachers. The CBA is still concerned about the training needs of archaeology, in particular the voluntary sector, and is involved in the work of the Archaeology Training Forum. On behalf of the forum it is establishing a website (the Training On-line Resource Centre, http://www.torc.org.uk) to enable people to search for training opportunities throughout the United Kingdom. The CBA was also consulted about the development of standards for archaeology NVQs by the Cultural Heritage National Training Organisation. A key interest for the CBA is to ensure that there are opportunities for training in archaeological methodology for members of local societies and non-professional archaeologists in general, and the 16+ sector in particular. The area of training is now receiving a much higher profile, both within archaeology and the work of the CBA. As a result the Education Committee has decided that it would in future be known as the Education and Training Committee of the CBA.

Providing advice and information

The CBA is in a good position to be able to monitor archaeological education nationwide and compiles databases of courses at all levels. It has also organised surveys; for example, a survey of education work within the Standing Conference of Archaeological Unit Managers (SCAUM) and the Association of County Archaeological Officers (now the Association of Local Government Archaeological Officers, ALGAO) was undertaken in 1985–1986. A great deal of the information held by the CBA and CSA is used to answer enquiries from the public. Information from the database of courses is published regularly in the Briefing section of the CBA magazine *British Archaeology*, and the database is used to answer a great many enquiries from the public. Around 6,000 such enquiries are received every year and include requests for information on excavations taking volunteers, courses available to the public, what A-level choices should be made by sixth formers, careers available, and information on teaching resources, etc. Information sheets have been produced by both the CBA and the CSA to meet this demand.[2] The CBA has also been able to advise archaeological organisations on organising education work, and teachers on how to include archaeology in their work.

The future

Future areas of work for the CBA and the CSA Education Committees will need to take into account the development of new technologies; for example, increasing the educational use of the Internet for archaeology. There will also be a need to be more socially aware by dealing with issues of social inclusion – expanding archaeological learning opportunities for economically disadvantaged groups, ethnic minorities and for those with disabilities, for instance. Tackling these issues may not be possible with existing resources, and will probably not be a matter for the CBA or the CSA alone. Finding new sources of funding and making links with wider networks will be a key part of any future success. A new CSA Education sub-group is very much in its infancy, but it is hoped it will act as a useful advisory body and help develop an education strategy within the CSA's overall forward plan. The development of a strategy will help focus the CSA's educational role to allow a proactive role to be taken in promoting archaeology and education in Scotland.

Notes

1   The Lloyds Bank booklets were as follows:

Adams, B. (1985) *Archaeology and the Sea*
Corbishley, M. (1982) *Archaeology in the Classroom*
Corbishley, M. (1982) *Archaeology in the Town*
Croft, R. (1982) *Archaeology and Science*
Dale, F. (1982) *Archaeology in the Primary School*
Dyer, J. (1985) *Archaeology and Death*
Powlesland, D. (1985) *Archaeology and Computers*
Steane, J. (1985) *Upstanding Archaeology*
Steane, J. (1982) *Archaeology in the Countryside*

2   The CBA factsheets are:

- Getting started in archaeology
- Metal detecting: advice for users of metal detectors in England and Wales
- Training in archaeological science
- Archaeology in higher education
- A job in archaeology
- Part-time university adult education courses in archaeology
- GCSE and A-level archaeology syllabuses

- Everything you always wanted to know about excavations but were too afraid to ask
- The CBA and buildings in England

■ ■ ■

References

Austin, D. (1990) *Guide to Undergraduate University Courses in Archaeology*, London: Council for British Archaeology.

Corbishley, M. (1979) *Archaeological Resources Handbook for Teachers*, London: Council for British Archaeology.

Corbishley, M. (1992) *Archaeology in the National Curriculum*, London: Council for British Archaeology.

Cracknell, S. and Corbishley, M. (eds) (1986) *Presenting Archaeology to Young People*, CBA Research Report 64, London: Council for British Archaeology.

Fox, A. (1949) *British Archaeology: A Book List for Teachers*, London: Council for British Archaeology.

Halkon, P., Corbishley, M. and Binns, G. (1992) *The Archaeology Resource Book 1992*, London: Council for British Archaeology.

Henson, D. (1996) *Teaching Archaeology: A United Kingdom Directory of Resources*, York: Council for British Archaeology.

Henson, D. (ed.) (1997) *Archaeology in the English National Curriculum*, York: Council for British Archaeology.

Henson, D. (1999) *2000 Guide to Archaeology in Higher Education*, York: Council for British Archaeology.

Heyworth, M. (1995) *British Archaeological Yearbook 1995–96*, York: Council for British Archaeology.

Howell, R. (ed.) (1994) *Archaeology and the National Curriculum in Wales*, York: Council for British Archaeology, Cadw: Welsh Historic Monuments and the National Museum of Wales.

Pearson, V. (ed.) (2001) *Teaching the Past: A Practical Guide for Archaeologists*, York: Council for British Archaeology.

Richardson, W. (ed.) (1987) *CBA Education Bulletin* 6, London: Council for British Archaeology.

Roe, F. (1979) *Guide to Undergraduate University Courses in Archaeology*, London: Council for British Archaeology.

Roe, F. and May, J. (1983) *Guide to Undergraduate University Courses in Archaeology*, London: Council for British Archaeology.

Steane, J. and Cox, B. (1978) *Peopling Past Landscapes*, London: Council for British Archaeology.

Chapter 10

THE YOUNG ARCHAEOLOGISTS' CLUB:
ITS ROLE WITHIN INFORMAL EDUCATION

Pippa Henry

Introduction

Three questions are frequently asked when the subject of the Young Archaeologists' Club (YAC) enters into conversation: What is it? What does it do? Who benefits? For those of us who devote a considerable amount of time and energy to the Club it is easy to forget that it is not a universally known organisation. As soon as these three questions are asked, however, the answers are instantly and enthusiastically forthcoming. This chapter is thus intended to explain and describe the Club, its benefits to young people, and the very important role of the volunteer network of adults that makes the organisation possible.

The Young Archaeologists' Club

What is the Young Archaeologists' Club?

It is the only organisation exclusively dedicated to introducing young people to archaeology, and extending their knowledge in an informal and exciting way. As such it holds a unique position in British archaeology. The club has been undertaking this highly enjoyable and valuable task since 1972, when it was known as 'Young Rescue', and is primarily designed to meet the interests of young people between the ages of nine and sixteen, although younger members are also included in some activities.

Who runs the Young Archaeologists' Club?

The Club was the brainchild of Kate Pretty, who with Mike Corbishley ran and developed it into a highly successful organisation. It was co-ordinated from Cambridge by Kate during the period 1972 until 1987, when the running of the club was taken over by the York Archaeological Trust. Since 1993 it has been run from the CBA, where the YAC co-ordinator and YAC assistant are employed to administer the organisation. Volunteers have always been the mainstay of the Club, and continue to form an essential part of its organisation and running. The YAC National Advisory Committee, consisting of branch representatives and a Chair, and the leaders and assistant leaders and helpers who help run the branches, are all volunteers and currently number in excess of two hundred adults. Without them, the club could not exist.

How does the Young Archaeologists' Club work?

There are two interlinked strands to the Club: the United Kingdom membership system and the branch network. Currently the membership stands at approximately three thousand, with nearly seventy branches throughout the United Kingdom.

Membership

The membership system enables young people with an interest in archaeology to experience it at first-hand via the branch network and the annual holiday. In addition, members receive the Club magazine, *Young Archaeologist,* four times a year; they can also take part in various competitions, including the Young Archaeologist of the Year Award, purchase the Club merchandise, and have discounted entry to many heritage sites and museums throughout the United Kingdom. Finally, the Club website provides an up-to-the-minute source of Club and archaeological information.

Branch network

The branch network is primarily for Club members, although some branches include non-members. Branch and assistant leaders are drawn from archaeological and educational backgrounds providing a range of skills and areas of expertise. They are all volunteers and devote a considerable amount of time to the branch system. Branches run from a wide range of venues, including museums, archaeological units, university archaeology departments, schools and heritage sites. The differing areas of experience of branch and assistant leaders, and the range of venues which provide differing facilities, affect the activities undertaken by each branch. Most leaders try to ensure a balance of activities, while some concentrate on field trips, others place emphasis on experimental archaeology, and others on the acquisition of archaeological skills.

All adults involved in the branch network are trained via training sessions within each branch and through the United Kingdom Club training weekends, which include all aspects of the skills and requirements of working with young people. As well as an essential element of working with young people, training enables leaders and their teams to exchange activity ideas, which are backed-up with activity sheets and advice from the Club office. Most branches make use of the expertise of local potters, basket-makers and textile workers, etc. The end result of both training and the use of local expertise provides young people with a wide variety of archaeological experience and the opportunity to acquire archaeological skills.

Club activities

The Club offers a wide variety of activities, some are passive while others are participatory. Some of the activities are also open to non-members: the Young Archaeologist of the Year Award, the website, merchandise, and in some instances branch membership (although we try to ensure that all branch members are also Club members).

The magazine

The Club magazine has been in place from the outset, although its title has changed over time from *Young Rescue Newsletter* to *Young Archaeology* in 1981, and currently, since 1993, *Young Archaeologist*. The aim, however, has always been the same, to provide the Club members with up-to-date archaeological news, as well as offering quizzes, competitions, offers and 'how to make' sections, centred around replicating excavated artefacts or recreating dishes using ancient recipes. One of the much-looked-forward-to sections is the interview with well-known or influential people working in, or who have an interest in, archaeology and heritage. Recent issues have featured Mick Aston and Julian Richards who head *Time Team* and *Meet the Ancestors* respectively, as well as being eminent archaeologists in their own right; Lloyd Grossman, who as well as presenting *Masterchef* and *Junior Masterchef* is an English Heritage Commissioner and a keen supporter of museums; and Kate Pretty, who featured in the 25th Anniversary issue.

Young Archaeologist of the Year Award

This award has been one of the Club activities since 1978 when it was known as the Young Rescue Award; in 1982 it was renamed the Young Archaeologists' Award and is now known as the Young Archaeologist of the Year Award. In every other year since 1980 the award has formed part of the British Archaeological Awards. The award is split into a junior (9–12) and senior (13–16) section, with a different challenge every year. In 1994 the competition was to design a cartoon character which would become the club mascot; the overall winner was Matthew Lovatt (aged 10) who created Norman Helmet, the archaeological worm (Figure 10.1). Other awards have included archaeological studies of a locality or monument, archaeological posters, stained-glass windows, inventing a machine to help archaeologists with their work, and a millennium time capsule. The award is very popular and normally creates a great deal of interest. It is an enjoyable way of encouraging young people to put their archaeological skills, knowledge and imagination to the test.

National Archaeology Days

The beginning of the National Archaeology Days (NADs) goes back to 1979 when, in conjunction with the London and Middlesex Archaeological Society, activities were laid on to encourage young people and their families to take part in various aspects of archaeology. In 1982 the event became a nationwide one involving ten sites. Nothing else happened until in 1990 Geoffrey Cole of the Southern Central England Branch of YAC co-ordinated a nationwide day of activities known as National Archaeologists' Day; in 1992 it was renamed National Archaeology Day. The annual event proved to be so popular with the public that in 1993 an extra day was added. An average of 130 sites take part in England, Northern Ireland and Wales over a weekend in July (during September in Scotland), offering a wide range of archaeological activities from passive to hands-on, excavation to experimental archaeology, and archaeological games. The weekend attracts in the region of 90,000 visitors and has become a well-established, looked-forward-to, aspect of the archaeological calendar. It is an ideal way to introduce archaeology to young people and their families.

Discounted entry

Members of the United Kingdom Club benefit from free, discounted or privileged entry to a range of heritage sites and museums, including English Heritage, Historic Scotland, Cadw and National Trust sites.

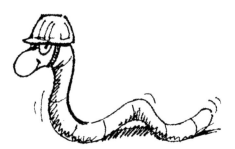

Figure 10.1   Norman Helmet

Merchandise

Way back in 1972 the Club produced the first items of merchandise: T-shirts displaying the Club emblem. The Club now has an extended range of branded merchandise ranging from sweatshirts and T-shirts to baseball caps and bum-bags. Mick Aston is often seen sporting a YAC T-shirt on the *Time Team* programmes!

Holidays

The highlight of the year for many of our members is the YAC holiday. The holiday was an annual event from its inception in 1975 until 1992. It was geared primarily to those young members without access to a branch. In the early days, two one-week holidays took place in the summer holidays, with the addition of a third week in 1978. The timing of the holidays subsequently changed but continued every year, with some being specifically organised for the older members of the club, aged 14–16. The holidays explored a different part of the country every year and even went to Denmark for one holiday.

In 1996 the holidays were reinstated following the pattern of the earlier ones: an annual event in which different parts of the country were visited each year, targeting those members without access to the branch network. Initially only one week was offered, but in 1999 demand was outstripping places so a second week was added. From 1996 to 1999 the group size per holiday was limited to fourteen; for the year 2000 holiday sixteen were being accommodated in each group. The groups are purposely kept relatively small to ensure that each young person benefits from individual attention and can get the most out of the activities offered. Since 1996 the holidays have taken place in Cornwall (twice), Snowdonia, Northumberland and East Anglia. In 2002 the holidays were expanded to three venues: Cornwall, East Anglia and Scotland. The residential centres that act as the holiday base are archaeological/ historical wonderlands in their own right – an upland farm with reconstructed Bronze Age village, castles, and Victorian mansions, etc.

The ethos of the holiday is to give young people an opportunity to encounter as wide a range of archaeological experience as possible from prehistory to nineteenth- and twentieth-century industrial and defence archaeology. As well as 'looking' and 'doing' we encourage debates regarding the ethics of excavation, interpretation, heritage, etc. The emphasis is on *holiday* so there is no compulsory note-taking or diary-keeping; the aim is to soak up the knowledge in an informal and enjoyable way. Judging by the questions fired at leaders and helpers, and the debates that rage throughout the holidays, this is more than adequately achieved; many adults could learn a thing or two!

The aim of the holiday is to encourage as much hands-on participation as possible, involving the survey and planning of building and earthworks, pottery making, textile working, roundhouse building, flint working, corn grinding, basket-making – in fact as many aspects of archaeology and experimental archaeology as we can arrange (Figures 10.2, 10.3). As well as hands-on work the groups are introduced

Figure 10.2   Surveying Black Middens Bastle House, Northumberland holiday 1998

Figure 10.3   Rigid heddle weaving at Trewortha Farm, Cornwall holiday 1999

Figure 10.4 Looking at buildings: Lindisfarne Priory, Northumberland holiday 1998

to buildings/structures and landscapes of different phases and periods, and are shown how to look for the evidence, and decipher and interpret it (Figure 10.4). Where possible we visit an excavation and have now been able to arrange a hands-on session at an excavation site for at least one of the holiday venues. The activities vary from region to region to ensure that the archaeology of each holiday locality is exploited to the full. To do this we invite local experts with various archaeological specialisms to work with the groups, ensuring that they get access to the best knowledge on offer, and introduce them to the wide range of disciplines that make up archaeology and to the characters who form part of the archaeological family!

The branch network

The seventy plus branches covering the United Kingdom range from relatively small groups of members to large groups with waiting lists. Branches hold a minimum of ten meetings a year, which include field trips and fieldwork, experimental archaeology and re-enactment (Figure 10.5), learning about aspects of various periods and cultures, and acquiring archaeological skills. The emphasis is on a high standard of learning in an interesting, exciting and informal way. Branches produce their own programmes of activities, many of which are requested by the branch members.

Field trips tend to take place during the spring to autumn months, with the winter months used for indoor activities. The range of activities and ways of presenting them are endless and dependent on the expertise and interest of the

Figure 10.5 Experimental industrial archaeology at Killhope Lead Mining Centre, Durham Branch

leaders and their teams. Some branches take a themed approach, examining aspects of one period or area of archaeology over several meetings; others examine individual aspects of archaeology or different periods to give a wide-ranging experience of archaeology. A few branches have access to archaeological equipment, as well as having the expertise to operate it. These branches often carry out archaeological surveys (Figure 10.6), and occasionally excavation and post-excavation work. Experimental archaeology is always popular with branch members, with a wide range of activities carried out, either undertaken by branch leaders and assistants or experts who are brought in (Figure 10.7). In general though, branch leaders ensure that many aspects of archaeology are explored and that branch members develop their knowledge and skills in an informal way.

The benefits to young people

Young people are under increasing pressure in the formal education sector, via the National Curriculum and the rise in the number of tests. In addition, archaeology and pre-twentieth-century history is being squeezed out of the school timetable in many instances. The Young Archaeologists' Club therefore not only acts as an antidote to the pressures of formal education, it also goes a long way to replacing many of the gaps in the archaeological and historical education of young people caused by the narrowing of the school curriculum.

Figure 10.6   Resistivity survey at Coxhoe Hall, Durham Branch

Figure 10.7   Experimental ladder making at Trewortha Farm, Cornwall Branch

Young people have always been excited by the past, which increased with the advent of large-scale urban excavations during the 1970s and 1980s, and the resulting interpretative sites built in their wake such as the Jorvik Centre in York. The 1990s witnessed a huge increase in interest, largely due to television programmes like *Time Team* and *Meet the Ancestors*, and archaeological discoveries such as 'The Ice Man' in the Austrian/Italian Tyrol, with the resulting media coverage it engendered. In addition, through the increase in use of imaginative interpretations and the use of reconstruction in museums such as the Museum of London, the utilisation of reconstruction at excavated sites, and the development of a more enlightened approach to informing the public at heritage sites, the last three decades of the twentieth century, and its continuation into the twenty-first, have brought about a far greater awareness of the past and a hunger to know more.

The founding of the Young Archaeologists' Club coincided with these developments and has continued to evolve to encompass new archaeological discoveries, thinking and ways of interpreting the past. As such, the Club ensures that all interested young people are not only taught the relevant skills of archaeology whilst learning about the past but are also kept up to date with developments and new ideas. The acquisition of the many skills and disciplines that make up archaeology also prepare young people for other areas of study, leisure activities and life in general.

In addition, some members, through the support of the Club and their local branch, have utilised this experience and knowledge to achieve success in the Duke of Edinburgh Award scheme, and have been able to undertake periods of work experience in archaeology units and university departments. A relatively large minority have also gone on to study archaeology at degree level, having a head start on their colleagues who have not experienced the advantages of membership of the Young Archaeologists' Club. Those who leave archaeology behind when they move on from the Club will always have the experience to look back on, and may even use the knowledge gained to influence decisions within various areas of business: development/construction, banking, sponsorship, etc.

It can be seen that the benefits of the Club to young people are extensive: from the simple enjoyment and excitement of learning about the past, to the more serious processes that can lead to a career in archaeology or related disciplines. As such it holds a unique position in archaeology and an essential place in informal education.

Conclusion

Returning to the commonly asked questions about the Young Archaeologists' Club: What is it? What does it do? Who benefits? It can be seen from the above discussion that the Club is an organisation that is dedicated to introducing young people to archaeology in an informal and enjoyable way, primarily aimed at the 9–16 age range. To achieve this the Club operates two interrelated strands: the membership system and the branch network. Within each strand archaeological skills and information are taught and presented to young people in a way that encourages the desire for more knowledge. The branch network and holidays in particular – only possible due to the dedication of the volunteers who run them – enable members to experience archaeology at first-hand, with activities covering all aspects of archaeology: experimental; the learning of archaeological techniques; discovering the evolution, development and demise of particular archaeological/historical periods and cultures. The *Young Archaeologist* magazine, the Young Archaeologist of the Year Award, and National Archaeology Days enable members to keep up to date with current news, put into practice the knowledge they have gained, and introduce family and friends to the intricacies of archaeology in a relaxed atmosphere.

The aims of the Young Archaeologists' Club are therefore to encourage an interest in archaeology, to ensure that all teaching and learning is carried out in an informal way in an atmosphere of enjoyment and excitement, and to help the development of inquisitive and well-rounded young people. Are these aims being achieved? Judging by the continuing success of the Club, and the members' determined and non-stop quest for knowledge, the answer has to be a resounding YES!

Chapter 11

VOCATIONAL TRAINING IN ARCHAEOLOGY

Peter Lassey

Archaeology is a very small and diverse profession. Its very nature and history has meant that the educational and learning provision for those who are actively pursuing a career in archaeology is limited. This short chapter looks at learning, how it can be encouraged in the workplace and the importance of occupational standards in making learning effective.

Embracing change

We are living in a changing world with each generation having to adapt to greater and greater change in an ever-shortening time-span. Technological change is having an enormous impact on all our lives. Society today is far more sophisticated than the world that we were all born into. As the leaps in technology become greater and greater, our ability to predict future developments with any certainty becomes more and more difficult. Consequently, a difficulty in predicting the future creates a difficulty in planning for future change. Few of us would argue that we keep pace with world events, technological developments and the development of ideas, that we constantly analyse this information and change or adapt our activities and ideas in response to the changing world. In other words we learn. However, in our professional life it is less straightforward. Do we always strive to improve our skills and abilities; do we strive everyday to learn from our jobs? For some, even the idea of being successful is unsavoury. Success and achievement in the workplace is somehow not very British, even vulgar. Still, success can mean less stress, more efficient and effective working, more spare time and even more respect from colleagues – not to mention the opportunities that open up to you and the feeling of security that comes with knowing that you are good at what you do. People have the ability to change and adapt. Successful archaeologists are people who learn. There is a saying: 'If you always do what you always did, you will always get what you have always got.' Without change there can be no learning and without learning there can be no improvement. Is it not strange then that for many of us change is something to be suspicious of and even something that should be avoided wherever possible? For many, change means uncertainty, insecurity and a lack of stability. Successful people embrace change and development. Any individual can learn and develop themselves. The type of environment in which they work will either help or hinder their development. An organisation that is likely to assist in the development of individual staff would appreciate that its future is dependent upon the abilities of all its people and provides opportunities for the personal development of those people. It would also accept that people learn in different ways, and would help all its people to learn, innovate and contribute to its future.

Learning

What do we mean by learning? The generally accepted definition of learning is the changing of behaviour, not simply on a theoretical level but on the level of everyday experience. We talk about learning to walk, to drive, to accept criticism and to live with someone else. Indeed, as all parents quickly realise, all human beings are created not only with the ability but with an almost obsessive compulsion to learn. Yet the mechanisms employed by society to assist learning tend to cater for a specific type of learner. This often labels others as unable to learn. Evidently this is not the case, but the priorities of the education system and society's attitude to a particular form of academic learning mean that the whole issue of learning is value laden. Moreover, it is easy to form the impression that learning equates exclusively with increasing knowledge, and the education system with bestowing that body of knowledge. It would be wrong to underestimate the immense value of knowledge and understanding in the learning process, but, at the same time, the acquisition of knowledge is just one part of the learning experience. Alongside knowledge, an individual needs opportunities to practise as well as a willingness and confidence to attempt the new behaviour. It is an active and often co-operative process and is dependent on the willingness of those concerned. To maximise effective learning in the workplace it is important for others to understand and be involved in the learning activities of their colleagues. Surprisingly, many quite senior managers in organisations still view the development of staff, and especially the acquisition of qualifications, as a threat. Often there is an assumption that providing training and development or qualifications will mean investing in an individual who will eventually leave, as if this was something that should never happen. Healthy organisations recognise that a degree of staff turnover is not only a fact of life but also necessary to a dynamic, robust and adaptable organisation. It is our most important attribute, but just as everyone has different characteristics and traits they also have different learning abilities and, as such, respond to different stimuli. For most of us, the way we usually learn is to search out information and advice relating to the subject that interests us. Often this is a TV programme, a book, a friend or family member. Only rarely would we look to the educational establishment for the learning, and then mainly when we need recognition for that learning. The same is true for how we learn at work. Mostly, we find out how to operate new machinery or how to achieve new tasks by asking and observing other colleagues. Eventually, we become proficient, after much trial and error. However, because we learn out of necessity rather than as part of a planned development we are always 'fire fighting'. Learning through crisis situations from colleagues is a very efficient and cost-effective method. It means that only essential skills are passed on. It means that employees are still working – hence, there is no down time for the employer and no cost to the employer.

It is perfectly feasible for an individual to identify development goals and seek out training and development opportunities for themselves. The learning process is multiplied many times when the learner is conscious of the process, since they become a participant in the process rather than a recipient. In order to do this, the learner needs to be able to assess their current performance, set down goals and analyse (objectively) data about their performance, be open and honest with colleagues, and turn to colleagues as a resource for learning. Colleagues can encourage learning by acting as mentors or guides for learners. Their role would be to reflect and provide accurate feedback in a positive manner, and encourage empathetic thinking by asking probing questions. The ability of an individual to learn from their experiences is dependent upon the individual's ability to learn how to learn. However, the learner's ability to learn is only one factor in determining the learning of an individual. Other factors will include the organisation's structures, the opportunities made available for learning and the learning culture within the organisation. There are many professions where there is no well-defined or structured in-service training. The majority of in-service development is through on-the-job learning or coaching; so it is with archaeology. The art of coaching is providing learning opportunities, guiding the learner, providing encouragement and evaluating the performance of the learner.

Learning opportunities

The learning opportunities provided for the learner fall into two main categories: carefully chosen work activities that will become progressively more demanding and demonstrations from the coach. The skill of the coach is to provide genuinely challenging activities for the learner whilst at the same time ensuring that it falls within the ability of the learner. The coach should seek to provide opportunities that contribute to an overall plan for the development of the learner. For example, if the learner has a learning need for project management skills it would be sensible to provide opportunities where the learner could become progressively involved in the running of projects. It is especially useful in developing additional skills, perhaps to prepare learners for promotion or for elements of a qualification. These work activities or learning opportunities should arise where possible from the job role, but they could spring from special tasks or job swaps. No matter where the source of the learning opportunity, it should always be a 'real' situation. This means that after preparing the learner for the task, the coach should take a back seat, letting the learner make the decisions and manage the task. This way, the benefits of the learning experience are amplified because the learner proves to herself as well as to others that she can accomplish the task without help. It is important that there is an opportunity for the learner to fail in order for the learning opportunity to be 'real', yet the coach should ensure that the learner will not fail. One way to achieve this is to ensure that the learner is quite clear about their responsibility for the learning activity and is fully prepared for the task, something that can only be achieved through detailed and careful briefing from the coach. It is important that the learner is involved in agreeing their learning needs, but the tasks must be selected because the coach believes that they can be achieved. However, this is not something to be broadcast to others. It is enough to say that the learner is undertaking this activity because the coach wishes them to do it and the coach is confident that they can successfully achieve it. Possible mistakes should be avoided. However, mistakes are a fact of life and will occur. If the learner does make mistakes, it is important that they learn from them. This can only be done in an organisational culture where mistakes are identified and put right at the earliest opportunity, where mistakes are not punished and where the correction of, and learning from, errors is valued and encouraged. Coaches should not blame a learner for mistakes in a coaching situation. All coaching tasks should be challenging, and coaches should encourage learners to think for themselves, not solve the learners' problems for them. They should also argue that the development of staff is the key role of all managers, and be genuinely concerned about the aspirations of the learner.

The coaching process

A coach will be required to show the learner 'how to' perform a particular task. A good demonstration will not only clearly illustrate the particular skill but will also outline the situations in which it should be used and the rationale for performing the skill in that particular way. It should highlight to the learner the importance of each stage and the reason why the skill is performed in that particular way. A typical demonstration might take the following form:

- the coach ensures that the learner can easily observe the demonstration;
- the coach performs the activity, explaining each step and its significance;
- after the demonstration, the coach clarifies with the learner that they have seen and understood the activity;
- the coach performs the activity once again, but this time asks the learner to explain the significance of each step, repeating steps if required until the learner is confident to perform the activity;
- the learner performs the activity themselves, explaining the significance of each stage.

The effect of any development activity is multiplied if the learner is aware of the process and its outcomes. Therefore, the evaluation of all development is crucial to coaching, and good evaluation is structured into the way in which the development activity is planned. In order to properly evaluate the learning outcomes of any learning opportunity both the learner and coach need to be clear from the outset what the learning needs or goals are, since the evaluation of the learning event is first and foremost an appraisal of the learning in relation to those learning goals. The proper evaluation process can do much more than simply identify if the learning activity was effective; it can also redefine the learner's learning needs, identify new learning opportunities, insights into working methods, feedback on the effectiveness of work systems and procedures, and establish a strong and trusting relationship between the coach and the learner. That is to say, bad evaluation can be damaging to the whole learning and coaching process. It is important that an initial evaluation and its resultant feedback are provided to the learner as soon after the activity as is practicable. Some of the questions the coach could ask are: Does the learner feel she has learned through the activity? Was the learning activity appropriate for the learning goal? How well does the learner feel she did? What has been learned? Has the development need been met? How can the learning activity be improved for future trainees? Was the learner provided with appropriate support? What are the implications for training and development within the organisation?

Competence

People and successful organisations do not just learn, they plan their learning. The real skill is not to learn skills that you should already have but to develop skills that you will need in the future; in short, to be a proactive learner. To do this effectively an individual needs to assess the skills they possess accurately, identify the skills they are likely to need in the short and longer term, and plan a personal development path that will provide those skills. 'Skill' is probably the wrong word to use as it has rather a narrow usage in terms of personal development. A more accurate term would be one that has wide acceptance in the training and development sector already: 'competence', which infers far more than simply 'skills'. For someone to be competent they would need to be able to apply all the relevant skills and knowledge, in the right measure and at the right time, in a real work situation. As learners, this should surely be our aim – not to develop skills, but to develop competence. The learning needs of an individual are to assist them to perform competently in their current job, or to prepare them to perform competently in a future job role. The starting point should be the description of each job role in terms of what constitutes competent performance. This calls for a systematic approach in defining the roles and responsibilities of each job role and what constitutes competent performance for each job role. This can be achieved in a number of ways and can be described by a plethora of different documents such as job descriptions, personnel specifications, job specifications and standard procedures, to name but a few. There is always a danger that the large array of different documents can lead to numerous descriptions of performance, all of which are slightly different; not exactly a recipe for clarity. Yet, by using a standard component to describe competence across all these documents we can provide greater clarity and guard against differing standards. Moreover, by utilising national occupational standards, organisations can benefit from the work and investment already spent on identifying and describing performance. Most areas of industry have a national training organisation (NTO) with a wide-ranging remit to improve and develop their respective sectors through the development of their workforce. The NTO for the archaeology profession has been the Cultural Heritage National Training Organisation, covering museum, gallery and heritage sector. It has been working with the National Archaeology Training Forum to develop new standards for archaeologists. Defining occupational competence is a time-consuming and resource-intensive activity, however, as other industries have concluded. The effort is worth it since what results is a set of standards for job-related activities that are nationally agreed. The national training organisations are in the process of being reorganised and merged into larger sector skills councils (SSCs). As yet, the nature of the SSC that will cover archaeology is unclear.

What do we mean by being competent? We learn, we change our behaviour, but to what end? The goal of all learning is to improve the quality of the learner's actions, or in other words to develop behaviour which is more effective in achieving the learner's aims. What we are looking for is competence. What and how much someone learns is evident in their behaviour, therefore the measure of the improvement in that behaviour (the increase in competence) becomes a measure of the effectiveness of the learning process. The idea of competence is well established and has various definitions: the dictionary describes someone who is competent as being adequately qualified, but this simply begs the question of what we mean by qualified. Essentially, being competent means to possess all the skills, knowledge, ability and confidence to perform to a generally accepted standard. Yet the term itself is meaningless unless it precedes a task, profession or occupation, since people can only be competent in relation to something – often their job. We think of others as competent, we think of them as safe, able and trustworthy; in short, people whom we can rely on to work without supervision. The competent archaeologist not only performs to the accepted standard but does it consistently; they react to new and changing situations and still carry out their job; they manage their own time and act responsibly. For employers we are describing ideal employees. For individuals we are describing the colleagues of theirs who are widely respected, the colleagues to whom people turn when problems arise. It is important to remember at this point that when we talk about standards of competence we are not talking about producing a standard archaeologist with standard responses to situations. Not only is this an unrealistic goal but it actually acts against the creation of a learning culture. Innovative solutions to new problems or situations are found by the creative and enthusiastic teamwork of individuals from different backgrounds and histories, people who may address problems from different angles. What is really revolutionary about developing competence is that we look to develop abilities to operate without specifying a particular way of achieving the necessary outcomes. The flexibility for the individual to change the established way of operating is built into the actual concept of competence. What constitutes competence? Job competence is to be our development goal, the first step is to define what we mean by competence for a particular job. Some elements of competence are relatively easy to define: the key tasks and task-related skills. However, it is easy to see how a competence model based on these factors alone would not describe the competent individual. The competent (safe, able, trustworthy, respected) jobholder can do much more than simply possess the skills to perform the standard tasks required of the job. Why? Because they can do it and still answer the phone, respond to requests from clients, supervise the intern – in short, they can do it in a real (and changing) work environment. The work environment often means that the jobholder may have some degree of autonomy over the allocation of priorities to tasks and is responsible for contingency management. Surely, our competent archaeologist is someone who can successfully manage a number of duties at once and deal with any reasonable problem that may arise. Thus, if we are to develop a workable model of job competence it should include the skills required for the individual to function within the job; knowledge to adapt to new and changing situations; social and communication skills; understanding of the job, the organisation and the industry; numeracy and literacy; the positive attitude to the success of themselves and the organisation; and confidence and a will to act. If we are looking to develop an individual to a level where they are competent, we must create a measurable set of criteria from the above points. This will enable them (and others) to assess their current state of development and allow them to judge when they have achieved the required level of competence.

Occupational standards

If we are to measure learning, we must look at what learners do and assess this against a standard. In order for the standard of competence to be useful in staff development terms it needs to be measurable, and this is the big challenge. Luckily for archaeology, the development of national occupational standards has meant that many of the issues around the structure of the criteria have already been addressed. Practitioners with a broad model of competence in mind have produced occupational standards and these provide an excellent starting point. However, they do have drawbacks. They are designed for every organisation and 'occupational roles' rather than specific jobs. Consequently, they are generic in nature, making them sometimes a little difficult to read, understand and interpret into some job roles. Once the standards of competence have been determined for a particular job role they can be used as a basis for recruitment and selection, identification of training and development needs, evaluation of training and development activities and development of organisational systems and procedures. The power of standards of competence is that they can be measured objectively; at least more objectively than any other form of performance measurement. Measurement is the judging of an object in relation to a known object. In this case, the object for judging is an individual's performance and the known object is the occupational standard. If we use the driving test analogy, it is easy to see that the performance of each learner driver is assessed by an examiner against set criteria. It is assumed that the learner driver is aware of the criteria and is ready to perform a number of manoeuvres and answer questions on command in order to demonstrate their competence. In a sense, all competency standards are predicated upon the same assumption: that people know what is required and believe that they can perform to the standard. It is their responsibility to prove to another archaeologist assessing them that this is in fact the case. Vocational qualifications are one of many uses for occupational standards and they simply constitute a collection of standards that are assessed within a quality-assured network of professionals.

Current work in archaeological training

An Archaeology Training Forum (ATF) was established in 1998 with representatives from a range of organisations concerned with archaeological employment and education. The Forum has been involved in a number of initiatives to raise the level of debate in archaeology about its training needs. It has built upon a survey of archaeological jobs (Aitchison 1999) and has commissioned a project to undertake a functional mapping of archaeology and devise occupational standards for the profession. These standards may then be used as the basis for devising vocational courses and qualifications for archaeology in the future. To ensure that existing courses are widely publicised, the CBA has set up the Training Online Resource Centre on behalf of the ATF to provide web-based access to databases of archaeology courses and training providers in the United Kingdom. Training in archaeology has still a long way to go before it reaches the levels seen in other professions. However, the profession is now fully engaged in a debate on training and is developing a concerted approach to providing the training its practitioners desire.

■ ■ ■

Reference

Aitchison, K. (1999) *Profiling the Profession: A Survey of Archaeological Jobs in the United Kingdom* (ed. S. Denison), York, London and Reading: Council for British Archaeology, English Heritage and the Institute of Field Archaeologists.

PART THREE

The Educative Role of Audio-visual Media

Chapter 12

ARCHAEOLOGY AND TELEVISION

Alex West

Introduction

In this subjective review of the development of archaeology on British TV, my aim is to evaluate how the treatment and presentation of the subject have changed. I also want to make an attempt to evaluate how the archaeological content of British TV may expect to develop in the near future.

First a definition is required: the scope of this discussion is limited to TV documentaries or factual programmes that have archaeology at their core. A film about ancient history may be archaeological, but not necessarily. I would define a film that is archaeological as one in which archaeologists and their work is featured, and/or a substantial part of the narrative is archaeologically driven. I do not directly concern myself with the 'media' in more general terms. Experience shows that news media are often keen on an archaeology story – especially at local or regional level. This is the level on which the vast majority of working archaeologists interact with the media. The nature of this interaction and some of the challenges and pitfalls will be discussed at the end of this review.

Ever since the development of television as a mass medium in the 1950s, archaeology has been a staple of factual TV programming. It remains a popular subject, and channel controllers, commissioning editors and producers are regularly involved in research, development and production of new ideas and formats for archaeological programming. The reason is simple enough: producers (certainly those involved with the 'minority' channels BBC2 and C4) perceive that archaeology attracts a sizeable constituency of viewers. In the

1990s, archaeological programmes, broadcast in the main on BBC2 and Channel 4, have regularly attracted audiences of 2–3 million viewers, and audience shares of over 10 per cent. These numbers show that archaeology holds its own among viewers faced with increasing choices as the worlds of digital and satellite broadcasting come on stream. Even so, in terrestrial TV terms it remains a minority interest and as such will remain largely outside the remit of the major channels BBC1 and ITV. However, the plethora of TV channels the digital revolution represents is affecting the traditional landscape of TV and how the main terrestrial broadcasters are developing in response to this. This is already having an impact on archaeological programming. The future is likely to see a lot more archaeology on TV. The question is will it be any good?

Archaeology as entertainment?

At the core of any discussion of the quality of archaeology on TV is the issue of how the television treatment of archaeology reflects the perceived reality of archaeologists about 'their' subject and 'their' discipline. Do TV shows accurately reflect the realities of the world of archaeology? Do they need to?

In the past, archaeology, as an academic and professional activity, and TV, as an entertainment medium, have been strange bedfellows. In other ways they have been successful partners. Like any relationship, what archaeologists and TV producers expect of each other has been the source of conflicts, but over the last thirty years few research activities have attracted as much sustained TV interest and loyalty as archaeology. Of its kind archaeology is way out in front. Other science subjects such as medicine (health) are more likely to be TV perennials because they affect us all and therefore attract journalistic interest. More recently, subjects like cosmology and genetics have become favourite topics, the latter due to its perceived 'relevance factor' and the presence of several high-profile 'character academics' like Stephen Hawking, Steve Jones, Robert Winston and Steven Pinker. But those looking for a view on the status of archaeology on TV can make a useful comparison with geology or earth sciences. Until the last few years geology rarely figured on TV in its own right. It took until 1998, with the production of *Earthstory* and its sister programme *The Essential Guide to Rocks* by BBC Science, for it to have a series all of its own. Archaeology has had series of its own since the 1950s.

Indeed, in its early years, TV and archaeology were quite closely linked in the public mind. Back then, archaeologists like Mortimer Wheeler and Glyn Daniel became stars. These men won the accolade 'TV personality of the year' in 1954 for their archaeological parlour game *Animal, Vegetable, Mineral*. This is not to hark back to a golden age. Indeed I believe some archaeologists in the 1990s have been guilty of too much harking back to the good old days when 'proper' documentaries about the subject were thought to be a common sight on the schedules. In fact there is probably as much, if not more archaeology on TV as there has ever been. Times have changed but they remain exciting. No archaeologist (or scientist) today would win the sort of TV gongs Professors Wheeler and Daniel did. Times have moved on, and technical experts, as opposed to celebrities and entertainers, no longer have the power to dominate the hugely enlarged landscape of TV as they had been able to in its first generation. This is partially due to the fact that experts in many fields would not necessarily agree that being closely allied to the categories of 'celebrity' and 'star' is a desirable state of affairs. Today, however strong their desire to popularise, archaeologists, like others, strongly defend their status as experts – people to be taken seriously with serious points to make, not 'characters' whose main aim is to entertain. As archaeology on TV develops this will remain an issue. I now turn to that development.

Developments in the 1990s

TV is changing rapidly. So is archaeology. In the 1990s both expanded. Archaeology has grown a great deal. University departments have enlarged, and undergraduate numbers have grown (see Henson, Chapter 2; Hamilakis and Rainbird, Chapter 5). So have the numbers employed as archaeologists in the areas of cultural resource management and compliance with planning and environmental law. Archaeology is a big, busy subject.

Television has gone through even more profound changes and even greater expansion. The 1990s witnessed the introduction of satellite, cable and more lately digital broadcasting. So-called multichannel households are on the increase. This will have a profound impact.

Partly in response to this new multichannel environment, shifts in the perceptions of TV producers have meant archaeology on TV in the 1990s has been undergoing rapid change. At the end of the 1980s, the BBC maintained an archaeology and history unit. It was a production department under Network Features and later BBC South & East. It made two main series: *Timewatch* covered history, *Chronicle* archaeology. *Chronicle* had been in existence since it was set up by the first controller of BBC2, David Attenborough, in 1966. In 1991, this department was closed and absorbed into BBC documentaries. Prior to closure, *Chronicle* had already been decommissioned after the death of its last editor Bruce Norman. At the time there seemed little hope for archaeological output on the BBC, and many producers associated with the history and archaeology unit left the BBC in the wake of the 'merger' with documentaries. In my view, this was only partly to do with an increasingly freelance culture that overtook the corporation in the wake of the introduction of producer choice under former Director-General John Birt. The real reason was still cultural, but in other ways.

The 1980s had seen an increasing development of post-modern thought into mainstream culture, and TV was no exception. At the time archaeology was very active theoretically – questioning its role as a science, discussing the nature of its epistemology, and getting to grips with its own historiography, especially in relation to the politics of the production of knowledge, Marxism and feminism. In TV, this was echoed in a rejection of the formal approach to the documentary, especially those seen to be a platform for middle-class male academics to espouse their views. The canon was collapsing, and with it archaeology as an interesting and audience-winning subject for programmes was rejected or simply ignored. Ironically, this happened at the same moment that archaeology was more concerned with post-modern issues and its relationship to the wider society than it had ever been. Sadly the message never got through.

For TV producers there was a sense that the 'big subjects' had been done to death and a new period of 'quirky', radical and chic factual shows invaded the schedules. These were championed by *The Late Show*, but there were many others – notably *Small Objects of Desire*, *The Rough Guide to the History of Europe*, and *Signs of the Times*. Yet archaeology did not disappear and its green shoots were ironically preserved by Channel 4. Channel 4 began broadcasting in 1982 and quickly gained a reputation as the 'alternative' channel. Ironic then that it should be the place where apparently unfashionable, old-fashioned archaeology should carry on and prove so successful that by the mid to late 1990s the BBC would be desperate to compete.

Time Team and *Meet the Ancestors*

C4 had made one or two forays into the genre in the 1980s, notably with *Blood of the British* – the archaeology of the Anglo-Saxons – presented by Catherine Hills. Hills popped up again on *Down To Earth* (1990–1992), an archaeological magazine programme. But the turning point came in 1992 when the then commissioning editor for Education, Karen Brown, asked producer Tim Taylor to make a series in which a team of archaeologists travelled the country digging up sites against the clock. *Time Team* was born and archaeology on television began a new phase in its development and popularity.

As *Time Team* began, there was no archaeological output on BBC TV, apart from rare moments when *Timewatch* covered stories. It proved to be a great success with viewers. More importantly it marked a profound shift in the way TV treated archaeology and the way archaeologists treated TV. It was (and remains) a format show. Instead of going out into the real world and filming an archaeological story, *Time Team* makes up its own. The group are asked to find out what they can or solve a puzzle at a place of historic interest (at least to the locals). They have only three days to do it in. In their attempts to answer questions, they enlist the help of experts in related fields, geophysical teams, excavators, and so on.

We are all aware of the format. And format was the revolution. *Time Team* is not real archaeology. It is set up for a TV show – without the programme, most of the dozens of sites it has dug would have remained uninvestigated.

At the time it began, *Time Team* faced harsh criticism from some quarters in the discipline. Academics criticised the way it portrayed archaeology as a treasure hunt against the clock. Some also criticised the way it portrayed archaeologists as slightly eccentric bearded men who loved to run around fields. There were also ethical issues of digging on scheduled monuments, of curation and publication. For the critics, *Time Team* did not do 'it' the way it was meant to be done – it demeaned the subject and turned it into a gameshow. Yet it proved to be the most successful archaeological programme ever made. It is one of C4's highest rated factual shows, it has won prestigious awards, and spin-off books (e.g. Taylor 1999) and pamphlets have sold out to a loyal following who maintain their interest via unofficial websites.

Time Team, like any TV show, is unlikely to last forever, but it has changed archaeology on TV for all time. Its impact was immense. It was one of the first format shows, and many others followed. In many ways *Time Team* has a lot to answer for. In its wake, home improvements, gardening and old buildings have all been given the format treatment.

In terms of history or archaeology subjects, the BBC tried to jump on the bandwagon with *House Detectives* – which, while popular, has never hit the spot *Time Team* has. Then in 1997, BBC Science (the sole producer of the BBC's archaeology output today) developed *Meet the Ancestors*, presented by (or should that be starring) archaeologist Julian Richards. In many ways this programme is an antidote to *Time Team*. Richards follows his trail for many months, waiting for the results of lab research, forensics, and cranial reconstruction. Nevertheless, *Meet the Ancestors* is format TV through and through. The aim is to reconstruct the face of an excavated burial, and along the way learn about the world he or she inhabited. Like *Time Team*, this is not real archaeology. Burials are rarely subjected to expensive cranial reconstruction – what would be the point in research terms? But, like *Time Team*, it is very popular. When it first aired in 1998, *Meet the Ancestors* was given a prime BBC2 slot (Thursdays at 9.00 p.m.) and delivered high ratings which placed it well into the channel's weekly top ten.

In *Meet the Ancestors,* the BBC did discover a show that could compete with *Time Team*. But as they have grown and developed, archaeology and television have been mixing in other domains. *Time Team*, *Meet the Ancestors*, *House Detectives* and *Down to Earth* all share one thing in common. They are not full-length documentaries, and they are mostly British in their scope and more importantly their funding.

Co-production

Away from the domestic market, archaeology on TV has seen other important developments. Long format (i.e. one hour plus) TV documentaries are expensive to make – especially those shot abroad. For many years it has been impossible for any single broadcaster to fund programmes that routinely cost over £200,000 to produce. Hence the growth in co-production – normal and necessary in the business of documentary production. In America, where the vast bulk of co-production funding comes from, large Public Television stations such as WNET (Boston), have traditionally co-funded BBC projects. Yet as far back as the 1980s *Chronicle* was co-produced by one of the first American cable networks, Arts and Entertainment (A&E). The growth in cable, and now digital broadcasting, has had a profound impact and will continue to do so.

It is worth thinking about the nature of the US factual TV market because its outlook and programming needs are now heavily shaping the content and nature of archaeological programmes on both sides of the Atlantic. Despite common assertions that television is a globalising force that destroys cultural identity and diversity, it can be argued that in many ways television is one of the most culturally specific mediums – TV reflects the cultural outlook of the country that produces it very closely. This is why it is possible in Britain to produce light entertainment shows that gently poke fun at TV shows from other countries – who has not seen the endurance-style Japanese game shows served up as something to laugh at rather than with? Yet, do we ever ask ourselves what the Japanese would make of *Time Team*?

This is an important point, because in the world of co-production several international broadcasters with an eye on their home market must attempt to agree on the style and content of a programme much more than they normally would. Archaeology is one of the most popular subjects for co-production because it is perceived as culturally neutral. This may come as a shock to a discipline that (academically at least) threatened to be overwhelmed in its interest in the culturally specific construction of historical knowledge, and, in many ways, is a very place-specific and historically contextualised pursuit. Yet for the world of international co-production archaeology is timeless, non-political, non-contentious, and universal in its appeal. This is reflected directly in the choice of subjects mainly covering the 'great' civilisations of the past. In the last five years Rome (*I Caesar*), Egypt (*Testament*), the Maya (*Secrets of the Jaguar*), the Byzantine Empire (*Byzantium*) have all had their own series on TV. Lately the upper palaeolithic has also featured (*Secrets of the Stone Age*), there have been forensics (*Secrets of the Dead*), ancient religions too (*Ancient Voices*). All of these series have been co-productions, and more are being developed and produced. Ultimately, TV is interested in narratives. Good stories are what it is all about, and the growth of multichannel TV has increased the demand for programmes on archaeology. National Geographic, Discovery Channel, The Learning Channel are all keen on the subject. And while editorial interest may ebb and flow, archaeology is the stuff of these so-called 'infotainment' channels.

The main danger in this expansion comes from a blurring of the boundaries between science and pseudo-science. Sadly, myth, legend and mysteries have long gripped American producers and, as archaeology has always had a fringe, this has started to creep into the enlarged coverage of the discipline. Perhaps the worst example of this was the fact that fringe best-seller Graham Hancock – the man who espouses hyper-diffusionism, lost races, and a mesolithic date for the Sphinx

– had his own series on Channel 4 at the beginning of 1999. Thankfully this was balanced by two programmes debunking Hancock *et al.* in BBC's Horizon series later in the same year: *Atlantis Uncovered* and *Atlantis Reborn*.

Conclusion

These battles will continue to be fought. Perhaps the best defence is for archaeologists to make sure they complain vociferously when TV gets it wrong. C4 science and the BBC have to be seen to have credibility. If the discipline lets the broadcasters know it is unhappy I believe this can have an influence if the criticism is constructive and shows awareness of the realities of TV production. Too often criticism can be seen as sour grapes or academic elitism.

Whatever happens, archaeology carried out in exotic faraway places, covering those themes of enduring interest, will continue to have a much greater chance of being covered than purely domestic research. The day-to-day business of archaeology – watching briefs, evaluations, desk-based assessments and so on – is not the stuff of national and international TV. I think this is fair enough. However, it should not discourage archaeologists from involvement and interaction with local media. Local stories have strong appeal, and archaeology by definition provides great coverage. Archaeology has a strong bedrock support as something worth while. However, getting 'the message' across can be frustrating when the local angle sees the archaeological dig as a form of novelty story. Equally, archaeologists can often be embroiled in controversy, especially regarding environmental issues. This can lead to bad press, and difficulties keeping news media away from sites due to sensitivities with clients, or the possibility of looting and vandalism.

Relationships with local media are important and need to be sustained. While a big TV series may reach large numbers of people, by their nature such series are very ephemeral and people rarely remember what they have seen in detail. Local interaction with fewer people can be sustained and be much more meaningful. An hour with a group of schoolchildren can change lives more than any TV show. I believe it is the responsibility of archaeologists to make and nurture those contacts. Try to write features in local papers about the archaeology of the area. Publicise sites; where possible go on the radio, and so on.

There have been a great many success stories in this way. And as a result I believe that in this country archaeology is held in high esteem. It is popular, it has endured, and, as it enters a new century, television continues to show a strong interest in the subject.

■ ■ ■

Reference

Taylor, T. (1999) *The Ultimate Time Team Companion: An Alternative History of Britain*, London: Channel 4 Books.

Chapter 13

THE USE OF LEARNING TECHNOLOGIES IN ARCHAEOLOGY

Graham McElearney

The revolution afforded us by information and communication technology (ICT) is transforming every sphere of life. The fact that this chapter exists at all is a testament to the importance of ICT to both archaeology and education. In archaeology, its impact ranges from field-recording techniques to academic publication and presentation to the wider public. In education, it is a highly visible icon that represents a much wider paradigmatic shift.

In a subject overrun with TLAs (three-letter acronyms), learning technologies (LT) can be defined as the application of ICT for the enhancement of learning, teaching and assessment. This chapter, aimed mainly at those who teach archaeology in FE and HE, looks at how the principles and practices of LT can be applied to archaeological education.

Much of what is described below does not lend itself well to conventional textual description (a bit like using an old black and white television to advertise DVD). Rather than litter the text with dozens of web addresses, I have provided an online section containing links to examples and other relevant resources. This is available at:

http://www.shef.ac.uk/learningmedia/cba

Pedagogy – the *learning* in learning technology

Pedagogy is the theoretical basis that underpins the use of LT. Without pedagogy, LT has the potential to be, at best, expensive and ineffective, and, at worst, a counter-force to learning. Its implications can be distilled into some broad pragmatic and practical considerations.

A pedagogical crisis for United Kingdom universities?

Quite apart from any technological revolution, FE and HE in the United Kingdom are both undergoing a major shift in culture. There are increasing government initiatives in widening access to HE and increased emphasis on lifelong learning. University senior managers are preparing to combat non-traditional competitors such as broadcasters and other commercial concerns. It is claimed that students will be from increasingly diverse social backgrounds, although current university admissions data suggest we simply have more students from the traditional sectors. It is envisaged these students will require and expect similarly diverse and flexible provision of teaching.

Traditional didactic approaches to university teaching have been criticised for a number of years for various reasons. Most importantly here, because:

- they do not adequately 'scale up' to the new demands;
- they are arguably flawed anyway.

Many universities have responded to widening access by just doing 'more of the same'. More lectures are given to more students, tutorial group sizes have doubled, and the same practical classes have to be repeatedly run each week to 'process' the numbers. Inevitably there has followed a 'loss of quality of learning experience for students', and a 'need to find *pedagogically acceptable combinations of teaching methods* and cost structures to sustain increased student numbers', as reported by Dearing (cited by Ryan *et al.* 2000; emphasis mine).

Pedagogically, the traditional model is criticised for being (increasingly) reliant on the notion that academic learning can be instilled in students by the simple transmission of facts and knowledge. Students have little interaction with the teacher or each other, and many activities, where they exist at all, are so decontextualised that they lead to knowledge which is 'inert' and effectively useless. Students come to think of facts as things to be memorised, and cease to explore them as tools to solve problems (Grabinger and Dunlap 2000).

So, whether we like it or not, it looks like university education will *have* to change. While the wholesale adoption of LT will not solve all our problems, its appropriate use may offer a very positive step forward into the ever-chaotic mêlée.

Models for learning, strategies for teaching

Rather than just negating the principles of didactic teaching, current pedagogy provides a series of complementary models and strategies for the effective use of LT.

The constructivist model of learning (see Copeland, Chapter 3) opposes much that is implied in the traditional model above. In constructivism, learners construct knowledge and understanding; they do not just have it thrust upon them. Fundamental to constructivism is the notion that learning should be active, and that this activity be directed towards the solving of realistic and relevant problems. Where possible these activities should be performed in collaboration with other students. The role of the teacher in this environment is as a facilitator. The constructivist teacher will typically encourage dialogue with and between students, use a wide variety of teaching resources, guide students through open-ended questions, and accommodate various subjective and individualistic learning styles.

In the conversational model, the structure and format of learning replicates that of a conversation between student and teacher. The teacher offers some description of the world to the student, who then discusses with and reiterates back their version. The teacher adapts their descriptions to the students and sets an appropriate 'task goal' (this could be anything from a ten-minute tutorial presentation on human origins to an entire landscape survey). The student and teacher then reflect upon the student's performance of the task. The important point is that the whole process is supported by two-way dialogue throughout. Teaching methods and materials that support the conversational model are discursive, adaptive (to the student's needs) and interactive.

Neither of these models are particularly new, the conversational model originates with Socrates. They have not just been made up to justify the salaries of people like me!

Resource-based learning (RBL) is a strategy for teaching that is compatible with the two above models of learning. Ryan *et al.* (2000: 30) follow the basic definition as stated by the Australian National Council of Open and Distance Education:

> Resource Based Learning is defined as an integrated set of strategies to promote student centred learning in a mass education context, through a combination of specially designed learning resources and interactive media and technologies.

RBL is not a strategy for making lecturers redundant, it is a strategy for making sure the most important resource – lecturer time – is used best.

The ethos of RBL identifies the following uses for LT (Ryan *et al.* 2000):

- delivering courses;
- identifying and using resources;
- communication and collaboration;
- activities and assessment;
- student management and logistics.

These map well on to the more elaborated claims that LT can:

- allow students to work at their own pace and place;
- provide access to rich and diverse multimedia/teaching materials;
- simulate real world problems and test scenarios;
- facilitate communication;

- be easily updated compared to books and videos;
- encourage active learning through discovery.

How many more platitudes can you take?

How does it work?

In looking at how different media and techniques can be applied to real educational contexts, or 'Learning Scenarios' (Conole and Oliver 1998), we can start to see how LT may achieve its goals.

Interactive multimedia

LT can provide access to rich and diverse teaching materials via the use of multimedia. Multimedia is the combined use of text, graphics, sound video and other 'new media' within a single integrated digital environment. There is nothing particularly new about combining these media types together into one seamless world – educational television has been doing it for years. Computer-based multimedia has one key difference: it is normally interactive, providing at least the ability for the user to navigate through the information at a pace they choose. Other possible forms of interaction are discussed below.

The educational applications of these media types has been extensively discussed by Laurillard (1993), and latterly Conole and Oliver (1998), so will not be repeated here. However, a few specific points regarding their application to archaeology are worth considering:

Text and hypertext

Despite its highly visual component, we must accept that the vast majority of archaeological thought is conveyed via text. We create extensive volumes of text ranging from detailed descriptions of excavation data to highly involved debate over complex theoretical issues. But reading large quantities of text is much easier from paper than from screen, so how can electronic text be of value in teaching; why do the students not just print it out?

The first point here is that they can do just that – they can get access to, and print out, far more complete versions of, say, lecture notes than the maniacally scribbled documents they create themselves.

Second, using hypertext links, documents can be linked together like nodes in a network – web page hyperlinks are the classic example. This provides the ability to create non-linear or 'polysequential' documents. In true hypertext scenarios there is no predetermined sequence of documents, only associations between documents. Whilst forcing the user/learner to be active in determining their own narratives may be very desirable, in many situations providing a clear narrative structure really matters (Laurillard 1999).

In many educational applications, hypertext is used to reveal supplementary information rather than allowing a complete departure into another document. So in archaeology a text describing certain long barrows could provide links to the full text of excavation reports or photographs, diagrams and other multimedia information.

The wider implications of hypertext in various forms of publication are not lost on the archaeological community. For Holtorf (1999), it was the power in 'making connections' that he wanted to exploit as an interpretative tool. For Hodder (1999), it is the 'placing side by side of specialist and public interests' and the opportunities for dialogue that are key attractions of the media. Both are creating constructivist prototypes which could be harnessed for education.

Finally, electronic text can be searchable, and anyone who has access to the enormous range of bibliographic databases and on-line journals supported by college libraries will appreciate the value of this.

Images

Apart from the narrative primacy of text, much of archaeological explanation resides on the use of images – images are constantly referred to in the description and interpretation of excavation evidence, artefact types, extant monuments and scientific specimens (e.g. pollen grains), etc. Traditionally, students' interaction and exposure to these images is largely constrained to slide display in lectures or what illustrations can be provided in textbooks. Making images available to students via the web, for example, allows students access to these resources outside of that which is afforded by the time and space of a lecture or the library textbook resource.

As well as being liberated from much of the constraints of cost in conventional publishing, digital images have the power to be interactive. Image maps allow different parts of the same image to trigger different hyperlinks or other events. The image itself can change when the student interacts with it via the mouse, for example revealing captions or other forms of explanation (often known as 'rollovers'). These and other techniques offer powerful tools for conveying the educational message.

Video and animation

Video uses the power of the moving image to convey its message. Video has the ability to modify both the passage of time, and the sense of relative physical scale. Both are of obvious concern to archaeologists. It is also very valuable in demonstrating procedural activities that are extremely repetitive to teach, or are precluded because of reasons such as cost, or health and safety. This has obvious benefits for teaching both lab- and field-based skills, though can never be a real substitute.

Digital video is easier to 'control' than its broadcast or tape-delivered equivalents, with readily accessible controls to stop, play, rewind/fast forward, etc. Video can be 'authored' to interact with other elements on screen such as text or graphics, so could, for example, stop at certain points and ask the student to answer questions, or perform some other activity (e.g. group discussion).

Most of the above is also true of animation. The key difference between video and animation is that animation can depict events and processes not readily observable in the real world – for example, environmental change, ditch sedimentation or the spread of the 'Carolingian revolution'.

New media

We can define 'new media' as that which has no analogue counterpart outside the digital domain. The fact that a multimedia package may allow the combination of the above in ways not used before may itself constitute a new media. The forms of new media that have most attention focused on them by archaeologists have been those of visualisation, and, more specifically, virtual reality.

QuickTime VR is a form of virtual reality which places the user at the centre of photo-realistic panoramas (nodes) in which they can navigate using keyboard and mouse. Whilst users can jump between nodes, they are constrained to them. This is not the case using Virtual Reality Modelling Language (VRML), where full 3D models can be freely navigated without such constraints. Neither can be adequately described here and should be experienced first-hand (Edmonds and McElearney 1999)!

A broad critique of these media in archaeology is well discussed by Bateman (2000), who comments that an 'enlarged group of practitioners . . . are following ways of moving beyond purely textual projections of their interpretations eg Edmonds and Seabourne'. The educational potential for the use of VR is enormous (Sanders 1997). VR techniques offer the potential for investigations that range in scale from individual sites to the wider landscapes beyond. Archaeologists have finally got the message from architects that monumental (if not all) architecture, in its very spatial configuration, is symbolic of meaning, whether political or spiritual. This is an important message that has to be taught. A QuickTime VR model may enable an interactive experience of an extant monument or landscape in photo-realistic detail. A student exploring Virtual Stonehenge can experience how moving through that architectural form articulates those meanings and helps structure the proceedings that may have taken place therein (Barrett 1994). The lack of photo-realistic detail need not necessarily detract from the experience of embodiment, and the addition of 3D spatial sound could ameliorate the attention to visualism (Pollard and Gillings 1998).

A taxonomy of learning technologies

Although some degree of overlap exists, it is possible to classify LT into broadly functional types.

Tutorial systems

Although very diverse in scope, tutorial systems are basically designed to 'teach something', originating in the idea that the computer can emulate the role of the teacher or some other component of the educational experience (Laurillard 1993). Whilst employing many of the interactive multimedia techniques above, they may often follow a fairly prescribed linear narrative.

Simulations

Simulations are computer-based abstracted models of the world that allow the learner to interact with them and control parameters that affect their behaviour or state. Typically embedded within tutorial systems, simulations are often used to replicate practical (e.g. lab-based) procedures, but can equally be used in broader scenarios (e.g. 'how much of this site can be excavated within our budget?'). (See the BBC's *Hunt the Ancestor* game for an excellent example of this.) The utility of such interactivity can sometimes be questioned: the student can just sit there and manipulate parameters at random until they get the right result, rather than actively constructing alternative models and testing their validity.

Structured resources and information retrieval

Structured resources are designed to allow random access, sequential browsing and, most importantly, effective searching of electronic data. On-line bibliographic databases and journals are one classic example of these – as well as gaining skills in efficient searching and data retrieval, increasingly students can gain access to the actual article. The multimedia capabilities of on-line systems allow images, video clips and other types of data to be accessed in the same way, allowing access to 'virtual teaching collections' of materials that would otherwise be impossible to maintain.

Computer-mediated communications (CMC) and collaborative learning

The importance of discourse in the 'conversational' model of learning above has contributed to the increasing interest in computer-mediated communication and collaborative learning (McConnell 2000). It is of increasing relevance to campus-based as well as distance-based students. CMC systems are described as either synchronous (enabling real-time discussion) or asynchronous (where there is an inherent delay between sending, receiving and replying to messages). Asynchronous communications are not dependent on everyone being on-line at the same time, and are logistically more flexible. In addition, in many asynchronous CMC systems (e.g. bulletin boards) past messages remain visible and accessible for future reference, and in this sense the students can be actively and collaboratively involved in creating their own educational resource. Constructivist heaven!

Computer-aided assessment (CAA)

CAA allows students the opportunity to perform formative, self-assessment proce-dures, enabling them to evaluate their own learning. Typically this is mediated through multiple choice questions – the computer presents a question with possible answers, the student makes a choice, and the computer provides some feedback. Ideally the computer is non-judgemental, and can allow the student as many goes through the test as they want. CAA is often used in tutorial packages as a means of maintaining student motivation. The normal multiple choice question (MCQ) type format is necessarily fairly 'closed' and is arguably too prescriptive for some disciplines.

Virtual learning environments

If a course is more than just a series of lectures and other events, then an on-line course should be more than just a set of web-based lecture notes. Virtual learning environments (VLEs) aim to replicate the holistic nature of a real course by inte-grating many of the above techniques into a single environment (Diercks-O'Brien 2001). Typically, VLEs will provide bulletin boards, synchronous 'chat' areas, an infrastructure for navigating through course content, self-assessment MCQs, student management and tracking, and other infrastructural tools. All are accessible from one single point of entry.

Practicalities: when to use learning technologies and how to get started

Where in the curriculum can we utilise LT? Whilst the specifics of every context are unique, here are some very common general scenarios:

1   Practicals overloaded, field trips too expensive . . .
   - Reappraise the educational objectives of the practicals – does everything have to take place in the lab?
   - Use simulations in the lab to cut pressure on equipment and materials, and/or cut down the number of sessions offered.
   - Use tutorial systems to better prepare the students in terms of background knowledge, use of basic equipment, etc.
   - Replacing expensive, non-durable reference material with a structured resource (e.g. an image database).
   - Could a 'virtual field trip' adequately replicate the activities and experi-ence of the real thing?
2   I waste hours repeatedly explaining the same thing . . .
   - Institute office hours and encourage/insist the students contact you by email.

- Set up a bulletin board and encourage the students to discuss the problem between themselves (you may need to moderate the content to stop 'group error propagation' here!).
- Place answers to 'Frequently Asked Questions' on the web, and direct the students to them.
- Use a multimedia tutorial system to provide alternative explanations (the current one does not seem to be working!).

3   My lectures feel boring, and I have little interaction with my students . . .
- Use multimedia materials to liven up the lectures.
- Use LT to cut down the amount of lectures by providing introductory materials and other forms of straightforward content.
- Use lectures to provide the narrative overview, use tutorial systems and on-line notes to fill in the details.
- Use the saved contact time to spend on tutorials and small group activities.
- Use CMC systems to prepare the students for tutorials, and facilitate discussion outside the tutorial.

4   Students are ill-motivated, have no sense of research ethos and cannot work in teams . . .
- Get the students to work collaboratively, for example by sharing and discussing real world laboratory data via email (Doonan *et al.* 2001).
- Get the students to research seminar topics by searching through biblio-graphic databases and on-line journals.
- Try and get them to actually talk to each other!

Using learning technologies: where to go next

Assuming that you want to go ahead and use LT, the following is intended as a (far from exhaustive) quick guide as where to go next:

- First, establish your educational objectives: What do you expect the students to learn or achieve from the LT? How does it fit into the rest of the course? You will never pass 'Go' until this is done!
- Seek some advice – this could be from a colleague or an adviser at faculty/institutional level. At the very least they should help you get the first bit right, and establish what use of LT is appropriate to your needs.
- Gain access to some resources: Does what you want already exist? Subject specialist advisers from the Learning and Teaching Support Network will have a good overview of what is out there. If you want to search the web your-self, use subject-specific directories maintained by academic institutions, or other general directory sites like Yahoo.
- If you find some resources, you will need to evaluate them on several grounds: Do they meet your objectives? What is the cost implication? Will the soft-ware run locally (many web-based interactive material requires the correct

'plug-ins' to be installed)? If possible test the material with your colleagues or a small group of students before introducing it en masse.

- Integrate the LT into the rest of the course – failure to do this is the largest source of dissatisfaction with LT. Make sure the students know exactly how to access the material and what they are expected to do with it. This should be documented in the course handbook. Devise specific exercises that require the materials to be used, preferably providing opportunities for both group and private study.

- Finally, be prepared to evaluate the outcomes of using the technology (this may be a requirement if the software has been produced as part of a consortium). Evaluation is essential – it is the primary data that informs our pedagogic strategies (Oliver 2000).

If you want to create your own LT materials, all the above and more apply. Producing learning technology resources can, but does not have to be very time consuming. Irrespective of the degree of interactive multimedia you use, you will need to plan out the contents of your materials very carefully, paying particular attention to how the students will navigate through it. It is quite likely that you will need to buy and learn specialist software for creating the materials, unless you are lucky enough to have the appropriate resources and skills in house. Seeking advice at the institutional level is crucial here. Be aware that sources of funding do become available for developing LT, and that gifted students can achieve an awful lot by way of projects.

Conclusion

Evaluation data have shown that LT can achieve many of its goals, but rarely without some problems (see e.g. Diercks-O'Brien 2001). The penetration of LT into archaeological education in FE and HE has not been that great, partly due to its perceived and actual cost of development. Perhaps the greater barrier to its adoption is in embracing the changing roles of teacher and learner. Constructivism, whilst great for those students who *know how to learn*, pays little attention to those who do not (Tam 2000). School leavers have not generally spent the last thirteen years of their lives in a very constructivist educational environment! Despite claims that LT can enable wider access to higher education, an increasing reliance on students' ownership of computers may simply re-enforce existing social disparities.

In what is becoming an increasingly globalised education market, LT will remain of considerable importance in years to come. Glorious visions of virtual universities exist, comprised almost totally of granularised 'learning objects', shared internationally by consortia whose lecturers can pick and choose between the resources available, having merely to supply the narrative as 'glue'. This is not necessarily an institution in which many of us may wish to work. LT may well help solve some of the problems we are in now, but it is only an educational tool, not a panacea.

■ ■ ■

References

Barrett, J.C. (1994) *Fragments From Antiquity*, Oxford: Blackwell.

Bateman, J. (2000) Immediate realities: an anthropology of computer visualisation in archaeology, *Internet Archaeology* Issue 8: http://intarch.ac.uk/journal/issue8/bateman_toc.html

Conole, G. and Oliver, M. (1998) A pedagogical framework for the embedding of C&IT into the curriculum, *Association for Learning Technology Journal* 6(2): 4–16.

Diercks-O'Brien, G. (2001) Approaches to the evaluation of networked learning, *International Journal for Academic Development* 5(2): 156–165.

Doonan, R. *et al.* (2001) The use of soil studies in defining the spatial articulation of Iron Age metallurgy, *Proceedings of the 1st International Conference of Soil Science and Archaeology*, Szazhalombatta, Hungary.

Edmonds, M.R. and McElearney, G.F.X. (1999) Inhabitation and access at Gardom's Edge, *Internet Archaeology* Issue 6: http://intarch.ac.uk/journal/issue6/edmonds_toc.html

Edmonds, M.R. and Seabourne, T. (2000) *Prehistory in the Peak*, Oxford: Tempus Publications.

Grabinger, R.S. and Dunlap, J. (2000) Rich environments for active learning: a definition. In D. Squires, G. Conole and G. Jacobs (eds) *The Changing Face of Learning Technology*, Cardiff: The University of Wales.

Hodder, I. (1999) Archaeology and global information systems, *Internet Archaeology* Issue 6: http://intarch.ac.uk/journal/issue6/hodder_toc.html

Holtorf, C. (1999) Is history going to be on my side?, *Internet Archaeology* Issue 6: http://intarch.ac.uk/journal/issue6/holtorf_toc.html

Laurillard, D. (1993) *Rethinking University Teaching: A Framework for the Effective Use of Educational Technology*, London: Routledge.

Laurillard, D. (1999) Multimedia and the learners experience of narrative. *Computers in Education* 31(2): 229–242. www.sciencedirect.com/web-editions/journal/03601315

McConnell, D. (2000) *Implementing Computer Supported Collaborative Learning*, London: Kogan Page.

Oliver, M. (2000) An introduction to the evaluation of learning technology, *Educational Technology and Society* 3(4): 20–30.

Pollard, J. and Gillings, M. (1998) Romancing the stones: towards a virtual and elemental Avebury, *Archaeological Dialogues* 5(2): 143–164.

Ryan, S., Scott, B., Freeman, H. and Patel, D. (2000) *The Virtual University*, London: Kogan Page.

Sanders, D.H. (1997) Archaeological virtual worlds for public education, *CSS Journal* 5(3): http://www.webcom.journal

Tam, M. (2000) Constructivism, instructional design, and technology: implications for transforming distance learning, *Educational Technology and Society* 3(2): 50–60.

PART FOUR

Examples of Good Practice

Chapter 14

THE LIFE AND DEATH OF AN EDUCATION SERVICE

Vikki Pearson

From 1988 to 1999, the Northamptonshire Heritage Education Service (NHES) provided advice, assistance and resources for schools, teachers and pupils who wished to explore the educational potential of the historic environment of the county.

From its inception in 1988 to its demise in March 1999, the nature of the service, its scope and organisation underwent many changes in response to local government, education and financial pressures, including changes in funding, organisation, location, name and personnel. By 1999, the Education Service was located within the Environment Department of Northamptonshire County Council and was run by a full-time education officer and a part-time education assistant working closely with county council heritage management officers. It had come a long way from its first days as a short-term, temporary education project aligned to a specific archaeological investigation.

The educational programme

As archaeologists our interest was in the study of the past – the artefacts produced by human societies, the places where they lived and the effects they had on the landscape – and our role in seeking to develop our understanding of our heritage and also in its future preservation. As educationalists our role was to inform and educate teachers and pupils as to the nature of the archaeological record, as contained in the historic environment, and to demonstrate its importance both to our knowledge of the past and to the landscape today.

Throughout the lifetime of the NHES, we sought to develop up-to-date, accurate and innovative ways of disseminating knowledge about the historic environment to a wide audience, thus providing opportunities for schools, teachers, pupils, parents, local interest groups and landowners to develop their knowledge and involvement in their heritage through the use of the local historic environment. To this end, a number of specific aims were set which formed the underlying framework for the development of a wide-ranging programme of educational opportunities for all interested parties:

- To make accessible the richness and variety of the historic environment to the widest range of educational audiences and as a result promote a deeper understanding and appreciation of the county's heritage.
- To carry the message of the importance of the conservation of our heritage into the educational community and to foster an understanding of the need to protect our historic environment for both our own and future generations' enjoyment and knowledge.
- To introduce teachers and pupils to the local historic environment through site visits, resource materials and training opportunities.
- To provide up-to-date, relevant, accurate and cost-effective resource materials based on local sites and archaeological material for all educational audiences.
- To encourage an active participation by the educational community in the archaeological investigation of our past through provision of local opportunities, advice and information.

During its eleven-year lifetime, NHES developed a wide programme of educational opportunities focused on the archaeology, ancient landscapes and sites, historic buildings and artefacts of the county. This programme was continually being evaluated, changed and extended to reflect the shifting educational, organisational and financial environments but sought to fulfil the Education Service's stated aims through the provision of an educational programme which contained a number of key elements:

- *School visits* – a range of classroom sessions were provided for pupils of all ages from artefact-handling sessions for five-year-olds, slide talks about the role of archaeology in finding out about the past to the consideration of the role of buildings as a primary source of historical evidence at A-level.
- *Teacher-training* – regular courses aimed at developing teacher knowledge of and confidence in using local historic sites and archaeological resource material, including artefacts and the Sites and Monument Record. In addition NHES was able to provide individual school-based advisory and planning sessions.
- *Fieldwork activities* – working in partnership with landowners, developers and schools, practical fieldwork activities at a range of historic sites, including excavations, were made possible, including a regular summer Sixth Form Fieldwork Week.

- *Artefact loans* – high-quality resource material was developed to enhance in-school teaching. This included provision of an extensive archaeological handling kit scheme whereby archaeological material from a range of periods was made available to pupils.
- *Resources* – a wide range of resource and teaching materials was developed for teachers and other organisations, including site guides and teaching packs. We were able to respond quickly to teachers' requirements and specific local activities such as excavation discoveries to produce low-cost resource materials.
- *Recreational opportunities* – we were also able to provide informal opportunities for children and adults to learn about and enjoy the historic environment and archaeology through public events, displays and the launch of a local branch of the Young Archaeologists' Club (see Henry, Chapter 10).
- *Making connections* – working with landowners, local organisation and district councils to develop educational aspects of historic sites or material in the county through publications, meetings and training sessions.

From Stanwick Roman villa excavations to the Northamptonshire Heritage Education Service

The NHES began life in response to requests from schools and teachers for help and advice in developing the educational opportunities provided by the large-scale, long-term archaeological investigation of an area in the south-east of the county – the Raunds Area Project. The result was joint funding of an education officer (initially part-time) by English Heritage and the local education authority, who was based in the Northamptonshire Archaeology Unit.

At the start, education work was focused on the site of Stanwick Roman villa which was being excavated over several years. Educational visits for pupils of all ages were developed which allowed children to participate in hands-on archaeological activities, including excavation. To support these visits, it was obviously necessary to provide training sessions for teachers and resource materials that could be used for preliminary and follow-up work. It also became possible for the education officer to visit the schools to further enrich the archaeological experience for pupils.

This work took place during the summer term, but it was also decided to take advantage of the wealth of archaeological materials being accumulated by the Raunds Area Project – plans, desktop survey material, unstratified archaeological material – to produce resource materials that would continue to be of use to schools, teachers and pupils once the excavation and the education project ended. As a result, a number of artefact handling kits and an archaeological teachers' pack (the Quest Pack) were produced by the education officer during the autumn and winter terms.

As the excavation at Stanwick drew to a close in 1991/2 it became clear that schools that had taken advantage of the educational opportunities it had offered were anxious to continue to include educational activities relating to archaeology and the historic environment in their curriculum, especially in relation to the new demands of the National Curriculum. A number of new activities and site visits were therefore developed to provide this – most notably the development of educational visits to Kirby Hall, a sixteenth-century English Heritage property where excavations of the gardens had also been taking place. Educational work at Kirby Hall concentrated on the archaeology of the site rather than the historic nature of the house and involved study of the landscape features of the gardens and the superb earthworks of the adjacent deserted medieval village. Educational visits to Kirby Hall proved very popular with schools in the county, becoming a fixed part of many schools' history schemes of work.

By this stage the education officer was being employed full-time (term time) and an education assistant was needed on a part-time basis to assist with field visits and administration of the handling kit loans. It seemed, however, that the NHES was unlikely to survive following the withdrawal of, first, English Heritage funding (following completion of the Stanwick excavation) and then the introduction of Local Management of Schools and the consequent inability of the LEA to continue support of the education posts.

After discussion within the County Council it was agreed that support for the project would become the responsibility of the County Environment Department but that the Education Service would have to be partly (ideally wholly) self-funded through the introduction of charges for schools using the service. Until this point provision of all educational resources – visits, kit loans, teacher-training – had been completely free of charge. Thus a subscription scheme for schools was introduced whereby schools paid an annual fee in order to take advantage of the resources provided.

Shortly after this, a further strain was placed on the continued viability of the NHES when the organisation of local government archaeological and heritage management services was restructured in the wake of the introduction and implementation of Planning Policy Guidance Note 16. The Northamptonshire Archaeology Unit was divided into two separate organisations – a contracting side undertaking the actual archaeological investigative work (Northamptonshire Archaeology), which was expected to be financially independent, and a curatorial body consisting of the planning functions, the Sites and Monuments Record, as well as Historic Buildings and Conservation team (Northamptonshire Heritage). It was decided that the NHES, since it was not fully self-funding, would be better placed within Northamptonshire Heritage.

By 1993, the NHES had been established as a permanent organisation provided by the County Council with financial assistance from English Heritage, with a funded full-time education officer at a cost of around £21,000 per annum. The post of education assistant was to be funded through the subscription scheme and the hope was that eventually the whole project would become self-financing (though it quickly became evident that this was unlikely to be achieved).

From 1993 to 1999 the Education Service continued to develop its role as a provider of high-quality educational advice, information and resources for those wishing to develop educational work in the field of historic environmental education. Areas of development included work with secondary schools in the production of GCSE Schools History Project Schemes of Work, production of new resource materials, including teachers' packs based on aerial photographs, Northamptonshire castles and the discovery of an Anglo-Saxon boar helmet in the county, development of educational aspects of the Countryside Stewardship Scheme (Grenville 1999) on historic sites and a widening of the target audience for our work with the launch of a Northamptonshire branch of the Young Archaeologists' Club, summer playscheme activities and weekend events. These developments were in addition to the provision of an annual subscription scheme to a steadily increasing number of the county's schools (and some schools outside Northamptonshire), which included a programme of teacher-training courses, handling kits and artefact loans, a range of school visits and fieldwork activities at a number of different sites, as well as provision of advice and information both by telephone and face to face.

The strengths and weaknesses of the Northamptonshire Heritage Education Service

The fact that the NHES was able to develop from a temporary part-time education project to a permanent service employing full-time dedicated education personnel was a reflection of a number of particular strengths that were developed over its lifetime:

- The education personnel had strong links to both education and archaeology – both the education officer and her assistant being archaeology graduates and practising teachers. In addition close links were forged with the Local Education Authority and their advisory teachers as well as with the English Heritage Education Service (see Corbishley, Chapter 7). This meant that the credibility of the education programme provision in terms of its relevance to the educational curriculum and the school teaching environment was maintained throughout – teachers felt that the Education Service understood the classroom situation and that the resources we provided would reflect both their needs and the constraints placed upon them.
- The location within Northamptonshire Heritage allowed easy, quick access to archaeological information and resources. For example, close contact with the Sites and Monuments Record, Northamptonshire Archaeology and the County Archaeologist allowed the development of a teachers' pack based on the discovery of the grave containing an Anglo-Saxon boar helmet within days

of the discovery making the local and national press and the resulting enquiries from schools for more information.

- Collaboration and input from other areas of Heritage management such as Historic Buildings and Planning widened the scope of the Education Service and the provision of information we were able to provide.
- Location within the County Council, with close links to the Local Education Authority personnel, meant good contact with local schools could be developed and maintained.
- Employment of full-time education personnel and additional administrative support provided the time and resources necessary to ensure exploration and planning of a wide variety of educational projects rather than being tied to a specific time-restricted or site-related archaeological investigation.
- The commitment by the County Environment Department to the funding of the project enabled not only the opportunity for long-term development of the Service but also ensured that we did not have to charge schools, teachers and pupils the full cost of the provision of the educational programme.

However, there were also a number of weaknesses within the Education Service which caused concern and also ultimately led to its demise:

- The split in archaeological services provided by Northamptonshire County Council into separate contractual and curatorial organisations led to a weakening of the links between the Education Service and the actual on-site archaeological investigations. Coupled with the rise of 'developer pays' archaeology, this led to fewer opportunities for on-site 'real archaeology' (i.e. excavation-related) opportunities for teachers and pupils.
- The introduction of a subscription service meant there was increasing pressure to provide an Education Service that was specifically tailored to attract schools – i.e. catering solely for their stated needs/areas of interest. There was less scope for provision of development of material that primarily reflected the concerns of archaeology and heritage management.
- Continuing changes within the National Curriculum led to a shrinking curriculum scope within schools and their increasing difficulty in incorporating archaeological education projects within their schemes of work.
- There was continuing financial pressure on schools, especially with the development of funds for management within the individual school – each school had to pay for their own service and not all could afford or justify expenditure on the Northamptonshire Heritage Education Service. This led to increasing numbers of schools and teachers who wished to take advantage of our services but were unable to do so because of budgetary limitations.

As a consequence it became obvious that NHES would never be able to charge the full cost of providing our services to schools and that charging schools at a reduced level of cost would never enable the NHES to be financially independent. It was this weakness that eventually led to the withdrawal of the NHES.

The end of the Northamptonshire Heritage Education Service

In the final full year of the NHES, nearly 30 per cent of the county's schools subscribed to an annual programme, we made 35 school visits, over 120 handling kits were lent, 34 training sessions were held and 25 days of educational fieldwork were undertaken. Demand from Northamptonshire schools and others outside the area was high and growing, and the NHES was working with around 2,500 children and teachers of all ages each year.

Despite this undoubted demand for the NHES, a decision was made in January 1999 to withdraw support from the Education Service as part of wide-ranging budget cuts and reorganisation of policy priorities within the County Council. It appeared that the NHES was not seen as contributing to the Council's stated policy objectives – although the reasoning behind the decision to abolish the service was never clearly explained except in terms of the need to cut budgets and reallocate funding to other areas. Despite many protests from schools who used the service, and from outside organisations such as the CBA and English Heritage, the NHES ceased to operate from April 1999 with the education officer and assistant effectively being made redundant. The resources built up by the Education Service over eleven years, including over thirty artefact handling kits, were distributed to other organisations within the county such as local museums so that they would still continue to be available for use by local schools.

What lessons can be learnt?

First, that the need for such an education service is there, even in the days of the National Curriculum, Literacy and Numeracy Hours, and Citizenship. Schools and teachers rely on the expertise of others to enhance their teaching and pupils' experiences in education. However, it takes time to establish a successful education service – to make contact with schools, convince them of the relevance of your educational provision and to develop and expand the scope of the educational opportunities you are providing.

Second, any successful project will work closely with both sides – the archaeologists and the teachers. Such projects need to forge strong links with both to ensure that the educational provision being delivered reflects not only the aims of the archaeologist and conservationist but also the educational requirements of the teacher and pupil.

Third, education work is not generally a profit-making opportunity – normally the true cost of such an education service is not affordable by individual schools. Therefore funding of education work is an area that needs exploring carefully.

Fourth, big oaks from little acorns can grow – it is better to start education work on a low-key, low-cost level and hopefully be able to develop and expand it over time than to demand a full-blown, full-time dedicated education service at the outset and not get started at all!

Fifth, focus on your local links/resources – there is an increasing variety of resource materials being produced by large organisations such as English Heritage and commercial publishers whose resources and finances you cannot hope to match. Concentrate on providing high quality (in terms of educational relevance rather than necessarily production) that makes the most of your local resources – sites, artefacts and people.

Finally, above all remember what the aims of your education work are. Get your message across to as many people as you can in as many different ways as you can; be bold, innovative and fight to establish a permanent need and place for your educational work.

■ ■ ■

Reference

Grenville, J. (ed.) (1999) *Managing the Historic Rural Landscape*, London: Routledge.

Chapter 15

ARCHAEOLOGY AND EDUCATION IN CAMBRIDGESHIRE

Caroline Malim

Cambridgeshire County Council's Archaeological Field Unit (CCCAFU) is one of two locally based contracting units, although up to twenty other organisations also operate in the county. As a trading arm of the County Council, the CCCAFU must bring in all funds to cover its costs, and, as with other contracting units, must compete for its work. Therefore, its education service has had to run on a zero-based budget since 1994.

Introduction and background

In the early 1970s, the post of county archaeological officer was established with a brief that covered not only advice to the planning authority and the creation of a Sites and Monuments Record, but also to raise the profile of local archaeology, involve the public and bring archaeology into conventional education within the newly formed county of Greater Cambridgeshire (Malim 1997). It was as a result of Alison Taylor's appointment and her development of the educational side that a number of initiatives were introduced over the following twenty years:

- The writing of popular publications on the county's archaeology
- Display panels for use in schools, libraries and public events
- Artefact-handling sessions at the East of England shows and other public events
- Close co-operation with museums in Cambridge, leading to joint displays

- The production of permanent interpretation boards for monuments around the county
- Active encouragement of amateur involvement in archaeology
- The compilation of artefact packs for schools to borrow
- Talks to schools, colleges and societies
- Secondment of teachers to write educational resource books for different periods
- Guided walks around historic towns, villages and monuments
- Archaeology activity days at selected monuments
- An annual leaflet, *Archaeology For All*, to publicise forthcoming events
- Acquisition of standing buildings for County Guardianship in which a series of ancient music concerts were given in order to promote public interest
- The Cambridgeshire Monument Management Programme

Linked to the educational initiatives, Alison's pioneering efforts in the management of monuments included aspects such as site access and interpretation. The County Council owns a considerable amount of land itself, which includes a large number of listed buildings, scheduled ancient monuments and other archaeological sites. The County Farms estate is the largest in the country at 46,000 acres, and in 1989 Alison received financial backing from English Heritage to undertake a survey of the estate which was published as a formal report (Malim 1990). This report included not only valuable recommendations but also a variety of illustrative material, which was included to make the report more attractive to farm managers, tenants and the general public.

One of the main recommendations of the survey was a project to reverse the destruction of one of the estate's scheduled monuments, Stonea Camp Iron Age fort, by reinstating its banks and ditches and converting it to pasture, with public access and a series of interpretation boards. The success of both the County Farms Survey and Stonea Camp led to agreement from English Heritage to fund a rolling programme of evaluation of county farm land in order to achieve more beneficial farm management for important archaeological sites. This helped in preserving monuments, enabled better public access and interpretation for the general public, as well as providing locations for public and schools events, and 'hands-on' activity days. Sadly, after Alison Taylor's retirement in 1997, the county archaeologist post was not re-filled. Resources had been constantly cut back over recent years and budgetary constraints meant that the education service, built up over twenty-four years, was no longer seen as a priority, although the Development Control and SMR responsibilities continued to be funded.

The CCCAFU had for a long time provided Alison Taylor with the support and expertise required to produce some of the educational materials and lay on activity days and other events. The conviction amongst its staff that, as part of the County Council, the CCCAFU should not only be a contracting unit but also a County Council service for the public was the main reason behind its 'full adoption' of the education service. The service (Table 15.1) runs on a zero budget with the result that all education work must either be funded by the recipients of the service or written off as an overhead to the unit. This was a brave decision because competition for developer-led projects makes funding very tight and therefore places the CCCAFU in a disadvantageous position for commercial tendering. However, the importance of an education service run from a field unit should not be underestimated, with its ability to provide a holistic service linking the immediacy of fieldwork with interpretation, presentation, access, SMR and development control. In the long term archaeology will only be seen as important if the public sees it as such and supports us. To reach schoolchildren and convert them at an early age is an essential part of any archaeologist's role.

The CCCAFU had already produced its own *Education Review* (Gait Utime 1994), setting out why an education service was desirable, how such a service could interface with other departments in the County Council's Libraries and Heritage Service (which included libraries, archives, arts and museums), how the existing archaeological education service could be enhanced, and how the venture was to proceed. The bulk of the *Review*, however, was concerned with eight aims (each accompanied with their own objectives) identified as crucial to the service:

1   Enable the general public to gain knowledge of and involvement in the archaeological heritage as encountered by the CCCAFU
2   Make this knowledge accessible to both adults and children
3   Provide a service which is relevant/appropriate to the needs of the customer
4   Instil in staff of the CCCAFU the importance of imparting knowledge to the public

Table 15.1   **Educational services of the Cambridgeshire Archaeological Field Unit**

Adult oriented	Family oriented	School oriented
Talks	Excavation open days	Teaching packages/worksheets
Conferences	Hands-on activity days	Free artefact-handling boxes for loan
Courses	Exhibitions	Displays
Volunteer opportunities	Display boards	School talks/handling sessions
	Leaflets	Free guided tours to county farm monuments
	Excavation information sheets	Work placements
	Training excavation	Hands-on activity days
	Storytelling events	Excavation open days
	Popular publications	Free archaeology road show
	Public events programme	Schools events programme
	Guided walks	
	Permanent interpretation boards for sites and monuments	

5   Provide an integrated education and information service which complements and builds upon those already provided within the County Council's Heritage Service
6   Promote related activities and services of other sections within the County Council's Heritage Service wherever possible
7   Provide a quality education and information service
8   Provide funding for the education service

Efforts to secure funding for an education officer post to run and organise the service were unsuccessful. As a result of this the 'post' is jointly run by two staff members who must find time to co-ordinate and divide the education work around their own respective posts of senior illustrator and project officer. In retrospect the complementary skills and abilities of each officer (one with a teaching qualification and experience in design and presentation of information, the other with practical field experience, report writing and monument management) has proved highly successful. There is, however, a heavy reliance upon the goodwill of other CCCAFU staff without whose help many of the public or school activities and events could not be achievable – particularly those held during bank holidays and weekends.

Although the CCCAFU aims to reach adults as well as children it still finds that those who use the service most are primary schools, due to areas they cover under the history curriculum, and schools with children with severe learning difficulties who benefit from the very 'hands-on' nature of some of the CCCAFU's classroom sessions and activity days at monuments. Secondary schools also use the service from time to time but find that time, money and/or curriculum requirement can make justification more difficult.

A knowledge of school pressures, workloads, current educational trends (such as the emphasis on literacy and numeracy), curriculum changes, dates for school holidays and term times (the prospects of getting schools to come to an activity during the first week of the school year are unlikely), and contact names is essential. It is not easy keeping up to date with all this information, especially when different schools start and break up at different times, are following different themes, were allowed extra spending for history last year but foreign languages get it this year, etc. This all has an impact on how well different aspects of the education service will fare at different times.

The fact that the CCCAFU found the same schools coming back year after year led to the introduction of an Archaeology Road Show whereby handling sessions could be taken to different schools in the county or a museum nearby free of charge. This gave schools an opportunity to get some experience of the education service, and us an opportunity to talk to teachers. Unfortunately the fact that many of these schools were either very hard up and/or located in distant parts of the county has meant that any hope of them coming to CCCAFU activity days usually proves to be too expensive as coach travel costs per pupil match and in some instances exceed the cost per child normally charged by the CCCAFU for any given event.

Occasionally a developer-funded project may include a specific element for education or promotion, but such events are more often associated with publicly funded projects such as County Council or English Heritage schemes. However, the CCCAFU successfully integrates public archaeology on several commercially funded sites.

Following this necessary introduction, which gives an understanding of how the foundations of the education service were laid, the following sections will give a flavour of the kind of site-based activities that the CCCAFU undertakes as part of its education programme.

Excavation open days

Introduction

For the developer, archaeology is required as no more than part of the planning process, and archaeologists are in the tricky position of selling a service which, in effect, the developer does not want to buy (and in some cases does not pay for) – their main concern lying with how quickly and cheaply the archaeological work in question can be done. The archaeologist must normally bid for the work, win it and then, where appropriate, discuss the possibility of funding to include an educational aspect to the project. This might, depending upon the nature and scale of the archaeology, consist of any or all of the following: school talks, open days for schools and the public, teachers' packs, leaflets, booklets, temporary and/or permanent interpretation boards, and permanent displays, etc. (Figure 15.1).

Figure 15.1   Cambridgeshire County Council Archaeological Field Unit signage

Some excavations attract plenty of local public interest, and the CCCAFU has on many occasions successfully managed to integrate an educational element to both commercially and publicly funded sites. However, not all developers are sympathetic to the idea and some can even be quite hostile, despite the fact that community involvement can act as a good public relations exercise for them.

Willingham Anglo-Saxon settlement 1997, in the centre of present-day village

This excavation provided the largest opportunity ever to investigate the early Anglo-Saxon settlement in the area, and was carried out in advance of a housing development. Features were clearly visible and consisted of the post holes of timber buildings, rubbish pits, wells, ovens, hearths and ditches around house plots. For the benefit of visitors the houses were outlined with white paint. The site's large area and extensive visual features made it ideal for the public to visit. Posters were put up in the local area and a press release sent out advertising a site open day, which was held on a Sunday and staffed by CCCAFU members volunteering their time; schools were invited to visit in the week. The open day was free of charge and provided guided tours of the site, information sheets, and a visitor hut with an exhibition which included artefacts and reconstruction drawings of the site. Over a thousand visitors came to the open day. Public and school involvement was made possible without the developer's financial support. Rather, it was paid for through the unit's overheads and voluntary support from staff members. The developer had already made it clear that they were not interested in community involvement.

Barrington Anglo-Saxon cemetery, 1990–91

This site was found as a result of metal detecting and ploughing and was funded by English Heritage, Cambridgeshire County Council and South Cambridgeshire District Council. Over one hundred pagan Saxon burials were excavated, the cemetery population representing a good cross-section of the community with their associated grave goods. For two of the three summer seasons, excavations were planned so that the site could be open seven days a week to schools and the public. A series of worksheets and handouts were written for schools. Children as well as older volunteers took part on site excavating and pot washing, and they were also shown how to record features (Figure 15.2). Guided tours of the excavation were given and a visitor hut was installed with displays and artefacts, which developed as the excavation progressed (Figure 15.3). The excavation received over 7,000 visitors and further people had the opportunity of visiting an exhibition laid on at Wimpole Hall, a National Trust property a few miles away. Numerous talks to local schools and societies were given, and repeat talks about the excavation continue to be requested by teachers covering the Anglo-Saxons at school.

Figure 15.2 Child planning features at Barrington

In conclusion, although many sites are not suitable for public access because of their cramped conditions, sometimes surrounded by heavy machinery and posing a health and safety nightmare, nonetheless other sites might have the potential for involving the local community. Sadly, tight deadlines and tighter budgets can often preclude taking such action, but even in these situations, if there is a will to inform the local public there is always, at the very least, the possibility of sticking up a small, basic information board and/or offering an evening talk to a local society.

Community archaeology

This includes talks to local societies, guided walks around monuments, site tours, information leaflets, displays and volunteer involvement. Sometimes one project can offer the opportunity to include all of these and more. An example of this is the Ramsey Project.

The Ramsey Abbey school excavation project (a PPG16 development) carried out in 1998 was seen by the CCCAFU as a good opportunity to launch a combined programme of events, bringing together for the first time many different parts of the newly formed Community Services Division of the County Council's Education, Libraries and Heritage Service. The different elements of this programme included: *community education*, with a four-week course of evening classes and a day school;

Figure 15.3   Looking at an excavated grave at Barrington

libraries, with displays and a coffee morning at Ramsey library using materials from Archives and Archaeology; *museums*, with a joint opening of the site to the public with that of a craft fair at the Rural Life Museum on a bank holiday Monday; *arts*, with an ancient music concert held at Ramsey Church; and also the creation of a web page by the CCCAFU which tracked development of the excavations and related events. The catalyst for all this was the excavation itself at Ramsey Abbey School which already had its own programme for getting involvement from both the primary and secondary schools on the site through talks, displays and visits. Subsequently the CCCAFU received a Royal Society and British Association Millennium Award to undertake a programme of geophysical surveying which involved the pupils.

Activity days

Introduction

'Living in the past' and hands-on events are a very popular format for bringing archaeology alive to the public. Cambridgeshire County Farms estate are keen to promote public access on their monuments and therefore sponsor the CCCAFU's hands-on activity days and free school guided walks which are held on the estate. The decision was made early on that, as an archaeological organisation, the CCCAFU is better placed to share its first-hand knowledge and expertise about the prehistoric, Iron Age, Roman, Anglo-Saxon and Viking periods, and would therefore concentrate activity days primarily upon these periods.

Stonea Camp

Stonea Camp Iron Age fort is situated in the depths of the Cambridgeshire fens, on the edge of what was at one time an island. It lies within the territory of the Iceni, and remains of a Roman town lie in a field adjacent to the fort (Jackson and Potter 1996). Anyone familiar with the fens will know how cold and windy they can be even on hot days, and Stonea Camp is a long way from anywhere, exposed to the elements, difficult to get to, and has no toilets.

Amazingly, despite all this, the 'hands-on' activities at Stonea since 1992 were very well attended, with events advertised in the local newspapers and on the radio and television. Activity days for schools are held over a period of a week during the summer term with one day over the weekend for the public. The hands-on activities include cooking, spinning and weaving, making coil pots, iron smelting, and daubing; a site tour is also given, and a session about early farming techniques and animal breeds is provided by one of the rangers from Hinchingbrooke Country Park, Huntingdon. Daubing was introduced as an activity once the decision was made to build a round house in the activity area next to the monument. Children were able to build on these activities back in school (Figure 15.4).

Hinchingbrooke Iron Age village

The CCCAFU's work at Stonea Camp with the rangers from Hinchingbrooke Country Park ultimately led to the creation of Hinchingbrooke Country Park Iron

Figure 15.4   Child's drawing of an Iron Age warrior

Age farm in 1994. Here a number of structures have been built, including a completed roundhouse, granary, a bank and ditch, pens for pigs and sheep, a herb garden and a turf kiln. Activity days for schools are held at the farm twice a year over a period of about three weeks (Figure 15.5), and both the rangers and CCCAFU staff take part in running the events which are similar to those run at Stonea, but also include wood-turning, basket-making (using willow from the park) and storytelling. The concern that overemphasis on the Iron Age might deter schools from coming, as the period does not feature in the National Curriculum, has sometimes led to promotion of the site as Romano-British, a period which does feature, and including wherever possible visits from members of Roman re-enactment groups. Pupils' enjoyment of their visits has been apparent (Figures 15.6, 15.7).

Figure 15.5   Children at the Hinchingbrooke Iron Age village

The training excavation

Introduction

The CCCAFU, in its *Education Review* of 1994, had already identified the desire to run a training excavation which would give local people the opportunity to become involved in archaeology through a course of structured, practical fieldwork. The training excavation also provides a useful link with adult education courses in which some CCCAFU staff members are engaged. Thus a Certificate in Archaeology accredited by Cambridge University's Board of Continuing Education provides the academic background, whilst the training excavation provides a practical application which is locally and conveniently placed. The training excavation is run over a four-week period and participants have a choice of attending for as many of those weeks as they wish. It has been funded by South Cambridgeshire District Council, Cambridgeshire County Council, English Heritage and other commercial sponsorship, with fees paid by the trainees.

Figure 15.6   Letter from a school pupil (1)

Credit accumulation and transfer scheme (CATs)

For those over 18 who elect to join the scheme, the accredited training excavation allows credits towards a degree to be collected. Participants in the scheme are expected to complete specific assignments along with relevant CATs and CCCAFU documentation. Ten credits are awarded for successful completion of each week of the training excavation.

Figure 15.7 Letter from a school pupil (2)

Training excavation course aims

The training excavation has three main aims:

1   Systematic excavation and recovery of buried archaeological deposits and the recording of primary data.

2   Opportunities for each participant to carry out archaeological excavation in a safe and effective way, and give participants an understanding of why particular tasks are undertaken (Figure 15.8).

3   Opportunities for participants to learn a variety of excavation and related techniques (Figure 15.9).

Figure 15.8 Group with surveying staff at the training excavation

Documentation

Participants and their supervisors complete a daily record sheet indicating the day's work and progress towards learning outcomes (Table 15.2) which are scored against the assessment criteria (Table 15.3). At the end of the course, assessment records are completed for each participant who then receives a certificate based upon the daily record sheet and assessment record. Those who enrol on the CATs scheme must also complete set assignments and documentation.

Figure 15.9   Surveying with a tape at the training excavation

During the excavation each participant is responsible for their own feature from start to finish, planning, excavating, recording and photographing, etc.; they are allowed to take home copies of the work they have done.

Initially, trainees from the age of twelve were accepted but it was found that for most of them training was too intensive. The minimum age now accepted onto the training excavation is fourteen, which has proved to be more successful. The training excavation attracts participants from all over the country and overseas. Some return on a regular basis whilst others make a family holiday of it. To date at least eight participants have gone on to degree courses, their places at university helped by completion of the training excavation.

Conclusion

It is becoming increasingly difficult for the general public to take part in site-based archaeology, due, in no small part, to the nature of the large numbers of developer-led projects. Competitive tendering for fieldwork, and the rising numbers of projects carried out by 'roving' archaeological organisations, is making it hard to provide people with opportunities to get involved with, and obtain information about, their local archaeology.

The extra time and expense required to cater for education is, on the surface, unacceptable for commercial businesses which are competing for work more likely

Table 15.2 Training excavation learning outcomes

After one week

Gain an understanding of health and safety matters specific to the excavation, to include an awareness of individual responsibility to self and others when participating in practical excavation, particularly when using unfamiliar tools and equipment.

Attain a basic level of excavation skill and satisfactorily excavate simple, discrete features under supervision.

Learn to recognise common types of artefacts and ecofacts such as pottery and animal bone; learn to identify obvious archaeological deposits.

Gain an understanding of why and how finds are cleaned and stored in order to prevent further deterioration. Demonstrate ability in a practical session devoted to the curation of finds.

Gain an understanding of the context number and understand the importance of matching finds to contextual information.

After two weeks (plus all the above)

Gain an understanding of the site grid, how it is constructed and how it relates to the Ordnance Survey. Use the grid in order to contribute to the primary record.

Draw sections through simple archaeological features in order to contribute to the primary record; the finished drawing should be a clear and accurate representation of the excavated deposits.

Gain a basic understanding of the archaeological and historical background to the project, why the excavation is taking place and what is hoped will be gained from the excavation.

Use a dumpy level to measure accurate and comparable heights on archaeological deposits; gain an understanding of how these measurements are achieved and how they relate to the Ordnance Survey.

Cross-reference drawings and finds to context forms and index; gain an understanding of the importance of keeping clear and accurately cross-referenced records as part of the primary record.

After three weeks (plus all the above)

Use the site grid for drawing archaeological deposits in plan at a variety of scales. Define and draw simple deposits.

Photograph archaeological features for archive records and display purposes using a 35 mm camera; ensure that all documentation is completed.

Gain an understanding of why and how environmental samples are taken. Select deposits to be sampled in consultation with supervisor and practise taking and recording a variety of different sorts of sample.

Gain an understanding of the processes involved in preparing samples for microscopic analysis and assist in the flotation of bulk samples.

Be able to assess how simple, discrete features should be tackled in consultation with supervisor and be able to tackle simple, discrete features with a minimum of supervision.

Table 15.2 continued

After four weeks (plus all the above)

Be able to record observations of deposits and cuts on the context recording form in consultation with supervisor. Discuss and interpret archaeological deposits.

Learn what the total station surveying instrument is used for. Gain a basic understanding of the instrument and participate in practical exercises under close supervision.

Be able to excavate more complex deposits, such as intercutting features, to a satisfactory standard in consultation with the supervisor.

Be able to differentiate and recognise finds belonging to broad periods from the site; for example, prehistoric and modern pottery.

Gain an understanding of stratigraphic matrices and how to construct them. Complete context form by ensuring all cross-referencing and indexing is done.

Table 15.3 Training excavation assessment criteria

1 Participant has been shown how to carry out a particular task
2 Participant has successfully carried out the task under direct supervision
3 Participant has understood why and when the task needs to be carried out
4 Participant has carried out the task with little supervision
5 Participant has appropriately and successfully carried out the task without any supervision

to be won on lowest cost than 'value for money', but it would be a serious error to imagine that this situation can be sustained indefinitely. Archaeology relies upon the support it receives from the general public – teachers, parents, politicians and the developers themselves. Without adequately engaging the public we will ultimately be starving archaeology of the lifeline it needs to survive. We cannot ignore our responsibility towards public archaeology without serious consequences for the longer term future of our past.

Since the writing of this chapter, Cambridgeshire County Council reinstated the position of county archaeologist in 2002.

Acknowledgements

My thanks to Aileen Connor for providing me with details of the training excavation programme, and to Tim Malim for his information about the history of the education service under Alison Taylor and helpful advice on the content of this chapter.

■ ■ ■

References

Gait Utime, C. (1994) *Education Review*, Cambridge: Cambridgeshire County Council Archaeological Field Unit.

Jackson, R.P.J. and Potter, T.W. (1996) *Excavations at Stonea, Cambridgeshire, 1980–85*, London: British Museum Press.

Malim, T. (1990) *Archaeology on the Cambridgeshire County Farms Estate*, Cambridge: Cambridgeshire County Council.

Malim, T. (1997) Alison Taylor, FSA MIFA: Cambridgeshire County Archaeologist 1974–97, *Proceedings of the Cambridge Antiquarian Society* LXXXV: 5–10.

Chapter 16

OUTREACH AT WESSEX ARCHAEOLOGY

Pippa Smith

Introduction

In 1996 the Trust for Wessex Archaeology decided to appoint a community officer with the aim of expanding their existing outreach work. Initially the post was part funded by English Heritage but in 1998 the Trust decided to continue funding the post in full. In 1999 the post of community officer was made permanent.

The responsibilities of the post are wide ranging and are not limited to formal education. The Community Officer is available to help anyone with an interest in the subject to learn more and to discover ways in which they can become involved. Groups are given lectures on aspects of the Trust's work: these groups range from local archaeological societies to village groups and organisations. Other groups visit Wessex Archaeology's premises to look at post-excavation work and many groups are also invited to visit excavations (where this is safe to do). Individuals are given advice and answers to their queries, and many individuals work as volunteers with Wessex Archaeology either as part of formal placement schemes or simply because they are interested in our work. The Community Officer also started and continues to run a branch of the Young Archaeologists' Club and organises large-scale events for National Archaeology Days (see Henry, Chapter 10). During the tenure of the post, the popularity of archaeology seems to have risen, possibly as a consequence of successful television programmes such as *Time Team* and *Meet the Ancestors*.

Work with schools

The work carried out by Wessex Archaeology within the formal education network covers schools, further and higher education institutions and adult education groups. A set of examples will be given below which concentrate on activities with children from Key Stage 2 (ages 7–11).

Classroom visits

One reasonably formal part of the activities with Key Stage 2 is linked to the National Curriculum for History and is usually requested by teachers as part of a topic on the Romans. A small charge is made for these visits but they are heavily subsidised by Wessex Archaeology. The Community Officer visits the school taking a travelling kit of artefacts and other materials. The session starts with discussion with the children to find out what they already know about archaeology. The discussion is steered around to the idea that much of what archaeologists find is rubbish (i.e. what people threw away). The children are then divided into groups and each group is given a sack of clean, modern rubbish and asked to find out about the people who threw this material away. They are then told that one of the sacks belongs to the community officer and each group can ask one question of her to try and decide which sack this is. The pupils usually manage to track down the correct bag. This is a useful confidence-building exercise which demonstrates to the children that they can use deductive logic to reach the correct interpretation.

At this stage, real Iron Age and Roman artefacts are introduced. Mystery objects are given to each group and they have to decide what these objects might have been used for. The objects are quite large (for example a quernstone) and the group is encouraged to look, touch and even smell the objects to gain some idea of their function. Trays of mixed artefacts are then given to each group and a series of sorting, drawing and counting exercises done, tailored according to the age and ability of the group.

Looking at Old Sarum

Other one-off projects have been undertaken and one such was a project requested and funded by English Heritage involving the local guardianship monument of Old Sarum. This activity took place as part of SET 2000 week (Science Engineering and Technology) and was linked to the National Curriculum for Technology. Each class was divided into three groups and each group given a different challenge. The first part of the challenge involved observation on site, including estimation and measurement.

One group worked within the gatehouse and considered defending the main entrance to the castle. They were asked to estimate the original thickness of the walls of the gatehouse and their original height. The bridge was looked at and

Figure 16.1   Children showing their colleagues a solution to drawing water out of a well at Old Sarum

photographs of the surviving stonework beneath the present wooden bridge were shown as it was thought to be too dangerous for the children to lean over to look at the stonework. This group was asked to investigate different types of drawbridges and provided with materials in order to make models to test their ideas.

Another group worked at the keep and was again asked to estimate the thickness and height of the walls. The defensive importance of the keep was discussed and this group was then asked to work out why the keep wall is sloping, or stepped. They were given material to build different types of walls (e.g. straight sided, steep sided) and to test the strength and stability of these different-shaped walls. If time allowed they were also asked how the stones could have been moved and lifted into place.

The third group looked at the well after discussing the importance of a water source to a castle under attack. They were asked to estimate the depth of the well and then given materials to measure the depth. This group's challenge was to work out how a bucket full of water could most easily have been drawn from the well (Figure 16.1). All of the groups were given materials with which to build models to test their ideas. These were very simple and consisted of:

- Several lengths of rope
- String
- Dowel poles 3 feet in length
- Wooden blocks
- Short lengths of wooden planks
- Pulleys
- Soft balls to throw at the model walls to test their stability
- 30-metre tapes

Each group demonstrated their models to the rest of the class and explained the different steps that they had taken to arrive at their ideas (Figure 16.2).

To finish the session, the children were shown reconstruction pictures of parts of Old Sarum and asked to look at the different ways of bridging gaps – for example,

Figure 16.2   Children looking at a model of a medieval drawbridge at Old Sarum

arches, straight lintels. Using a model arch provided by English Heritage, the strength of the shape was demonstrated by the Community Officer standing on the keystone. The final activity was to get the children into small groups and ask them to stand as shown in Figure 16.3 and lean forward. The Community Officer then pushed down where the children's hands were linked and easily broke the link. The children were then told to stand as in Figure 16.4 and lean forward, in this position the link was impossible to break and the children started to understand the direction in which the forces travelled and what gives the arch shape its strength.

Ten classes visited the site for these sessions and feedback from the teachers was generally very positive, apart from some adverse comments on the weather!

Visits to excavations

Wherever possible Wessex Archaeology, with the consent of the relevant landowner or client, invites local schools to visit their excavations (Figure 16.5). The process starts with the community officer visiting the site to undertake a risk assessment specifically for the school visits. If the site is considered safe for access then the community officer contacts nearby schools to offer guided visits. Once on site, the children are divided into small groups, depending on the size of the site and how

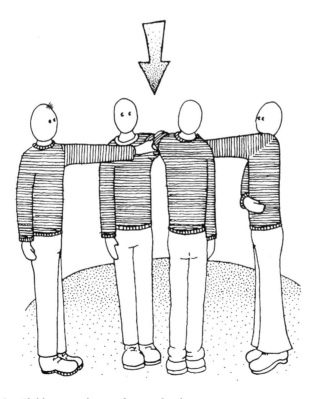

Figure 16.3 Children standing with arms level

Figure 16.4   Children standing with arms raised

many children can safely look around at any one time. Some children are left under the supervision of their teacher, either to look at artefacts or to wash some of the finds from the site, whilst the other children visit the site. The groups are then swapped around so each child sees both site and finds.

The costs of such visits are generally met by Wessex Archaeology and the schools are not asked for any contribution. Clients would only be asked to fund such access if it was specified in the brief.

Between 7 and 18 June 1999, Wessex Archaeology undertook an archaeological excavation in advance of development at 69 Greencroft Street, Salisbury, Wiltshire. The site lies in the north-east quadrant of medieval Salisbury within what was known as the Griffin Chequer. Greencroft Street was formerly Melemonger Street (1361), 'the street of meal sellers'. It was decided that although the site was small this was a good opportunity to involve a local school.

Two trenches were excavated and a series of features found dating from at least the thirteenth century to modern day (see Table 16.1 for a summary).

Figure 16.5   Local schoolchildren visiting the excavation of medieval remains at Greencroft Street, Salisbury

Although the excavation was small, it was possible to make it safe for children to visit once all heavy machinery was no longer needed on site. A local school was studying Salisbury as part of their local history project, so a visit to the site fitted in very well.

On site, the children were shown the sections where the stratigraphy was very clear, starting with modern tarmac and progressing down through several well-delineated layers. They also looked at the walls, doorways and hearths that could be seen in plan. The children looked at the different types of measuring and recording taking place on site and discussed how important the labelling of finds is. The groups were told about the original name of Greencroft Street and what it meant. They were also shown some of the finds, including a medal commemorating Queen Victoria's Diamond Jubilee of 1897. This find particularly involved the children, as we had some record of who lived in the properties at around this time, and they started to make a connection between the finds and real people from the past.

The census returns for 1871 and 1891 had been researched so that this information was available and this again helped to make a link with the idea of people leaving evidence behind them, not least because some of the surnames still occur in the town (Table 16.2).

The children enjoyed their visit to the site and were fascinated to discover just how much evidence lay beneath the streets of Salisbury. The teachers were delighted with the extra dimension that this visit gave to their local study and have since asked the Community Officer's advice on other ways to use archaeological evidence in teaching.

Table 16.1 Phasing at 69 Greencroft Street, Salisbury

Phase	Activity/event	Date range
1	The earliest activity on the site was a buried soil, either plough or garden.	13th century or earlier
2	A north–south ditch in Trench 1 and a shallow pit, possibly truncated.	13th to early 14th century
3	A build up of soils predominantly in Trench 2, possibly ground levelling prior to construction.	13th to early 14th century
4	First phase of building, a single-roomed structure approximately 10 square metres with a mortar and crushed-chalk floor. Constructed of flint and mortar walls with an east–west drain exiting the building in the south-west.	13th to early 14th century
5	Possible rebuilding after demolition or substantial repair work to Phase 4. Includes extension to the north.	13th to early 14th century
6	Build up of rubble to rear of Phase 4 in Trench 2, more than likely associated to Phase 5.	13th to early 14th century
7	Hearth near west wall. Completion of extension, and contemporary build up of soils to rear (Trench 2).	13th to early 14th century
8	Minor alterations within structure, including a mortar floor and associated post hole both within extension Phase 5. General build-up of soils and some rubble to rear of structure.	17th to early 18th century
9	Repairing/rebuilding of internal wall and new mortar/chalk floor on rubble levelling. Small wall to rear of building (Trench 2) and rubble deposition.	17th to early 18th century
10	Major demolition Phase 4 and construction of brick terrace house with brick floor support walls and hearth in south-west corner.	18th century
11	Demolition of terraced house and levelling of ground for construction of garage and car showroom.	Modern

General enquiries

Wessex Archaeology receives a large number of requests for advice and information and the community officer deals with many of these. The range of enquiries can be broken down into four basic types:

- Children, young people and adults who want information about a career in archaeology
- Students at college and university asking for help with projects
- Enquiries about opportunities for fieldwork and other involvement in practical archaeology
- Queries about fieldwork or monuments in the enquirers' locality.

Table 16.2 Census returns for 65–69 Greencroft Street, Salisbury

Name	Age	Status	Occupation	Birthplace
Census returns for 1871				
65 Greencroft Street				
Jonathan Tiger	67	Husband	Retired farmer	Hampworth
Elizabeth Tiger	66	Wife	Retired farmer's wife	Salisbury
Elizabeth Woodhouse	33	Married niece		Shoreditch
Susan Woodhouse	3	Niece		Peckham
George Churchill	66	Visitor-widow	Hawker	Britford
67 Greencroft Street				
Issac Luther	47	Father-widow	Slate layer	Alvediston
Charles Luther	13	Son	Errand boy	Salisbury
Emma Jo Luther	11	Daughter	Scholar	Salisbury
Arthur Luther	10	Son	Scholar	Salisbury
Henry Luther	8	Son	Scholar	Salisbury
69 Greencroft Street				
Mary Darrington	37	Mother-widow	Washerwoman	Salisbury
Jane Darrington	13	Daughter	Undermaid	Salisbury
Albert Darrington	4	Son	Scholar (deaf)	Salisbury
Elisa Darrington	48	Sister-widow		
Census returns for 1891				
65 Greencroft Street				
Henry Harding	29	Husband	Labourer	Salterton
Elizabeth Harding	35	Wife	Cook	Ilfracombe
Alfred Jones	22	Nephew	Plumber	Ilfracombe
Edith Mary Jones	20	Niece	Dressmaker	Ilfracombe
Elizabeth Jones	15	Niece	Domestic servant	Ilfracombe
William Jones	14	Nephew	Weaver	Ilfracombe
67 Greencroft Street				
John Werne	40	Widowed	Tailor	Devonport
Christina Werne	4	Daughter		Salisbury
69 Greencroft Street				
Richard Bolwell	63	Widowed	Bricklayer	Salisbury

The Community Officer has collected, and continues to collect, information from local societies, information sheets on archaeological careers, leaflets on local and national organisations, information on courses for undergraduates and part-time study, and information on field schools and training excavations. Using this, she is able to respond to many requests for information immediately. Other queries may be satisfied by referring people to other organisations such as English Heritage, the CBA, the local SMR or museum. In other cases, the Community Officer may have to do some research in Wessex Archaeology's library or by asking other members of staff in order to answer the query. It is very rare that no advice can be offered, and even some unusual queries such as 'what can I give my husband for his birthday' have been successfully answered by suggesting membership of one of the national organisations as a gift.

Outreach in a professional context

There are some drawbacks to developing outreach within a large practice. One is that some clients are reluctant to allow general access to their sites, or to allow any publicity to be generated, as they are concerned about adverse reaction. Thankfully, this is becoming less and less common as clients become more used to the fact that archaeology has to be a part of the planning process and assume that many of their developments will require some form of archaeological intervention. As clients become more used to the involvement of archaeologists on site they also become more aware of the general interest in the subject and see the benefits of allowing access.

Perhaps the biggest drawback to working within a professional practice is the problem of involving people directly with our excavation work. Many sites are simply too dangerous to allow this, either being working building sites, demolition sites or quarries. Other types of archaeological intervention simply do not allow sufficient time for the involvement of volunteers – for example, watching briefs and evaluations. If we have longer-running excavations, then, where possible, we will take volunteer diggers. However, this is not always straightforward and a delicate balancing act is sometimes needed to ensure that we comply with professional ethics and do not use volunteers to substitute for contracted staff. Volunteers must do additional work to that which is specified, thus giving added value to a project. If we do take volunteers then we must undertake to offer them some training or run the risk of exploiting them, which is not acceptable. However, if we are to spend time training volunteers then we like them to spend a reasonable amount of time on site rather than just visit for a day to 'have a go'. The number of people who would like to be involved in excavation is increasing all the time and there is a serious question as to whether the large professional practices are the most appropriate groups to meet this need. Perhaps the professional supervision of research excavations that are not the consequence of development is the best way to move forward.

Although I have outlined some of the drawbacks above, there are many advantages to working within a large professional practice. There is always a wide variety of archaeological work undertaken, from desk-based assessments to large-scale excavations and post-excavation work. This opens up a wide variety of opportunities for outreach, although the best opportunities are usually provided by those projects undertaken towards the larger end of the scale. The community officer also has access to all of the back-up services that such a large practice uses: computing, illustration, photography and a large literature and photographic bank. The variety of expertise available within Wessex Archaeology also provides a great deal of back-up to the community officer should she need advice on any specific projects or queries. Finally, being a part of Wessex Archaeology allows the Community Officer to keep up with developments in archaeological practice and changes in guidelines and policy relevant to archaeology.

Chapter 17

USING OBJECTS: THE YORK ARCHAEOLOGICAL TRUST APPROACH

Andrew Jones

Introduction

The York Archaeological Trust (YAT) has a long history of using archaeological objects in an imaginative and creative way in order to stimulate public interest in archaeology and better educate the world about past cultures. This chapter presents a brief overview of the way the Trust has experimented with the display of objects over the last twenty-five years in order to meet its central objective of 'educating the public in archaeology'.

Like all museums, the glass-case display has been an important arrow in the quiver of presentation techniques (Merriman 1989, 1991). The Trust, however, has sought to use the glass cases in unconventional places. From the earliest days of the YAT in 1972, finds were put on show in caravans used to explain archaeological projects to site visitors. Once the Trust was better established, displays were placed in shop windows in central York containing objects and graphics specially designed for building society windows, shop displays in high streets and shopping centres. Museum displays, at the Yorkshire Museum and throughout the world, have also included objects from the Trust's excavations. This work continues to be an important activity.

There has always been a readiness by YAT staff, including the Director Dr Peter Addyman, to show visitors finds when they come to YAT buildings. The first head of finds administration, Chris Clarke, and more recently Christine McDonnell have always been prepared to put on temporary displays of objects for special interest groups. Similarly Jim Spriggs, head of the conservation laboratories, has always welcomed small numbers of visitors to view finds being conserved. Indeed the conservation laboratory's Behind the Scenes tours were nationally advertised in the National Science and Technology Week 2000 (SET 2000) programme. Visitors no longer explore one cramped basement laboratory, but view three large laboratories where the Trust has developed an international reputation of excellence in research and conservation of organic and bio-organic materials. There is little exceptional in the activities described so far. In this respect the York Archaeological Trust acts in a manner accepted as normal in most archaeological organisations.

Taking objects to the people

Experience gained in the late 1970s during the fund-raising campaign to extend the excavations at 16–22 Coppergate and later to build the Jorvik Viking Centre (Addyman and Gaynor 1984; Addyman 1994) saw the Trust embark on a different campaign – that of taking objects to the people. Under the expert guidance of the York Archaeological Trust conservation and finds administration departments, selected robust and visually attractive objects were packed into an attaché case with inert foam and carried around the world by Magnus Magnusson, Peter Addyman and others to show potential donors and others the quality and nature of artefact excavation at Coppergate. At the same time Sheila Goater, then schools liaison officer, put together a small collection of objects to implement her work visiting schools and preparing educational groups for visits to excavations.

These initiatives are not unique to the York Archaeological Trust, but they demonstrate the organisation's commitment to 'access'; that is, enabling more people to view, appreciate and understand material cultures from excavation contexts. It is this positive attitude to public presentation and exposition that enables the Trust not only to carry out major excavations but eventually to build the permanent museum displays. A large loan was received from and repaid to a consortium of Scandinavian banks allowing the installation of shoring, and therefore safe conditions, to undertake deep excavations at 16–22 Coppergate (Hall 1994, 1996). This willingness to show finds to people was also influential in development of the Jorvik Viking Centre which has so far received over 15 million visitors. Research into visitor reaction to the Jorvik Viking Centre has demonstrated that it is accessible, attractive and alters visitors' understanding of the Vikings (Blud 1990; Watkin 1988).

The Trust has also been quick to realise the potential of replica objects as a source of income. At first this was a small cottage – or garage – industry carried out by York Archaeological Trust staff and sympathisers. Soon the demand outstripped supply and specialist replica-making companies were commissioned. Currently the Trust shops sell replicas valued at several thousands of pounds. This is now a major funding item supporting research and publication.

By the late 1980s when the Trust was planning the conversion of St Saviour's church into the Archaeological Resource Centre (ARC), it had experience of working with archaeological finds with large numbers of schoolchildren and the general public. It was clear that while members of the public are impressed by spectacular and rare finds, especially those made of precious metals or decorated with intricate motifs, in the hands of informed archaeologists common bulk finds, such as fragments of large mammal bone, oyster shells and medieval roofing tiles are exciting and useful props for talking about how people lived in the past and how archaeologists make sense of buried evidence. These experiences led the Trust to create a series of interactive hands-on displays for the Archaeological Resource Centre (Jones 1995, 1999a, 1999b).

During 1989, in a phased period of development, staff undertook 'front-end evaluation' on possible activities devised for the ARC. In these sessions, target groups (mainly teachers and pupils) were invited to try out activities such as sorting finds, weaving, measuring and recording finds using a computer database (Figure 17.1). Meanwhile, YAT staff assessed the success of the activities, the likely consequences for objects involved and the reaction of teachers and group leaders to the tasks.

In 1990, the ARC opened to public and archaeological acclaim with a range of interactive hands-on displays using both ancient and modern replica material to enable visitors, mostly educational groups in term time and families at weekends and holidays, to understand more about archaeology.

After a seven-minute introductory video, visitors were introduced, by trained and mostly voluntary demonstrators, to a tray of mixed bulk finds: tile, non-human bone, shell, etc. The task for visitors was to sort the materials, think about the sorted material with the demonstrator, and then bag and label the finds following conventions and codes used on site. This activity was designed to introduce visitors to the nature of archaeological finds – very often it is their first opportunity

Figure 17.1 Using a computer to input data on objects at the Archaeological Resource Centre, York

to handle such ancient material – and to learn the basic principle of archaeological work: creating order from chaos. It is in effect a microcosm of the civilising process – going from a disordered mixture of disparate finds to neat, carefully labelled and bagged materials ready for further research.

The ARC first opened for a trial period of two months free of charge to all school groups booked. The ARC was open seven days a week and had a staff of three full-time members, centre manager, deputy manager and one general assistant. It had already been anticipated that volunteers and others would be helpful, and a modest campaign was begun to build a team of voluntary workers, both retired people and younger members of the community. The team recruited people of as many age groups and backgrounds as possible: sixth formers, students on full-time courses, parents of young families wanting work experience, and those who had been ill for long periods wanting to ease themselves back into work.

A training programme was devised and over the next few months more formal recruitment procedures, inviting references and interviews, were put in place. Paid and voluntary staff worked together according to their abilities and interests: running the shop, giving introductory talks, demonstrating activities, teaching groups through the displays.

The ARC was divided into five main areas, termed 'archaeological activity areas' (Figure 17.2). The first activity was listening to and watching an audio-visual presentation. At the start this was delivered as a slide presentation, later transferred to video. The text, narrated by the TV presenter John Craven, and the images showed archaeologists at work in preparing for excavation, on site, in finds research and preparing publications.

The second activity area consisted of a group of eleven trays of mixed bulk finds. The aim of this activity was to enable visitors to sort, bag and label finds following conventions used on site. This served as an introductory activity, allowing visitors to become familiar with large robust finds.

After this activity was completed the group would move to the third activity area and would be divided into three and rotated around three activities. Some began sorting sieved soil residues for fish bones, seeds, finds, etc.; others compared broken sherds of pottery with illustrations of pots presented in small back-up flip-charts; a third group worked with mammal bones. Here visitors compared Viking Age cattle bones and modern cattle bones, noting differences in colour and size. The activity challenged visitors' ability to match objects in three dimensions. They were also encouraged to arrange the bones so that they formed the lower limb of a cow. The display, with the help of demonstrators, made the point that Viking Age cattle were already the product of several millennia of intensive breeding. Until the fourteenth or fifteenth century, farmers preferred to produce rather small general-purpose cattle suitable for milk, leather, meat and other products. It is only since the agricultural revolution that cattle have been bred for either beef or milk.

The next activity area was based on modern replicas and enabled visitors to investigate various aspects of ancient technology. Over ten years of operation, staff

Figure 17.2   Overview of original interactive displays at the Archaeological Resource Centre, York

and students developed a range of 6–8 activities. The central and permanent focus was a warp-weighted loom and hand spinning using a drop spindle. Other activities included opening a replica of the Viking Age chest fitted with barrel padlocks – this chest contained wooden bowls turned on a pole lathe and other objects. A complete tanned cow hide formed the background to a shoe-making activity where visitors sewed together a replica Roman one-piece shoe. Other activities included writing in runes, using large carved runes on magnetic tiles and making numbers with Roman numerals.

The fifth and final activity area of the ARC was a bank of computers – in 1990 an important and innovative tool in education and society as a whole. Systems were specifically designed and built by York Archaeological Trust under the leadership of the head of computing, Jeff Maytom, to show how archaeologists use computers to catalogue objects, and how new technology – first laser disk players, later CD-ROM or, most recently, disk-based images – can be used to manipulate images.

It was at the cataloguing station that York Archaeological Trust put a series of five important objects on open display – small finds, each individually packed in inert foam. These were:

- an antler tine
- a bone skate
- a leather shoe sole
- a whetstone
- a grindstone

All but one of these objects have survived ten years of handling by 500,000 visitors. The only object damaged was a fourteenth-century shoe sole which lasted
three years before it was slightly torn. It was removed from the display to be
replaced by leather off-cuts. Although many visitors handled objects, there was
remarkably little damage: a little handling polish or accumulation of perspiration
on the most handled objects. No small finds were stolen in ten years of operation.

However, close observation of visitors has made it clear that visitors did not
always investigate objects in the way we had hoped. For example, at the cataloguing
display, where visitors were encouraged to investigate objects and then type relevant data into a computer, many visitors simply typed the data presented on the
label rather than closely observing the actual objects.

This activity – placing small objects outside the glass case for visitors to handle,
and monitoring visitors using these objects – has been pivotal in the development
of the current displays at the ARC and greatly influenced the thinking of the team
who planned the redevelopment of the ARC in 2000.

Loss and damage to archaeological material

Although properly packed objects were not removed from the ARC by unautho-
rised visitors, a small amount of display material, including archaeological finds,
has been taken by visitors. One of the first things to disappear from the displays
was a group of small card labels identifying replica pots, on pottery displays. It is
interesting to note that in the introductory talk staff informed visitors that they
could touch anything on the benches but to ask a demonstrator if they were interested in any of the objects on grey shelves. These can be handled with the help of
staff. It was the labels on the grey shelves that were the first materials to be stolen.
None of the replica pots have been stolen and the only broken one was damaged
when a member of staff used it in an experimental bread-making display when it
was cracked because it was heated too rapidly.

In the first month of operation the number of staff in the archaeological activity
areas was often low (one or two). On one spring Sunday – a particularly quiet day
when a very small number of visitors attended (fewer than ten) and only a few
members of staff were on duty at the ARC – two pieces of Roman pottery were
stolen from the pottery display. This experience emphasised the need for staff to
be conspicuous at all times.

Over the ten years of the ARC, a small number of bones were lost from bone
displays. Robust bones and pot sherds have gradually become rounded, but the

number of fragments removed by visitors has been negligible. At the sorting activity using sieved soil residues there is also some loss of material – groups of school-children are not always adept at using forceps, and fragments of stone gravel and occasional organic material such as charcoal, shell and bone have been lost to the floor to be removed inadvertently by the cleaning staff.

Hands-on activities do therefore cause some loss and damage to archaeological material, but as the Trust was careful to use unstratified material, or material that occurs in very large quantities, it is a small price to pay for improving access to our collections. Surely a small amount of damage by, and loss to, visitors should be seen against the losses caused when objects are loaned for display, and by poor curation and inadequate packaging of archaeological collections. In sum, the loss and damage of archaeological material has been negligible.

After ten years of use and several awards, culminating in 1999 when the ARC was honoured as the best archaeological presentation to the public in the history of British archaeological awards, it is clear to all that the approach taken to presenting objects has been a most significant success. There can be no doubt that the design implementation of Dominic Tweddle and the ARC Working Group led by the Chairman of the YAT, Gerald Dean, in the later 1980s has been highly influential.

Sagas and Sums

During the autumn of 1998 and spring of 1999, a special educational event entitled 'Sagas and Sums', sponsored by the Department for Education and Employment, was developed and delivered to five York primary schools. This project was devised in order to help raise standards in school. The government invited museums and galleries to bid for money for 'study support' projects in August 1998. Study support was defined as voluntary educational activities outside the normal school day. The applications were screened by the area museums councils. The initial dead-line was the end of August, final submission the end of September, and we were informed of our success in October.

The project was to develop interactive learning experiences based on the Icelandic sagas and archaeological finds related to Viking Age trade, and was designed to help build skills in literacy and numeracy. The target audience was children of year 6 (typically 10- and 11-year-olds), who had not yet reached National Curriculum level 4 for maths and/or English. The individual children taking part in the project were selected by the year 6 teachers, with assistance (as appropriate) from the headteacher and Local Education Authority educational social workers.

Real archaeological finds were an essential component of the project. A collection was put together using material from the Yorkshire Museum, a local metal detector, and the YAT research collections. All objects were individually packed in inert foam within plastic boxes, the boxes being carried in robust metal carrying cases fitted with foam.

Figure 17.3   Examining an object as part of 'Sagas and Sums', a study support project run as a series of after-school sessions, developed jointly by YAT and the City of York Department of Educational Services in 1999

Staff and children were instructed to wear gloves while investigating objects (Figure 17.3). Pupils prepared detailed drawings of objects and the staff referred to the objects throughout the other sessions. The details of the lessons were developed with the help of York teachers and advisers, and the sessions delivered by YAT staff from the Jorvik Viking Centre and ARC with the help of suitably qualified and experienced teachers selected with the help of the LEA. The project involved selecting and presenting finds from the YAT's collection for use outside of YAT premises, and the production of high-quality educational resource materials which involved staff in several departments of the Academic and Attractions divisions of the YAT. This project demonstrated that rare and important material could be used, given sufficient supervision, with children in schools.

Refitting the ARC

After six years of operation, the displays at the ARC were beginning to show their age. Benches had lost their finish in places and some of the hands-on activities had developed a handling gloss while other displays were looking a little 'tired and grubby'. At the same time the National Curriculum had been implemented and the government announced that it would be revised in the year 2000. Amongst the educational community and public there was a growing concern over 'failing schools', and comparison with children in other EU countries showed that achievement by British children often lagged behind their continental contemporaries. A new wind was beginning to blow in education – gradually there was more emphasis on the basics of education, English and Maths, and more talk about the desire for 'whole-class teaching'.

At the same time it was clear that although the ARC was not running at a loss to York Archaeological Trust, visitor numbers had ceased to rise as they had done in the first four years: 32,000, 55,000, 60,000, 65,000 (Jones 1995), but were showing a slow, steady decline. These factors are the background to the refit, implemented at the ARC in spring 2000, and led by Richard Kemp, Director of Attractions for YAT.

Two assumptions were taken as given:

- the ARC would continue to serve teachers and their pupils in term time, and independent visitors, typically families, in the school holidays;
- hands-on activities would be at the core of the visit.

During late 1998 and throughout 1999, consultation with ARC staff and teachers, although interesting, tended to get the response that all that was needed was to replace the carpet, put in new benches and refurbish the existing displays. The project team was not satisfied with this outcome and spent several meetings brainstorming to develop a new concept. What follows is one view of what happened.

Over the months we resolved to:

- put the archaeology of York central in the displays;
- link the ARC more emphatically to the Jorvik Viking Centre;
- abandon computers in the fifth archaeological activity area – too expensive to keep up and by then ubiquitous in schools;
- replace a host of experimental archaeological activities with finds observation and drawing based on the experience gained with 'Sagas and Sums';
- make management of groups easier by keeping groups of thirty together for a whole visit (more whole-class teaching);
- redesign the building so that face-to-face contact between ARC staff and teachers with visitors is facilitated.

During the development phase, the project team re-read several of the York Archaeological Trust publications on excavation at Coppergate, most of which were not available at the time of development of the ARC in the late 1980s, and hit on the idea that visitors should investigate specific contexts – for example, look at the hand-collected finds from that context, then look at the small finds recovered by sieving and the identifiable objects from that context. The aim was to allow visitors

to explore a limited amount of data gathered using different archaeological procedures, and to gradually assimilate those data to create their own interpretation. It
was decided that each school group would be divided into two cohorts, each investigating a single layer from a Viking Age pit – so half investigated one context,
half a second context.

Following a number of 'front-end evaluation' sessions with the Education Panel
of the YAT, local schools and families, it was decided that each context should
produce evidence for local crafts manufacture. One would contain the residues
from an antler comb-maker, and the other evidence for leather working.

Once this was in place it would be possible to adapt the approved form to
Roman, medieval and other periods. The visit begins with a visit to a 'virtual dig'
where a stratigraphic section is explained and objects – a piece of worked antler
and a cattle horn core – are removed from the two contexts to be investigated.
Next, visitors sort bulk finds and find for themselves pieces of leather and worked
antler amongst mammal bone, pottery and other domestic residues from a Viking
Age pit at Coppergate (Figure 17.4). Next trays of sieved earth, highly organic
material from unprocessed samples, are sorted for small biological finds.

The next activity requires careful observation and recording of some thirty small
finds. Each is carefully packed in inert foam. Some can be removed from their
boxes, others drawn through the transparent plastic lid. Visitors are provided with
recording sheets, measuring equipment, cotton gloves and drawing equipment. This
is a very successful activity. Children and adults (Figure 17.5) produce excellent

Figure 17.4 Examining bulk finds – bone, pottery and shell – collected from archaeological sites at the Archaeological Resource Centre, York

Figure 17.5   A voluntary archaeological demonstrator and a visitor investigate a cattle skull at the Archaeological Resource Centre, York

work which they take away with them to form the basis for displays at school or at home. Following this activity, visitors gather together with a demonstrator to discuss their observations and create for themselves an image of life in the past based on archaeological evidence.

Conclusion

This chapter explains how the York Archaeological Trust is achieving its mission to educate the public in archaeology, demonstrating to the museum world how it can use objects from its massive archive in a responsible manner in new and imaginative schemes. Future generations will judge for themselves how influential these activities have been within the museum and educational communities.

■   ■   ■

References

Addyman, P.V. (1994) Reconstruction as interpretation: the example of the Jorvik Viking Centre, York. In P. Gathercole and D. Lowenthal (eds) *The Politics of the Past*, London: Routledge, 257–264.

Addyman, P. and Gaynor, A. (1984) The Jorvik Viking Centre: an experiment in archae-ological site interpretation, *International Journal of Museum Management and Curatorship* 3: 7–18.

Blud, L. (1990) From horns to cooking pots, *Interpretation: the Bulletin of the Centre for Environmental Interpretation*, July: 18–20.

Hall, R. (1994) *Viking Age York*, London: English Heritage/Batsford.

Hall, R. (1996) *York*, London: English Heritage/Batsford.

Jones, A.K.G. (1995) Integrating school visits, tourists and the community at the Archaeological Resource Centre, York, United Kingdom. In E. Hooper-Greenhill (ed.) *Museum, Media and Message*, London: Routledge, 156–164.

Jones, A.K.G. (1999a) Archaeological reconstruction and education at the Jorvik Viking Centre and Archaeological Resource Centre, York, United Kingdom. In P.G. Stone and P.G. Planel (eds) *The Constructed Past: Experimental Archaeology, Education and the Public*, London: Routledge, 258–268.

Jones, A.K.G. (1999b) Arcane to ARC: the York experience. In J. Beavis and A. Hunt (eds) *Communicating Archaeology*, Bournemouth University School of Conservation Sciences Occasional Paper 4, Oxford: Oxbow Books, 65–70.

Merriman, N. (1989) Museums and archaeology: the public point of view. In E. Southward (ed.) *Public and Private Indulgence. Conference Proceedings Lincoln 1987* (*Museum Archaeology* 13), London: Society of Museum Archaeologists, 10–24.

Merriman, N. (1991) *Beyond the Glass Case: The Past, Heritage and the Public*, Leicester: Leicester University Press.

Watkin, J. (1988) Jorvik: some school children's reactions, *Teaching History*, January: 21–25.

Chapter 18

ARCHAEOLOGY AT WILSDEN, WEST
YORKSHIRE: A LOCAL FOCUS FOR
NATIONAL CURRICULUM WORK

Dave Weldrake

Introduction: a problem and its solution

Successive versions of the National Curriculum study units for
History at Key Stages 1 and 2 have made the demand that history
should be taught from a variety of sources, including sites and
artefacts. In fact the whole concept is highlighted on the cover of
current Qualifications and Curriculum Authority documentation
with its picture of two children studying what appears to be a Roman
mortarium (QCA 1998). There is, however, a problem associated
with this injunction: many of the materials used for the teaching of
National Curriculum History are influenced less by a need to offer
a balanced view of the past than by a desire to provide the most
lavish illustrations possible. This seems to be particularly the case in
material illustrating Unit 6A of the QCA scheme of work ('A Roman
Case Study'), where illustrations of Bath and Hadrian's Wall loom
large. Units 7 and 8, which are concerned with the Tudors, fare
little better. Here national publishers tend to concentrate on the
lives, habits and costume of the Tudor monarchy. Yet all these things
so familiar to us from our own childhood studies of history are
anomalies. It gives the young reader the impression that history is
something which happened somewhere else to someone else, not in
their town or village. Yet every community has its history, if only
an appropriate way can be found to bring it alive.

This in essence is the remit for the education officer of the West
Yorkshire Archaeology Service (WYAS). My job is to provide a local
focus for the teaching of National Curriculum History. Much of the
necessary data is readily available through a search of the Sites and
Monuments Record. It merely needs to be processed and packaged

so that it can be more immediate and accessible to the non-specialist. This can be done in a number of ways. The WYAS produces a newsletter, *Archaeology in West Yorkshire*, which appears twice a year. It has a web site (http://www.arch.wyjs.org.uk/advsrv/advsrv/html); but many organisations do these days. More important in reaching the general public is the personal touch, and a chance to talk with an expert. This may take the form of a presentation to a local adult group (local history/archaeology organisations, civic societies, Probus, the Women's Institute, etc.), but I also take activities into schools. This can be as a one-off visit or as part of a programme of work. No charge is at present made for school activities.

A range of subjects

School presentations may take a variety of forms. The most popular of these is the Roman pottery handling session in which unstratified material from the excavations at Castleford is used to demonstrate the role archaeology can play in illustrating various aspects of ordinary Roman life. Clearly this is not the material illustrated in most school textbooks. For one thing, all my specimens are broken. I may have samples of Samian pottery, but it is broken, fragmentary and cracked, not the glowing complete vessels that appear to leap out at us from the pages of a children's textbook; but it *is* primary evidence and it can do a lot.

Illustrating history is only one possibility. The National Curriculum insists on the acquisition of skills rather than the accumulation of facts. Much has already been written about objects and sites and their role in language development (e.g. Fines and Nichol 1997; Maddern 1992; Durbin *et al.* 1990; Weldrake 1999), but, as a glance at the range of English Heritage's teachers' guides will show, this is only one area of National Curriculum study which can be developed through archaeology. In my own work I tend to concentrate on materials (Which type of object will survive? Which will not?), technology (How was this made?), economic geography (The Romans brought these bowls all the way from Gaul) and food cultures (This amphora might have contained 'garum'). It is a sad reflection of the public perception of archaeology that I have never been asked into school to talk about any one of these topics, although of course I always do. 'I learned a lot', is a comment often made to me by teachers. Let us only hope the children did too.

The format of pottery-handling sessions

The format of a pottery-handling session is fairly standard. I begin by trying to explain to the class some of the principles of archaeology in what I hope is an appropriate language level for the age group. 'It's like looking into other people's dustbins really', or 'It's like a detective looking for clues.' 'Clues to what?' 'What ordinary people were doing.' I make the comparison with today's newspapers. The president of the USA may warrant a headline in *The Times* (or the *Sun*, *Mirror* or *Guardian* as appropriate), but the members of this class will not. It is just the same if you look at books written a long time ago. Agricola gets awarded pages in Tacitus, but there is nothing about his household slaves.

Having gone through this introduction I then get the pottery out. All it needs is a few pieces to each group of desks, and after a few prompting questions I leave them to get on with defining their own inspection of the artefacts. After a while I ask them to give me their impressions of the pieces. A word list can be assembled on the board, which can then be used as the basis for later written work. Gaining the children's impressions is vital. The intent of this part of the session is to enable the children to make their own deductions, which can be developed during the course of the session. Naturally, I will have to make my own input later, but to start with a format that began with 'This is a Samian bowl: it came all the way from France' would close off the possibility of pupils making their own investigations. I have already told the class that it is like being a detective. Now is their chance to do the detecting.

After this I throw the proceedings open to questions. The nature of these can vary greatly according to the interests and abilities of the children. Some are inevitably very basic: 'what's this part of?', 'why is this broken?', or 'do all these pieces fit together?' Others can be much more wide ranging. Among the most common ones are: 'have you ever found any armour?', 'have you ever found any dead bodies?', 'how do you know it's Roman?' and 'what's the most interesting thing you've ever found?' (The answers are respectively 'no', 'yes', 'stratigraphy' and 'a cesspit'.) Each can lead in turn to a discussion of some other aspect of the school curriculum, as noted above.

The session is then usually wound up with a chance for the children to make an observational drawing of one of the sherds, followed by writing a few lines of description about their selected item. Some pupils may need help with the latter. This is where the words we have already written up on the board may come in useful, both as revision and as a stimulus to composition. Further revision can come from such questions as 'can you remember how old I said this was?' or 'where did I say this came from?' The answers to these too could go up on the board. Pupils with difficulties in composition might be prompted further with provision of a writing frame such as:

- We found out that . . .
- The archaeologist told us that . . .
- I thought the most interesting thing was . . .

Wilsden

It was with some of these preoccupations in mind that in the autumn of 1997 I made my initial visit to Wilsden First School, near Bradford, with the presentation on Roman pottery. The history co-ordinator, Beverley Forrest, had already spent several lessons talking about archaeology in general and the Romans in particular. I was there to present the pottery and give an expert view. The visit generated a considerable amount of interest with the children involved. I left feeling that the job had been well done, but that that was the end of it.

Not a bit of it. Follow-up work was carried out in school. Beverley organised a simulated dig for the children. This is an exercise which can take many forms. Whithorn Museum, for instance, has an elaborate affair of plexi-glass cubes. At Saddleworth they have 'blanket digs'. Both are very good, but in the classroom 'economy' is a by-word and it is not necessary to go to such extremes of elaboration. Beverley's 'excavation' consisted of a number of plastic tubs which had once held ice-cream. These were filled with sand, and various objects were then buried in the sand. Each ice-cream tub was then divided into quarters by string before being given to the pupils. The 'excavations' were carried out as a teamwork exercise. Pupils took turns at excavating, recording and drawing, so that several skills were being developed at once. Questions relating to the nature of the evidence and what it could be used to prove were also discussed. Once again archaeology proved to be a success and I found myself being asked if there was any possibility of the children being allowed to take part in 'a proper dig'. Clearly this would be impossible within the constraints of modern contract-based archaeology. Opportunities for volunteers of any age are declining, and the number of times when I have to write a letter regretfully turning down requests for work experience placements is sadly all too frequent. The only feasible solution would be to carry out an excavation of our own.

The excavation

Documentary sources suggested that part of the school playing field had once been the site of the outbuildings to an adjacent factory. It was therefore decided to investigate a small portion of this area in an attempt to locate the exact site of these outbuildings. Parents were advised of the forthcoming activity by letter, and the need for up-to-date tetanus injections was stressed. The excavation itself was to take place on 19 and 20 May 1998.

A number of preliminary meetings were held between myself and school staff, governors and interested parents. It was decided to divide the three participating classes into groups of ten to ensure adequate supervision. Each group had one hour on site and most pupils had the opportunity to sample a variety of archaeological tasks (trowelling, mattocking, drawing and surveying, sieving soil, washing finds), which ensured that they had little opportunity to get bored and were on task all the time (Figure 18.1).

Two small (3.0×2.0 m and 1.5×2.0 m) trenches were opened up (Figure 18.2). In both trenches the topsoil was removed and sieved. At a maximum depth of 0.25 m in each trench the natural clay subsoil was encountered and excavations ceased. In neither trench was there any trace of a structure.

Figure 18.1 Children working together to clean the finds

Figure 18.2 Children from Wilsden First School at work on site

The finds

Despite the failure to locate the hoped-for buildings the finds recovered from the sieving enabled more classroom work to be developed. The pupils had already washed the finds and I then sorted them by type. Much of it was of necessity nineteenth- and twentieth-century material (pottery, broken glass, brick and stone fragments). One modern item did excite the children's interest however. This was a spent 9 mm centre-firing cartridge from a pistol or possibly a sten gun (I. Sanderson, pers. comm.). Older finds included some fragments of seventeenth-century Wrenthorpe ware (Moorhouse and Roberts 1992), a number of fragments of gritty ware (*c.* 1400; C. Cumberpatch, pers. comm.), and a quantity of flint, though none of the latter was worked. Other items of a geological, rather than an archaeological nature had been recovered by the children. It is perhaps a reflection on the decline in the use of open fires that many of the children did not initially recognise coal for what it was.

Back to the classroom

In the follow-up, archaeological finds once again became the focus for more class-room work. In our case the finds had been generated by excavation, but a similar effect can be gained by use of finds generated by a garden pottery survey. Once again you are in a position to highlight all these school curriculum subjects which had been touched on in the first pottery-handling session. However, this is not mere revision. These finds have been generated by the children themselves. In a very real sense they are taking a hand in their own education. They have begun, in a small way, to 'own' the process. In modern jargon they have become 'stakeholders'. Naturally enough it generates interest and enthusiasm.

In the case of Wilsden First School, the post-excavation session was followed by more formal work in which pupils were asked to make a catalogue of their finds

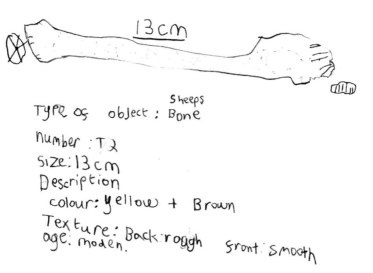

Figure 18.3   Example of a child's work describing an animal bone

so that the school would have a more permanent record of their work. Pupils were first asked to make an observational drawing of one of the finds (Figures 18.3, 18.4). They then had to fill in the following headings:

- Type of item
- Find number
- Size
- Description
- Colour
- Age
- Texture

In effect this is another writing frame, very similar to the Class Museum form given by Fines and Nichol (1997: 149). However, there is more here than language development. Classification and measurement belong to the world of maths. Putting the children's work together produced a finds catalogue to go with my rather duller

Figure 18.4 Example of a child's work describing a potsherd

analysis of the same material. The children's work, together with the finds and photographs of the excavation, was also used to make an exhibition in the school lobby for the benefit of parents and visitors to the school. It also featured prominently during the school's OFSTED inspection.

Conclusion

Archaeologically the excavation failed to meet its goals. The factory outbuildings were not located, but at least the presence of so much flint on a site from which it was previously unknown has given us something to think about. However, in terms of developing the understanding of a process the Wilsden project proved a great success. Essentially the children followed the whole operation through from posing an initial question ('what was there before the school buildings?'), establishing an hypothesis by reference to maps of the site, testing the hypothesis by excavation, and writing a report on what they had found. This would seem to me to be a textbook case of scientific method, and archaeology is, after all, a science, not just an adjunct to history.

During the process the children also had the opportunity to acquire skills with tools with which they were unfamiliar, to practise various aspects of language work, to categorise and to measure, to make observational drawings and scale plans. From this point of view it can be seen that archaeology is capable of forming a focus for a wide range of school-based activities at Key Stage 2. What is more, the children enjoyed what they were doing immensely. Their commitment to the project was high, and I am sure that the enthusiasm generated will last them the rest of their lives.

Acknowledgements

The success of the project was not solely due to the input of staff from the West Yorkshire Archaeology Service. We may have provided the stimulus which started the ball rolling, but many other people worked hard to make the project a success. The following perhaps deserve special mention: Beverley Forrest and the staff of Wilsden First School for co-ordinating and supervising the children; Peter Fawcett, school governor and local historian, for providing the historical background material; Dave Cowland and Steve Needham of Bradford University for providing some of the equipment and helping with the supervision; and Liz Weldrake for dealing with planning and photography. Finally, credit should also be given to the children who participated in the project. Their enthusiasm for the past made the whole thing happen.

■ ■ ■

References

Durbin, G., Morris, S. and Wilkinson, S. (1990) *A Teacher's Guide to Learning from Objects*, London: English Heritage.

Fines, J. and Nichol, J. (1997) *Teaching Primary History*, Oxford: Heinemann.

Maddern, E. (1992) *A Teacher's Guide to Storytelling at Historic Sites*, London: English Heritage.

Moorhouse, S. and Roberts, I. (1992) *Wrenthorpe Potteries*, Wakefield: West Yorkshire Archaeology Service.

Qualifications and Curriculum Authority (1998) *A Scheme of Work for Key Stages 1 and 2: History*, London: HMSO.

Weldrake, D. (1999) Archaeology at Beckett Park, *Archaeology in West Yorkshire*, no. 9.

Chapter 19

PUBLIC PREHISTORIES: ENGAGING ARCHAEOLOGY ON GARDOM'S EDGE, DERBYSHIRE

Bill Bevan, John Barnatt, Mike Dymond, Mark Edmonds and Graham McElearney

Introduction

> I like Gardom's Edge very much. I like drawing on the stone and looking from squares and drawing stones. I like it when we sat around in a circle and said a story. I thought that I would get a cold but I didn't. I like Gardom's Edge very much. Ta.
>
> Extract from a letter by a pupil

The Gardom's Edge project is an investigation of the inhabitation of a particular landscape over 4,000 years of prehistory, and ultimately up to the present day. A summer field season ran for each of five years from 1995 to 1999 and at the time of writing we are entering the initial phases of post-excavation analysis and publication. Since the beginning, the project has had two fundamental and interrelated aims: to produce a long-term narrative of prehistoric life in the area and to enable people to engage in various ways with the act of archaeology and interpretations of prehistoric life. The project is directed by Mark Edmonds of the Department of Archaeology and Prehistory at the University of Sheffield and John Barnatt and Bill Bevan of the Peak District National Park Archaeology Service.

As an exercise in landscape archaeology, the project has integrated a variety of forms and scales of analysis: excavation, remote sensing, metrical survey and the characterisation of environmental and soils data. Our research aim has been to explore how *individual* experience actively interrelated with wider social *structures* across space and time in prehistory. The definition of landscape used here being the meaningfully constituted world within which people act out their lives. It includes not only geology, topography, vegetational environment and built structures but all aspects of material traditions and relations between people. This sense of landscape as inhabited times and spaces is central to a great deal of recent research (Bender 1993; Ingold 1993; Gosden 1994; Tilley 1994). In our case we wanted to build on this understanding, not only in inter- preting the material but also in promoting particular forms of access to archaeology for people visiting and working on site.

In taking this path we have tried to acknowledge a variety of different 'commu- nities of interpretation' to be approached through a number of different media and allowing for different sorts of interaction. Public access has developed over the period of the project. Each year, we have built upon our experiences from previous seasons and experimented with different types of activities. We have also had to cope with relatively high numbers of visitors, so much so that we had to balance publicity and promotion of the project with the need to avoid long-term erosion of the moorland. Throughout, we have provided a variety of forms of engagement: from informal, and more formal, guided tours to co-ordinated projects with local schools and from an interactive website to the involvement of artists and theatre groups. We have also developed various forms of access for different special-needs groups. As a step away from a more conventional producer/consumer relationship, we also encourage people to participate 'in the field' in various ways. Our primary concern in this work has been to promote the recognition that a great deal of what people encounter in the landscape is as much a product of history as it is a part of nature. This is crucial in an area such as the Gardom's Edge moorland, which is often regarded and valued by visitors as being of outstanding natural beauty, and by some even as unchanging and timeless in character.

We also wanted to use that sense of discovery which is an important factor in people's interest in archaeology. Public excitement during the excavation of the Walbrook Mithraeum, the Rose Theatre, or the lifting of the *Mary Rose*, demon- strates a basic fascination with discovering something hitherto hidden from view. However, there is often a subsequent loss of interest in the same archaeological finds when presented as catalogues, displays or reports (Barrett 1995). We have tried to maintain the excitement of discovery while demonstrating that archaeology is about more than finding things or a simple process of uncovering facts from the soil; that interpretation is central to the writing of history and prehistory. On these foundations can be built a variety of different engagements.

Location and character of archaeological remains

> Life in the Bronze and Iron Ages centred around round houses scattered among the fields. As the house was abandoned the entrance was blocked by a stone bank. Was this field clearance or a deliberate act when the family left?
>
> Extract from leaflet handed out during guided tours

Gardom's Edge is part of the gritstone scarp which forms the eastern side of the Derwent Valley, Derbyshire (Figure 19.1). Behind the edge is a broad shelf which contains many archaeological features. Like other areas of the eastern moors of the Peak District, the Gardom's Edge shelf is remarkable for the sheer density of upstanding field evidence for settlement and other forms of activity during later prehistory (Barnatt 1986, 1987, 1999, 2000). The archaeological potential of Gardom's Edge has long been recognised. Preliminary surveys pointed to the presence of prehistoric field systems, cairns and other structures (Beswick and Merrills 1983; Barnatt 1986; Hart 1985). These observations have recently been augmented by the detailed 1:1000 survey of the dip slope behind the scarp (centred SK 273730) by the Royal Commission on the Historical Monuments of England and the Peak Park Joint Planning Board (RCHME 1987; RCHME and PPJPB 1993). About two thousand archaeological features have been identified across Gardom's Edge as a whole, most of which comprise subtle piles and linear heaps of stone, or earthen banks and lynchets, which for the most part lie hidden amongst the heather and bracken. On the face of it these piles of old stones would not appear to be greatly attractive to visitors – or so you may have thought.

Two very different phases of prehistoric activity have been proposed from the results of this detailed survey. The first is represented by a massive stone-built enclosure, probably neolithic in date (Ainsworth and Barnatt 1998; Barnatt *et al.* 2001), rather than Iron Age as postulated by Hart (1981). The enclosure is situated on the highest part of the Gardom's Edge shelf. It is defined by a rubble bank between 5 and 10 metres wide, up to 1.5 metres high and over 600 metres long. This bank delimits one side of a large area at the crest of the edge, the other being

Figure 19.1   Gardom's Edge from the north. The study area on the shelf above Gardom's Edge can be seen clearly, while the Derwent Valley is beyond

the precipitous natural scarp, and much of the interior is heavily boulder strewn. The enclosure has greater parallels with causewayed enclosures than it has with Iron Age hillforts (Edmonds 1999). A short distance outside the enclosure is a large earthfast slab with 'cup and ring' art. Three smaller examples of rock art have been found elsewhere on the moor.

Later in prehistory, sometime after the enclosure had fallen out of use, the Gardom's Edge shelf was occupied by families of farmers. Later prehistoric field systems can be seen across much of the better, if stony, land encompassed by the survey, associated with a rich variety of features, comprising house sites, clearance cairns, linear clearance features and lynchets, some defining small fields. Ceremonial monuments include a tall standing stone, a large burial cairn and a ring cairn. A linear rubble boundary and an embanked pit alignment cross the central area of the shelf, both apparently overlying early phases of one of the field systems. Subtle evidence for circular houses lies scattered amongst the fields, taking the form of slight platforms and stone banks. Artefacts and radiocarbon dates indicate that the settlements and fields on the eastern moors were used for upwards of a thousand years, from at least the middle of the second millennium BC if not earlier (Barnatt 1995). The patterned relationship of these ritual monuments to field systems throughout the eastern moors, and evidence from pollen cores, suggests that the farmed landscape may have been established as early as the earlier Bronze Age (Barnatt 1987, 1999; Long 1994; Long *et al.* 1998). If fields were not established until later, these monuments and more transient forms of agricultural practice were certainly heavily drawn upon. Pollen evidence and differences in field layout suggest that farming may have continued in more favourable areas into the later Iron Age (Long 1994; Long *et al.* 1998; Barnatt 1999, 2000; Bevan 1999, 2000).

Guided tours and time trail

> If I had paid £20 for this experience in a theme park, I would have thought it money well spent – Baldrick, eat your heart out!
>
> Comment by visitor on guided tour

The traditional guided tour formed a central element of interpretation for the majority of on-site visitors (Figure 19.2). The main focus for our work lies on the Gardom's Edge shelf at approximately 255 to 280 metres above Ordnance datum and over 1 kilometre from the nearest roadside access points. Most of the land is open access with well-defined footpaths leading on to the moorland from surrounding roads. We used two of these footpaths to create a circular trail over 2 kilometres long which took people from a National Park car park to the location of the excavations and back down again. The car park was chosen as the starting point to the trail because it appears on Ordnance Survey maps, we could

Figure 19.2 Dave Sainty leads a tour of 'drop-in' visitors around one of the trenches while a volunteer excavator shows a recent find

signpost the trail from it, there are adjacent bus stops and even more importantly a nearby public house! Temporary interpretation boards along the route not only acted as waymarkers to the excavation trenches but were also designed to emphasise the great time-distance from the modern day to prehistory; they illustrated elements of the surrounding historic landscape and encouraged people to read the landscape themselves.

We decided to have a range of different types of tours to cater for different levels of archaeological knowledge and different visitor needs. Full-time guides were available on site every day for visitors who could drop in at any time during the day for tours of the trenches. We also ran more formal and longer guided walks at weekends which incorporated the surrounding landscape as well as the trenches. For people with a knowledge of archaeology who wanted to discuss some issues in depth, there were walks led by the project directors. For those new to archaeology there were similar walks led by an actor who role-played characters from different periods of the past. Visitors comprised people from the local area and holidaymakers to the National Park, approximately 70 per cent visiting for the first time each year.

The interpretative nature of archaeology was emphasised during all tours and visitors were encouraged to make their own interpretations of features, based on the material evidence, instead of passively receiving a package of given facts. Encouraging discussion of viable options and interpretative problems was central to this approach. On the whole, this approach proved highly successful, with many visitors willing to voice their opinions and contribute to the interpretation of the sites. The tour guides achieved a balance between providing information and encouraging dialogue. Those who wished to participate actively could do so, while at the same time people who wanted to be more passive could opt-out of such contributions without having their experience diminished. We also discovered that there are certain areas where adults are more comfortable in making their own interpretations. There tended to be less offers of interpretation made about the trenches themselves, people with less archaeological experience being slower to 'read' the trenches and to offer comments. The layout of and activity within the trenches can also be perceived as a technical barrier to making contributions, though at the same time the somewhat unusual nature of the act of excavation does provide opportunities for questioning which can be turned into more of a two-way dialogue by the guides and excavators themselves. In contrast, there were lively discussions about the nature of prehistoric societies which occurred at the edge of trenches and as groups moved across the moor. Where people felt most empowered to offer their own interpretations was at the rock art. This abstract design pecked into a large earthfast slab seemed not to lie within a specialist area of competence and therefore visitors felt more comfortable about offering their own interpretations. The art of such interactive tours lies in understanding that the tour guide acts as a facilitator rather than simply as an authority.

Direct participation

> Have been taught how to measure co-ordinates and it makes a change from scraping. It's good to be outside with lots of people all working together. I have really enjoyed this dig (being my first) and look forward to my next.
>
> Comment by first-time volunteer

A proportion of visitors on guided tours returned in following seasons to join the excavation team. The potential to participate was stressed on the guided tours, and this, plus the emphasis we placed on discussing practice, helped some to move beyond the idea that work on site was the *exclusive* preserve of specialists (Figure 19.3). With the increasing professionalisation of archaeology over the last few years there has been some debate on the input of independent archaeologists into fieldwork and analysis. Some archaeologists do perceive fieldwork as the sole province of the trained professional and the independent as a threat to jobs. Others have argued that archaeology is not a discipline which can or should draw its boundaries so tightly, emphasising that independents have made significant contributions throughout the history of archaeology and continue to do so. At the same time there have been less and less opportunities for people with an interest in archaeology to get directly involved, while archaeological information from

Figure 19.3 Local people interested in archaeology from TV programmes such as *Time Team* have the opportunity to participate for themselves, some returning to dig after previously taking a tour

developer-funded projects has increasingly been deemed confidential for commercial and planning reasons.

We believe that to exclude the public from archaeology is detrimental to the profession in the long term and morally invalid. The case for professional versus independent cannot be so easily reduced to a simplified black and white argument. To do so is little more than the entrenchment of pre-existing positions, each of which partly defines itself in opposition to the other. The nature of archaeology as a discipline requires boundaries to be more flexible and permeable, where both professionals and independents can contribute to the benefit of archaeology as a whole. There are areas where archaeological investigation, conservation and management should be undertaken by paid professionals, and where the skills-pool needs to be maintained and enhanced through employment and training. Equally, there are areas where independents can undertake these activities, and where independents and professionals can co-operate. The whole Gardom's Edge project has been organised around an inclusive policy of enabling people from as wide a range of backgrounds and interests as possible to be involved in archaeology whether they have any experience or not. The majority of the participants are people from the surrounding area who know the region and the location well because they live or work there, or visit the moorlands for recreation. Some already have an interest in archaeology, often through membership of local societies or through taking extra-mural classes, and have been doing archaeology and running their own projects for up to forty years. Many others have never had any involvement in archaeology at all, Gardom's being their first opportunity to participate. Of these a number have gone on to study archaeology, or have joined local research societies and thus helped to strengthen the archaeological community in the region rather than diminish it.

Schools

> I went with Mike to draw a survey on the rocks. Let me explain. There was a wooden frame with string across it that made string squares. Then Mike gave us pieces of paper to draw on. And then we placed the board with the string on top of the rocks. Then we copied what we saw in the string onto the squared paper. Then we moved on to the actual cliffs of Gardom Edge. We soon came to something that looked like a circle. Amazingly it was actually the Earth Circle [ring cairn]. O forgot to tell you that I was given my archaeology degree when we went to the excervation [*sic*].
>
> Extract from letter by pupil, aged 8½

A module in environmental studies for seven- to twelve-year-olds based around Gardom's Edge was developed in partnership with the Derbyshire Educational Authority's Chesterfield Urban Studies Centre (Dymond 1998). Environmental studies proved to be a very successful route to introduce prehistory and archae-ology into the National Curriculum, which largely omits pre-Roman periods from history. The module incorporated lessons on environmental change over long periods of time, the impact of different intensities of land use and agriculture, how people perceive different landscapes, and skills of landscape investigation. Each participating school was provided with a teaching pack of information, materials and activity ideas for teachers. Introductory sessions for both teachers and pupils were undertaken by park rangers and project archaeologists. Schools then visited Gardom's Edge during the fieldwork season on educational 'discovery days'. A broad range of schools took up the module, including rural schools within the National Park, urban schools in nearby cities and special needs schools.

The aim of the 'discovery days' was to provide a dynamic opportunity for both pupils and teachers to see archaeology at work, to teach some of the skills of land-scape archaeology and interpretation. These stress observation and identification of the surviving prehistoric and historic remains, and encourage pupils to make their own interpretations based on the available evidence. Each school party had a tour of the trenches so that they could see at close-hand how archaeologists excavate and record an area, see the latest finds, ask the archaeologists questions and offer interpretations of what they could see (Figure 19.4).

Figure 19.4   Scholars from a special needs school get a trench tour from educational archaeologist Mike Dymond

In the final season, the tour was interspersed with a series of encounters with 'prehistoric people', in the form of the State of Flux theatre group. The group adopted the roles of farmer, hunter-gatherer and thinker to animate different themes and interpretations of life in prehistory, including seasonal movement across the landscape, the social significance of boundaries, dissemination of ideas, the meaning of the rock art and different perceptions of landscape including their contestation (Figure 19.5). They also encouraged the children to think about their lives and society today in comparison to prehistory, and to discuss whether they saw one right way of living or many different ways which had their own validity. Each encounter was followed by a question-and-answer session where pupils were encouraged to explain what they had just seen or taken part in. The key here was not to turn the children into a passive audience and present them with a single answer, nor to state that an interpretation was inherently wrong. Instead we encouraged the children actively to give their own interpretations to explore the difficulty and excitement inherent in establishing connections between the past and our present. At certain places, pupils were asked to give their own interpretations and at others they were presented with different interpretations, each using the same evidence which lay in front of the pupils, and were asked which they believed to be the most likely explanation. This exercise allowed pupils to see how archaeologists construct an understanding of the past and to see the basis on which they do so.

Figure 19.5   Pupils from a Sheffield city centre school discuss the meaning of rock art with neolithic people, aka State of Flux theatre group

It also empowered them to select the interpretation that they preferred and to develop their own interpretations, so putting into practice the ideas of multiplicity of interpretation.

There were also a number of hands-on activities for the children to take part in. These included the surveying of archaeological features using planning frames, and choosing places amongst the boulder-strewn landscape to draw rock art designs in chalk inspired by interpretations of prehistoric life. The most dynamic activities were those where they interacted with the 'neolithic people', including exchanging gifts and explaining modern objects and ideas. The finale involved each school being divided into three groups, farmers, hunter-gatherers and thinkers, who then learnt a song with lyrics relevant to their identities but sharing a common chorus. This they sang as they processed into the neolithic enclosure in their three separate groups; once inside the enclosure they met at a 'campfire' to take turns singing their own verses and communally singing the chorus. After a short 'gift exchange' session between the three groups, a final discussion rounded up the ideas behind the procession, and the use of the enclosure. The integration of theatrical role-playing and other hands-on activities into the educational project enabled greater stimulation of the children's imaginations and encouraged more participation in interpreting the past (cf. Stone 1986). The school parties were therefore much more actively involved than in those situations where children visit a site to receive information passively solely from lectures or tour guides. One consequence of the schools' involvement was the impact on the guided tours, especially at weekends. Children who had come with their class came back with their parents in tow, so broadening the range of people visiting the site.

Artists

> I'll look at the landscape in a different way from now. But painting time-depth? Now there's a challenge.
>
> Member of art group

During two of the field seasons two artists worked with the project: a photographer and a sculptor. They worked with visitors on the guided tours, with special needs schools and with art groups. Their brief was to use their chosen media to interpret and work with the themes central to the landscape and the theoretical approaches of the project.

The sculptor used materials local to the moorland (heather, bark and clay) and typical of those used on the excavation (for example, barrier tape) (Figure 19.6). The installations were all of a temporary nature, more so when attacked by cows(!), and would change during the period of the excavation subject both to their ongoing construction and to weathering. Her work was incorporated into the trench tours but was not overtly signposted. Instead, tour groups would pass by sculptures, some incorporated into trees and others set on the ground. These appeared as surprises or were seen in the distance along approach routes. Through this form of encounter, we encouraged visitors not to take everything at face value. People had to look closely at, and question, the surrounding landscape, to realise the richness and variety of its components and try to interpret its many features and meanings. This provided another set of contexts in which visitors could explore ideas about cultural meanings being incorporated into the landscape in prehistory.

Figure 19.6   Artist Alex Norman with a sculpture made from local clays. The sculptures were included in the guided tours as they slowly degraded during the field season

The photographer worked to two interrelated briefs (Bateman 1997). One was to produce images to aid interpretation to visitors. This was undertaken on the moorland itself through the production of Polaroid timelines of individual trenches over the period of the dig. These timelines were added to trees adjacent to the relevant trenches so that a visitor on any one day could see and discuss the stages of excavation leading up to the day they visited. This helped to get away from the static 'snapshot-in-time' experience of excavation that visitors usually get during a one-off visit to an archaeological site on a single open day. Photographs have also been incorporated into Gardom's Edge exhibitions off-site and included into the website. The photographer also worked closely with the archaeologists to explore the practice of excavation itself through images. He focused on how the layout of the site, use of materials and social relations influence the pasts that are created. For example the layout/positioning of trenches, participation in specific tasks, and use of certain tools all bear on interpreting the past rather than being an objective medium for producing facts.

www.shef.ac.uk/~geap/

I found you on the web!
                                    Visitor arriving brandishing a print-out of the website

Our motivation behind the website was to both expand and diversify access to, and engagement with, the place and our research on Gardom's Edge. This may be used to complement or as an alternative to site visits, so enabling access to those who are unable or unwilling to reach the excavations. It is also an ongoing resource which will continue to be developed now that the excavations have finished (Edmonds and McElearney 1998, 1999). Rather than seeing this as an electronically published version of a traditional interim report, we wanted to utilise a number of important opportunities provided by the medium: to make available interpretations as immediately as possible during the field to enable interactivity and to allow the website visitor to choose their own paths through the material (Poster 1995). A central aim for the website was one which is central to the archaeological process but which is often overlooked or actively masked in the presentation and dissemination of archaeology in the field – that of changes in both evidence and interpretation. Apart from the most dedicated visitor, most site visits are one-off events which produce snapshots of the evidence and of interpretation at a particular moment. Even though earlier phases of excavation and different interpretations were discussed on guided tours, the dynamics of how interpretations change during a project were difficult to grasp for someone making a one-off visit. The website allowed us to demonstrate more effectively the ways in which interpretations change and how ideas arise from new discoveries, dialogue and argument, over the period of field-work. Hopefully, we will be able to continue this process as post-excavation analysis and discussion are added to the website.

Structure

To expand the level of access to, and engagement with, the primary archaeological research, we needed to decide on a structure within which the story could be packaged. This structure is the prime means by which our visitor will navigate through the website. Using a very simple linear 'table of contents' style it is possible to move through the site relatively freely, gaining basic information about the project, its rationale, methodology and the Gardom's Edge landscape. At various points, it is also possible to branch off into more detailed discussions of specific landscape features and accounts of work on those features to date. This tiered approach allows the user to gain easy access to the level of detail that they are personally interested in without being overwhelmed with walls of thick description from the outset.

One of the first areas people access to familiarise themselves with Gardom's Edge and the range of archaeological features is a diagram of the area. Originally we used a copy of an archaeological plan but quickly realised that this was too cluttered and unfamiliar to many people not used to reading such plans. Rather than enabling access to information the plan was as likely to act as a barrier and potential turn-off for visitors who are not familiar with the conventions of archaeological representation. We have replaced this with a panoramic map from a bird's-eye view as a more accessible and familiar type of view, but have also left the old plan for comparison and to illustrate how archaeologists record such landscapes and features. The map is interactive: as you move the mouse over the key it highlights where those features are located and brings up photographs. A click on the mouse then gains access to more detailed descriptions and photographs if desired.

Excavation diary

During the fourth and fifth excavation seasons a regularly updated diary was the main focus for visitors to the website. In this section they could gain access to photographs of the dig in process, changing interpretations, and the latest finds. This was designed to help people to share in the excitement of the sense of discovery and the process of interpretation which is open to change as excavation continues.

Many of the diary pictures are interactive. For example, photographs of a group of post-holes under excavation or of buried soil layers appear like any standard site photographs. However, when the mouse is moved over the photographs, elements which are discussed in the accompanying text are highlighted with overlays. We wanted to incorporate such interactive pictures for two reasons: to enable a level of active input from the person viewing the website (again tying in to ideas of discovery) and to use web technology to aid the readability and interpretation of what can otherwise be unclear technical photographs.

Animation

The website also incorporates QuickTime VR pictures to provide online animations of views of the landscape and time lapse images of the trenches during excavation. With one series of QuickTime pictures we situate the visitor at the centre of a digital photographic panorama, wherein they can pan their field of view (left to right, up and down) and zoom in or out of the image. Using these panoramas, we have begun to explore how movement within images might provide a more satisfactory basis for conveying a sense of the topography, setting, character and associations of much of the archaeology. As interpretative concerns in archaeology embrace various strands of hermeneutics and phenomenology, so there is a requirement to think through the bodily experience of past material conditions. This inevitably involves thinking about the routine and more performative practices in which people were engaged at various places and times. It also requires a more thorough investigation of place itself, whether that be the character of the land, the forms and spaces of monuments and other features, or the shifting perceptions of space encountered when moving across the landscape. We are also developing animated walk-overs of the moorland so that you can get an idea of how the surrounding landscape changes with movement along selected paths.

Currently under development, at time of this publication, are the adaptation of the teachers' pack into an interactive learning resource and a series of time-lapse animations of the trenches during excavation. The former will provide on-line resources for teachers and interactive activities for pupils. The time-lapse animations, taken from the same viewpoint, allow people to see the process of archaeological excavation from start to finish. They will be annotated by text and overlays which highlight new evidence and ideas.

Conclusion

> Just came out to have a look around the site but seem to have been roped into a spot of trowelling.
>
> Visitor/volunteer cross-over

Overall, the public programme on Gardom's Edge has been inseparable from the archaeological research. Many issues, such as individual perceptions and interpretations of structures and phenomena, and relationships between individual and community, have crossed over. A notable aspect of the public programme has been the opportunity to experience the Gardom's Edge landscape with large numbers of people moving across it. In what is such a quiet area the rest of the year, this has sometimes fed back to our thoughts on the nature of social interactions made possible in this particular landscape during its inhabitation in prehistory. It has also helped many of our visitors consider similar issues.

The multitude of approaches and media utilised has echoed the multiplicity of interpretation and how ideas change over time as new discoveries are made and ideas discussed. This has enabled a range of people from different backgrounds, with varying knowledges of archaeology and prehistory, to engage with the Gardom's Edge prehistoric landscape in a variety of ways and depths. Interactivity and devolution of interpretation have produced a more active engagement than a traditional approach where the archaeologist situates him/herself as the authority figure passing on definitive and unquestioned facts, which only the archaeologist as specialist has the ability to produce in the first place. We have redefined the roles of the archaeologists and guides as facilitators and storytellers. We have also avoided the reduction of prehistory into a heritage experience to be consumed (no shops, no gifts to buy), instead sharing the excitement of discovery and the changing thoughts these have inspired.

There have also been many spin-offs from one area of public activities to another. The education programme has helped to foster a greater awareness of archaeology amongst primary school pupils and had the knock-on effect of encouraging parents to visit the excavations at the insistence of their children. Visitors on guided tours have returned later as excavators; first-time diggers have gone on to do night classes. Overall more people know more about the practices of archaeology and interpretations of prehistory, which must all be to the benefit of the discipline.

Acknowledgements

The authors would like to thank a range of organisations and individuals without whom the project could not have been undertaken. The Peak District National Park Authority and the Department of Archaeology and Prehistory, University of Sheffield backed the project. The Estates, Information and Rangers Services of the Park provided logistics and support throughout. Gavin Bell, Keith Clarkson and Caryl Hart raised funds for the interpretation projects and, with Jane Featherstone and Mark Simmons, helped organise school involvement. The Arts Council, Bass Limited, Chatsworth Trust, Chesterfield Urban Studies Centre, COPUS, Cox Accommodation, Derbyshire Building Society, Derbyshire Schools Association for Environmental Education, Global Environment–Landfill Tax, John and Ruth Howard Charitable Trust, Living Landscape Fund, Roy McGregor, NatWest Bank (Bakewell branch), Polaroid, Propix and SHB 4×4 Hire contributed grants or resources towards interpretation. Anne-Marie Heath and Dave Sainty guided visitors around the excavations. Jon Bateman, Steve Fox, Doug Fraser, Caroline Jackson, John Lord, Val Lord, Ray Manley, Alex Norman, Gary Short, Sheffield City Museum and the State of Flux Theatre Company worked on various aspects of interpretation. Kenny Aitchison, Tim Allen, Talya Bagwell, Olaf Bayer, Anne Marie Cadwallader, Adrian Chadwick, Anthony Dixon, Helen Evans, Chris Fenton-Thomas, Mel Giles, Anne-Marie Heath, Jamie Lund, Sarah Massey, John Roberts, Graham Robbins, Jim Rylatt, Alice Ullathorne and Graeme Warren were responsible for the day-to-day running of the fieldwork and supervising of volunteers. Finally we would like to thank all the people we have worked with during the project who have made it a successful, enjoyable and stimulating experience.

■   ■   ■

References

Ainsworth, S. and Barnatt, J. (1998) A scarp edge enclosure at Gardom's Edge, Baslow, Derbyshire, *Derbyshire Archaeological Journal* 118: 5–23.

Barnatt, J. (1986) Bronze Age remains on the east moors of the Peak District, *Derbyshire Archaeological Journal* 106: 18–100.

Barnatt, J. (1987) Bronze Age settlement on the gritstone east moors of the Peak District, Derbyshire, *Proceedings of the Prehistoric Society* 53: 393–418.

Barnatt, J. (1995) Neolithic and Bronze Age radiocarbon dates from the Peak District: a review, *Derbyshire Archaeological Journal* 115: 5–19.

Barnatt, J. (1999) Taming the land: Peak District farming and ritual in the Bronze Age, *Derbyshire Archaeological Journal* 119: 19–78.

Barnatt, J. (2000) To each their own: later prehistoric farming communities and their monuments in the Peak, *Derbyshire Archaeological Journal* 120: 1–86.

Barnatt, J., Bevan, B. and Edmonds, M. (2001) A time and a place for enclosure. In T. Darvill and J. Thomas (eds) *Neolithic Enclosures of North West Europe*, Neolithic Studies Group, Oxford: Oxbow Monographs.

Barrett, J. (1995) *Some Challenges in Contemporary Archaeology*, Oxbow Lecture 2, Oxford: Oxbow.

Bateman, J. (1997) Film and fetish: imaging the materials of excavation, Paper presented at the Theoretical Archaeology Conference, Bournemouth 1997.

Bender, B. (ed.) (1993) *Landscape: Politics and Perspectives*, Oxford: Berg.

Beswick, P. and Merrills, D. (1983) L.H. Butcher's survey of early settlements and fields in the southern Pennines, *Transactions of the Hunter Archaeological Society* 12: 16–50.

Bevan, B. (1999) Northern exposure: interpretative devolution and the Iron Ages in Britain. In B. Bevan (ed.) *Northern Exposure: Interpretative Devolution and the Iron Ages in Britain*, Leicester: Leicester Archaeological Monographs 4, 1–19.

Bevan, B. (2000) Peak practice: whatever happened to the Iron Age in the southern Pennines? In J. Harding and R. Johnston (eds) *Northern Pasts*, Oxford: British Archaeological Reports 302.

Dymond, M. (1998) Not just a day out! Archaeology and education on the Gardom's Edge project, *Assemblage*, http://www.shef.ac.United Kingdom/~assem/4/

Edmonds, M. (1999) *Ancestral Geographies of the Neolithic: Landscape, Monuments and Memory*, London, Routledge.

Edmonds, M. and McElearney, G. (1998) Web sites and public access at Gardom's Edge, *Assemblage*, http://www.shef.ac.United Kingdom/~assem/4/

Edmonds, M. and McElearney, G. (1999) Inhabitation and access: landscape and the Internet on Gardom's Edge, *Internet Archaeology*, http://intarch.ac.United Kingdom/journal/issue6/edmonds_toc.html

Gosden, C. (1994) *Social Being and Time*, Oxford, Blackwell.

Hart, C. (1981) *The North Derbyshire Archaeological Survey*, Chesterfield: North Derbyshire Archaeological Trust.

Hart, C. (1985) Gardom's Edge, Derbyshire: settlements, cairnfield and hillfort. In D. Spratt and C. Burgess (eds) *Upland Settlement in Britain,* 71–76, Oxford: BAR 143.

Ingold, T. (1993) The temporality of the landscape, *World Archaeology* 25(2): 152–174.

Long, D.J. (1994) Prehistoric field systems and the vegetation development of the gritstone uplands of the Peak District, Ph.D. thesis, Keele University.

Long, D.J., Chambers, F.M. and Barnatt, J. (1998) The palaeoenvironment and vegetational history of a later prehistoric field system at Stoke Flat on the gritstone uplands of the Peak District, *Journal of Archaeological Science* 25: 505–519.

Poster, D. (1995) *The Second Media Age*, Cambridge: Polity Press.

Royal Commission on the Historical Monuments of England (1987) Gardom's Edge, South Derbyshire, Unpublished report, National Monuments Record, NMR nos.: SK27 SE 29, 161–166, 175.

Royal Commission on the Historical Monuments of England and the Peak Park Joint Planning Board (1993) An archaeological survey of the northern halves of Gardom's and Birchen Edges, Unpublished report, National Monuments Record, NMR no. SK 27 SE 98.

Stone, P.G. (1986) Prehistory through ears, eyes and backs, *CBA Education Bulletin* 1: 8–11.

Tilley, C. (1994) *A Phenomenology of Landscape: Paths, Places and Monuments*, Oxford: Berg.

Chapter 20

KILMARTIN HOUSE TRUST

Damion Willcock

A single work of art contains a history of the consciousness of a whole people. It's a sculptural library. When removed from a land, it goes into permanent exile, which is to say, one half of it dies. The second thing that happens is that the people themselves are in a sort of exile. They are in exile from the repository of their dreams. They are in exile from the highest significance that years of ritual evolution have given rise to. One of the most effective and tragic ways of destroying a people's spirit is to, as it were, destroy the validity of their works of art. When that validity is destroyed, you have a kind of cultural schizophrenia. You have a sense in which people no longer know what they are, what they were and, therefore, what they can become.

Ben Okri, *Astonishing the Gods*

Introduction

Kilmartin House Trust is a pioneer ecomuseum (see Davis 1999) project in mid-Argyll, Scotland, founded in 1994 in response to the unusually rich environmental and cultural heritage of Kilmartin valley. A raised peat bog, Moine Mhor, is a National Nature Reserve, leading into salt marsh and estuary, part of a National Scenic Area. But it is the incredible concentration of prehistoric sites which is most startling. Within a six-mile radius there are 150 sites, including standing stones, cairns, and rock art, testifying to a long human occupation. Still apparent are many of the features, suggesting attraction and significance to a succession of ancient communities: a fertile valley floor, a plug of rock with commanding views, rocky shores with pools of limpets and mussels, much the same as when mesolithic people cast waste shells into midden piles.

The Trust provides a focus for this 'cultural landscape' by offering a museum with artefacts and interpretative displays, an information hall, audio-visual facilities and a study centre. The museum has attracted several major awards, including the 1998 Gulbenkian Prize and 1998 Scottish Museum of the Year. Its displays are complemented by a programme of events, courses and an evolving education programme. These are structured towards the central aim of improving awareness, particularly in young and local people, of the valley's rich landscape. A full-time education officer is employed for this purpose.

Development for the entire project, including purchase of property and conversion to a museum and visitor centre, has exceeded £1.5 million. Sadly, less than 2 per cent of this funding came from Argyll. In a poor tourism market, visitor figures are 40 per cent lower than anticipated and the result is a current reliance upon revenue support. This, unsurprisingly, is far harder to attract than development support. Fund-raising absorbs a great deal of time and we have had to be very proactive in our search. A trading company creates a small revenue for the Trust through the sale of museum tickets, a shop and café. Sales of books and our own prehistoric music CD are mainstays, and increasing numbers are also sold through the Trust website. E-commerce is seen as the way forward to achieving financial sustainability.

Education

So why bother with education? First, the childhood experience of David Clough, Kilmartin House Director. Having spent his formative years here he remained puzzled by the mounds of stones and strange carvings along the valley bottom. Little mention of these ancient relics was made in the classroom. Rather, Egyptians and Vikings were the favoured topics. Teachers, along with most local people, simply did not have access to information. In contrast to the static monuments, the removable artefacts – neolithic and Bronze Age pottery, jewellery and metalwork – had long since 'departed' by way of Victorian archaeologists to the national museums of Edinburgh and London.

Thankfully these works of art had not been destroyed, although all but lost from the consciousness of the Kilmartin community. Much of the Trust's work has been to secure the return of these displaced riches. The emotive power of artefacts is considerable, and engendering pride and interest in cultural heritage is a whole lot easier if identifiable objects are to hand.

The second reason for placing such emphasis on education – less idealistic but more pragmatic – is that many more funding opportunities become available. In 1997, the Trust gained a substantial Heritage Lottery Fund grant (approximately 50 per cent of total development costs) enabling purchase and conversion of

Kilmartin House from a former manse into a study centre with offices, library and collection store. The grant also covered staff wages for 18 months and financed development of a guidebook.

The education programme has a wide spectrum of audiences, including, of course, Argyll's primary schools. Teachers are assisted in their use of the museum's collection and the surrounding landscape. We receive visiting groups and also operate an outreach programme, increasingly through ICT (information and communication technology). Special relations exist with our closest schools and we do our best to ensure they benefit from any events; there cannot be many schools who have welcomed Swedish drummers, Stone Age flint knappers and Shropshire coracle makers.

Resources

The core resource is the museum display, which begins with a scale model of the Kilmartin valley, covered by a transparent dome, on which the sites of cairns, standing stones and other physical features can be illuminated. There are hands-on exhibits intended for visitors of any age; for example, stone querns with a supply of grain for grinding flour, a selection of animal furs and samples of different species of timber. Arrows and bone tools are among several wall-mounted objects held in position by velcro, allowing easy removal and inspection. Each room also includes a drawer of extra artefacts for use in supervised object-handling sessions. In addition there are 'sound posts' at which push-buttons select recordings of a variety of sounds, music and song, including the call of a stag, the sounds of a bone flute and pottery drum, and a chant for Saint Columba. Most activities which groups subsequently participate in (e.g. flint knapping, coracle making and pottery) have reference to some aspect of these displays.

Perhaps our most successful resource is a simulated archaeological dig. Resembling an excavation of a mesolithic site, its finds include seal bones, burnt hazelnut shells, a shell necklace and a bone flute made from a swan's wing. A skills-based approach is well served by the simulated dig: selecting relevant tools to excavate, sorting finds into categories, recording the evidence that is uncovered, identifying explanations for the position or state of their finds. Young excavators go on to investigate organic remains missing from the dig: birch bark containers, animal skins and wooden shafts for the mounting of flint points. An accompanying booklet develops artefacts into project material; so, for example, a piece of wolf skin provides the starting point for investigating living things gone from Scotland, and some, like the osprey, which are returning.

Activities

Some teachers with a particular interest in prehistory manage to bring a group several times, even from some distance. With a school roll of five, Ulva Primary on the Isle of Mull must be one of the United Kingdom's smallest. The whole school fits into the teacher's car. Their 'Early People' topic was, at the suggestion of the children, divided into a number of aspects: houses, food, tools, clothing and transport. They visited three times and on each occasion focused on one aspect. Looking at how objects change through time is a useful approach. How does a stone axe compare to a metal axe? How does a saddle quern compare to a rotary quern? When you have replica examples to hand there is only one way to find out. Whenever possible we also handle real artefacts; to grasp a 5,000-year-old axe-head really used by a Stone Age person is high-octane fuel to the imagination.

An extension to the activities at the museum is to use the wealth of archaeo-logical sites on our doorstep. We are fortunate in Kilmartin, being surrounded by the very archaeology we wish to celebrate. Through the museum windows one sees the cairns of the great linear cemetery – a string of five enduring structures begun in the neolithic. Investigation of artefacts in the museum can be followed two minutes later by a walk to the monument in which they were found. Once again, artefacts are an effective method of interpretation. I carry a rucksack of replica pots, jewellery, axe-heads, boar tusks and plant fibres. Why not lie down in a Bronze Age cist, draped in wolf skin, accompanied by engraved beakers and a jet necklace? Or storm the Dalriadan fort of Dunadd to search for clues of wars and walls, wild boar carvings and stone-etched footprints. Hear horns of bronze and be anointed king on the airy top, overshadowed by Jura's peaks. This is culture!

Experimental archaeology

> In a sense we grow up more helpless than ever before. Although collectively we have extraordinary – unprecedented – powers of control over the earth's resources, and have marvels of engineering available in every household, indi-vidually we have lost most of the skills common to our ancestors; building a home with family, friends or neighbours from local materials, the long but shared times producing and then preparing the raw stuff of food or clothing. Television seduces us with the illusion that we are participating in the world, and we probably have more surrogate experiences than the richest medieval kings and queens had real ones. But though more wonders pass in front of our eyes than ever before, we actually make and do less and less first hand.
>
> J. Keen, *A Teacher's Guide to Ancient Technology*

Our facilities are developing as we learn new techniques, often the result of a visiting craftsperson. This contact with other educators and institutions has been invaluable as a source of skills and ideas. During a tour of museums in France I was particularly inspired by the experimental archaeology used in education programmes: erecting standing stones, heaving a huge monolith laid on wooden rollers, working bellows to smelt bronze, firing pottery in earth ovens, painting rock-faces using quills, hollow bone and brushes of deer hair. Particularly impressive is the use of reconstructed prehistoric buildings, which provide wonderfully atmospheric venues for experimental archaeology and the perfect venue for storytelling.

Some of our earlier events capitalised upon the craftspeople commissioned to create the museum displays. One of the most memorable was the construction of Mighty Three Tails, a six-person prehistoric coracle. Local children had the opportunity to touch and smell lanolin, raw hide, cut willow and make their own miniature version in what was the first experience of its kind for many adults too. Thanks to a visit by two Swedish prehistory enthusiasts we now have an elk-skin container for boiling water 'prehistoric style'. The process begins by rubbing sticks to make fire, heating stones until red hot and placing them into the water-filled container. Within seconds the water boils, mint leaves are added and tea is on the way. Investigative skills are challenged and imaginations stretched in a participatory and fun experience. Such occasions can become abiding memories for many children.

Teaching at a distance

> I am worried about replacing artefacts with information about objects. There is a dimension of objects which resists interpretation. I've found some of the most exciting and enduring things when 'lost' in the V&A. It is very important that the technology should bring people back to the objects. What I'd like to do whenever I'm going around the V&A is to plug into the wall and be able to interrogate the artefact, have my questions answered, and to accumulate my own observations in a two-way process.
>
> Tim Benton, art historian, 1995

In an ideal world I would like every Argyll schoolchild to visit Kilmartin, to marvel at Bronze Age cists and towering stones. But our geography of islands and mountains means long journeys and high costs, and it is apparent that to provide for many schools we need an investment in communications technology.

Many schools have only one or two teachers, and in a dispersed rural area, access to Gaelic, French, PE and instrument tuition can be difficult to arrange. In an attempt to overcome the problem Argyll schools have used an internal computer network (a mini Internet) to facilitate distance teaching by specialists. Teachers are provided with, and exchange, support materials and resources. In 1996 Kilmartin House Trust joined the network providing information on ancient Argyll and its use in the curriculum. Later we contributed a children's version of Agenda 21, the 'forward plan' for Planet Earth drawn up at Rio in 1992.

The latest development for distance teaching is the use of video communication technology, now used by over half of Argyll schools to access specialist teachers.

Providing both a video and audio link is the next best thing to being in the same room as the person you are communicating with. The stuff of *Star Trek*. Again, the technology provides a great opportunity for museums and, following a successful pilot study, we now use it to link with schools. Pupils can interview a curator or watch a demonstration on prehistoric technology. Additional cameras can zoom in on an artefact's detail and, given an extension lead, permit a gallery tour. It is not only Argyll schools with which we can communicate, but anyone worldwide. Soon we hope to link with classes in North America.

Conclusion

For many years, public educational policy was based on the assumption that, for the majority of the population, the most important learning took place in the classroom. In recent decades understanding of learning and education has changed beyond recognition. Today learning is a lifelong process (see Lock, Chapter 6), growing out of our everyday experience, to which formal education at school and college and training contribute. I feel that museums have long been the perfect demonstration of this 'new-found' policy.

Having spent four years working to bring Kilmartin's history alive I can identify more and more with the words of educational psychologist Howard Gardner. He considers that museums have a vital and complementary role to play in children's education, and advocates in *The Unschooled Mind* (Gardner 1991) that all children should attend an intensive museum programme rather than, or in addition to, schools. He believes that the informal, enjoyable, contextualised environment of the museum and the apprenticeship model of learning are more relevant to the needs of today's children than the decontextualised environment and formal methods of the school.

At Kilmartin House, we have, through financial necessity, had to adapt our provision to a number of audiences: nurseries, after-school clubs, universities, special needs groups, retirement clubs and history societies. There are too few people living in Argyll to do otherwise. We have worked hard to secure these audiences and, in many cases, we have been responsible for making initial contact. What is needed is innovation, enthusiasm and, above all, a willingness to adapt one's approach. In 2000 we will begin a new project, part of a national initiative aimed at increasing youth participation in museums. The plan is to provide a number of apprenticeships relating to our displays, targeted at the young unemployed with the hope of creating jobs. A workshop where local talent turn out coracles, pottery, bronzework and jewellery may be some time coming, but like the return of Kilmartin's artefacts it is not an impossible dream.

■ ■ ■

References

Davis, P.S. (1999) *Ecomuseums: A Sense of Place*, London: Cassells Academic/Leicester University Press.

Gardner, H. (1991) *The Unschooled Mind: How Children Think and How Schools Should Teach*, New York: Basic Books.

Keen, J. (1996) *A Teacher's Guide to Ancient Technology*, London: English Heritage.

INDEX